A PROVENÇAL
KITCHEN
IN AMERICA

SUZANNE MC LUCAS

Johnson Books: Boulder

Johnson Publishing Company
1880 South 57th Court
Boulder, Colorado 80301

To Heather and Eric

Contents

Preface

Laughter, the friendly sound of wine glasses, the still air suddenly electrified by the buzzing of cicadas, the sweet heady fragrance of herbs, the pungent aroma of garlic teasing the senses—this is the homeland I remember!

I wish I could bring all this to you. At least I can convey to you a vital part of it through an understanding of the preparation of foods that were one main source of that early contentment. I have wanted to do this book for years, it seems, because good, honest French cooking—the real family type of cooking—is not well enough known in this country.

Certainly everyone has heard a great deal about the world of *haute cuisine*, the gastronomical achievements of chefs. However I think the average cook, man or woman, has often been intimidated by these extravagances or by the complex descriptions of mysterious dishes composed of ingredients too difficult to find or too expensive to buy. This is sad and misleading for all of us who love good food and enjoy entertaining, since it is so relatively simple for us to learn about the sensible, wholesome, nutritious, well-balanced, and thrifty meals that are served in French homes.

Does such simple cuisine lack in elegance? Not at all, for elegance is often synonymous with simplicity. A dish need only be tastefully prepared and pleasantly presented to become truly elegant fare. The personal touch has always been the secret ingredient that makes a dinner memorable—one that produces that atmosphere of well-being and conviviality that is the objective of every host and hostess. For what better way to enjoy life than to dine with those you love and enjoy? As the Provençal people would say:

"Sans une bonne table, il n'y a pas de plaisir."
("Without a good table, there is no pleasure.")

I have chosen to emphasize the cuisine of the South of France because it is sensuous in aroma, flavor, taste, and appearance, and being an incurable romantic, I love the South for its romance. The cooking of the South is a distillation, a symphony if you will, resulting from the contributions of successive waves of races and civilizations.

If you have visited this part of the country, you have no doubt come to agree with our legend which says, "The South is a microcosm of Creation." It is this South which has inspired the artists, poets, writers, mystics, builders, great chefs, and last, but not least, good home cooks.

This is my heritage, and to it I owe the love and respect for nature and its bounty, and the love and respect for good food. I want to try through this book to pass on some of the knowledge acquired through this heritage. But first, let me pass on one small piece of advice:

> Be honest in your cooking. Honesty is love. Do the best you can with what you have and what you can afford. Prepare it with love. Put *yourself* into it, your personal touch. You will be repaid!

And now, *je vous souhaite bonne table et bonne compagnie!*—I wish you a good table and good company.

—Suzanne

A Bit of History

After God created the sun, the earth, the mountains, the waters, and other good things, He realized He had a little of everything left over and decided that out of these He would make His private paradise. And this is the way the South came to be.

So goes the legend that the old people still tell. To one who has never been to Provence it would seem exaggerated, but to the native or the visitor it contains a great deal of reality.

The sun-drenched land of the South of France—the land bounded by the warm Mediterranean, the Alps, and the Pyrenees at the Golfe du Lion (named for its tumultuous waters) and carved by the majestic Rhône—is the kingdom of the olive and the garlic. It is a landscape of tall cypresses etched against a deep blue sky . . . an electrifying atmosphere dominated by the buzzing sound of cicadas . . . a mosaic of colors . . . a symphony of pungent herbs and spices.

It is the land of Oc, where "yes" was *oc*—as compared to the rest of France, where the language spoken was the *langue d'oïl* and "yes" was *oui*. Since antiquity the South has attracted hordes of invaders, barbarous or cultivated, warlike or peaceful, who left their imprint and molded the personality of its people—and contributed to the uniqueness of its cuisine, a cuisine as varied, spicy, and distinctive as the people who created it.

In prehistoric times the plateaus of Provence were already inhabited. Then the Ligurians and Celts came down from the North, following the Rhône valley. Traces of these invaders are observed to this day, blended with our Christian traditions and customs.

For example, the yule-log ceremony in Provence is tied directly to the ancient rite of the Druids—the renewal of fire for the winter solstice. Just before midnight the family assembles, and the head of the household (father or grandfather) pours the cooked wine over the new burning log, proclaiming the end of the old year and the coming of the new and asking for the blessing of his household, his crops, and his sheep. The family then goes to church to hear the Christmas mass, followed by the *Reveillon*, the long supper of fish, herb omelet, vegetable dishes, and the traditional thirteen desserts: dry figs, dates, black and white almond and honey nougat, tangerines, oranges, apples, raisins, delicious winter melon kept to ripen since September in the cellar, hazelnuts, walnuts, almonds, and the Christmas bread called *la pompe*, slashed in the center in the form of a cross and tied with a sprig of holly. The *crèche* (nativity scene) with little figurines called *santons* (little saints) is seen in a prominent place in the house. Also given prominence is the dish in which wheat has been growing since December 4 (feast day of Saint Barbe*) to bring good luck for the coming year's crop.

Six hundred years before the birth of Christ the Phocaeans came to the shores of Provence and established a series of trading posts, one of which was to become the most important—Massalia (now Marseille). A poetic story, part true and part legend, tells of the encounter between Protis, the young chief of the Greek navigators, and Gyptis, daughter of Nann, king of the Ligurians. The feast that followed their wedding gives us some idea of Ligurian fare: large dishes made of cork (which by the way can still be found in Provence) filled with fish boiled in sea water, flavored with wild fennel; platters of lamb and goat meat cooked in rancid butter; small fresh cheeses made of goat milk; sour milk and a drink made of barley resembling beer. The elixir called hydromel (mead) sealed the marriage. The next day the Greek sailors returned the favor by giving their hosts thousands of amphorae filled with olive oil and the wine of Samor. They later taught the Ligurians to cultivate grapes and olive trees and how to use wine, olive oil, and saffron in cooking. From then on, fish was cooked with this marvelous spice in a bouillon which has become our famous *bouillabaisse*.

Later, the Romans under Julius Caesar conquered Provence and Languedoc and ruled for four centuries, leaving behind some grandiose and well-preserved monuments, which are strewn all over the South. For example, Nîmes, in the Languedoc, was named Nemausus and was the capital of a tribe of ancient Gauls. It fell easily to the Roman domination. The visitor can still admire some of the Roman influence in the famous temple "*la Maison Carée*," built under Augustus in the first century B.C.; it now houses the Museum of Antiquity. The amphitheater is another well-preserved example of the work of the first century B.C.

---

*Legend has it that Ste. Barbe, patron of stone workers and protectress of crops, in answer to the prayers of the parents of a little girl who had no hair, sent a little bird down to tell her to hold some wheat in the palm of her hand during a rainstorm. This the girl did and soon grew a magnificent head of long, flowing hair!

Arles, in Provence, was the capital of the Roman *Provincia.* Its aqueduct, 75 kilometers long, is still in use. It boasts some of the best and most beautifully preserved curiosities of the ancient world: the arenas and amphitheater, the St. Trophime Portal and its cloister, the Alyscamps, which was a Roman necropolis celebrated in the Roman world.

Glanum, near St. Rémy de Provence, was a Greco-Roman city dating back to the sixth century B.C. First discovered in 1921, continuing excavations provide a moving trip through the past. Near by, the tourist can marvel at the artistic and powerful beauty of the mausoleum, built to commemorate a powerful Roman, and the municipal arch, one of the oldest of Roman monuments. Orange, in Vaucluse, and its formidable Roman theater, still in use, are somewhat to the north.

High above Monaco and Monte Carlo, *"la Turbie,"* an imposing Roman tower built in the fifth century B.C., commemorates the fall of the Ligurians to the Roman armies.

Rome was not only bent on conquest but on good living, and many of her citizens were gourmets of renown. In the first century B.C. Lucullus, a famous general and epicure, introduced cherries to the Empire which he brought back from his campaigns in Asia. In 63 B.C., Apicius, a famous epicure and writer of culinary books, spent millions of sesterces to produce rare ingredients and invented rare dishes. When he found he had only the equivalent of $360,000 on which to survive, he killed himself.

Aurius Camars, Roman moneylender who governed the alluvial land or delta lying between the two long arms of the Rhône where it meets the sea, gave his name to the great marshland la Camargue, the field or *domaine* of Camars. The wild bull played an important role in antiquity. Its cult was brought to the Camargue, where it remained in modified form. The capture of a wild bull is still a glorious and courageous feat and the *fé di biou* (celebration of the bull) takes place every year in many villages of the Camargue.

Today the Camargue is a flat, monotonous land, the lowest part lying two meters below sea level. It is a land of rice paddies, salt flats, wild horses, cattle, rare and beautiful birds—flamingos, herons, and egrets—a paradise for fishermen, as fish from sea and sweet water abound. This land of mirages has been chosen by the gypsies of Europe as their holy land, and they gather every year at Saintes-Marie de la Mer, a small town on the coast, to celebrate the feast of one of their saints, Sara la Noire. Rich in tradition, the Camargue has enriched the Provençal heritage and its cuisine.

The medieval era was also a time of conquest for Provence.

Hordes of Visigoths, Burgundians, and Franks brought anarchy in their wake. It was the bishops of the Catholic Church who restored order and kept the traditions. Under Charlemagne and Charles Martel, the Saracens came from Spain; later came the Infidels from Africa. Their influence still lingers in many of the names, in the physical appearance of some of the people, in the language, and of course in the cooking—for the invasions extended over a period of two hundred years.

After a brief episode of Italian influence under the reign of Jeanne, Queen of Naples, the South and especially Avignon became the center of Christendom for almost a hundred years. From 1300 to the end of the century, successive popes established residence in Avignon, which became not only the spiritual but also the gastronomical center of the South, as the popes were inclined to eat well and were highly appreciative of fine food.

There followed a dark period under the house of les Baux, which was a citadel of independence, political and religious, from the rest of France. *"Race d'aiglons, jamais vassale,"* sang the Provençal poet Mistral—"a race of eagles, never conquered." Life at les Baux was spent fighting and defending the land, until the people and the fortress were finally destroyed by enemies in 1791, after several heroic battles. In that precarious existence, food was only a matter of subsistence for the people. With the return of peace, the art of living also returned, and with it invasions of the wealthy. Provence and the Riviera became the playground of kings, queens, rich exiles, and artists, attracted by the brilliant light, the unique scenery, and the wonderful food. The rich and sunny countryside and the mild climate produce the most flavorful fruits, vegetables, and wines.

Marseille, capital of Provence and second city of France, is a true cosmopolitan port, and has been called the "door to the Orient" since the opening of the Suez Canal in 1869. Corsicans, Italians, Spaniards, North Africans, Indo-Chinese, Armenians, and of course French from all over France can be found rubbing elbows in its ancient and narrow streets, which resemble Mediterranean bazaars.

It is this kaleidoscope of sounds and colors that is the true spirit of the South. It has inspired poets and writers. Dante thought of writing his "Divine Comedy" in *langue d'oc.* The South of France has become a center of good food, a place where gourmets the world over come to sample this distillation of centuries of good cooking. It is one aspect of this cuisine, the home cooking of the South, essentially simple and straightforward but deeply influenced by this history, that is the subject of this book.

Introduction

I feel this introduction to be so important to the successful use of the book that I strongly recommend your reading it before you begin to explore the recipes. It has been designed to acquaint you with the procedures followed in presenting the recipes; it explains why certain ingredients are used; and it offers you some alternatives.

FORMAT

All the recipes have been classified according to degree of complexity by numbers appearing in the upper righthand corner of the pages. The three classifications are:

1 — very easy
2 — intermediate
3 — advanced

This identification makes it possible for the beginning cook to prepare interesting recipes without searching through the book for what appear to be simple dishes, and to help him or her to learn the basic skills not only of French cookery but cookery in general. The seasoned cook will also find some of the simpler recipes not only appealing but novel or different.

Each recipe bears its French title and the English translation. The approximate number of servings is shown for each recipe. Most have been designed for four to six persons in order to make the preparation easier, to minimize the chance of failure, and to cut down on cooking time and fuel.

The ingredients for each recipe are listed in the order in which they are used, even if that means that some items are repeated. Read through the recipe before starting; be sure you have all the ingredients together. If necessary, read the recipe a second time to acquaint yourself thoroughly with all the phases of its preparation.

Place the tools and utensils needed on your working surface and within reach. Measure in advance the liquids and solids needed.

Do the necessary processing — chopping, mincing, slicing, etc. — of ingredients and place them in individual bowls or containers in readiness for their use in the recipe.

In other words, organize your work before you start!

PROCEDURES

In many of the recipes olive oil is indicated. This is because it is used exclusively in the South of France, and I admit to being partial to its wonderful flavor. It is also rich in polyunsaturates and therefore very healthful. However, because of its high price you may wish to cut the olive oil by a half or a third by mixing it with a good vegetable oil such as corn oil or safflower oil. Then the beautiful flavor of the olive oil is still there, not as pungent but noticeable yet, and you can stretch it further. Olive oil may be kept in the warmest part of the refrigerator. If it congeals, bring it to room temperature. The flavor will not be affected.

In most recipes calling for butter I have offered the alternative of using margarine. I must stress the use of a margarine high in polyunsaturates, especially for anyone watching his or her diet. Moreover, I favor an unsweetened margarine. If butter only is specified in some cases, this is because I have found that the particular recipe does not respond well to margarine.

In some recipes you can make some substitutions. For example:

1 tablespoon butter = 1 tablespoon margarine = ¾ tablespoon
    vegetable oil or
1¼ cups butter or margarine = 1 cup vegetable oil

When deep-frying use polyunsaturated vegetable oil, and do not reuse the oil. This practice will cost a few cents more, but you will do yourself and your family a favor by protecting your good health.

Watch the salt in cooking. It is always better to undersalt. Respect the health of your family and guests. For this reason I have not provided precise salt measurements, leaving it up to you to taste at the end of the cooking process and decide what amount of salt you wish. But remember that the use of herbs in French cooking is a superb way to lessen the need for salting.

Don't let the lack of one ingredient, or the lack of funds, stop you from making a dish; use substitutes, as for example:

In place of shallots use the white part of green onions or even a small sweet onion.

Leeks in some recipes may be replaced by whole green onions.
Dijon mustard may be replaced by regular prepared mustard.
Cream in soups may be replaced by whole milk or even low-fat
milk.
Butter or margarine may be replaced by vegetable oil.

PRESENTATION

Make your meals and your table as appealing and colorful as you
can. One secret of successful chefs is their presentation of the food.
Some ideas that will help you:

Decorate a roast with watercress, parsley, or even curly endive
lettuce and some cherry tomatoes strewn on top.
Serve chicken or Cornish hens with grapes or orange slices, kiwi
fruit or apricot halves.
Try pork with apricot halves or kumquats, or thick apple slices
poached in brown-sugar syrup.
Garnish duck with orange or apricot halves or orange shells filled
with cranberries.
Garnish fish with fresh dill or fennel sprigs in season, lemon slices,
wedges, or twists.
Decorate lamb with watercress or fresh mint leaves and kumquats
or parsley sprigs.
Serve a vegetable or fish quiche with fresh tarragon, parsley sprigs,
or perhaps some cherry tomatoes.
Serve a slice of pâté on a lettuce leaf with a petaled cornichon or
small dill pickle on the side of some *radis roses* (petaled
radishes).
A sprinkling of parsley over a stew, ragout of meat, or poultry gives
a nice final touch.
A pretty way to serve a *ratatouille* or a *bohémienne* as an hors
d'oeuvre or vegetable is to present it in the hollowed-out shells
of the eggplants, the pulp of which you have used in a dish.
Poach the shell a minute or two in rapidly boiling water, drain,
dry, rub it lightly inside and out with olive oil, and place the
ratatouille in the little boats.
Serve vegetables such as peas, purée of squash, or lima beans in
pâte brisée shells or boats (*barquettes*).
Add a few slices or twists of lemon to asparagus *en vinaigrette*.
Serve creamed dessert or fruit in long-stem glasses.

Find out what is in season before you cook a dish; you will spend
less. *Then* look for a recipe. If you are a beginner, do not experi-
ment on guests; use recipes you are familiar with.

A typical French meal for guests would consist of *hors d'oeuvres* or *crudités* or a *potage*, one entrée*(fish, shell fish, egg, or cheese dish), a vegetable, a meat or poultry dish, salad, cheeses, dessert or fruits. But because most of us are unaccustomed to so much food at one meal, because we are watching our diets, or because we are yet new at entertaining, it is wise to make the meal light to start with. For example:

A *potage* or some *crudités*
One dish of either fish or meat or poultry
A vegetable or two
A salad
One or two cheeses
A light dessert (especially if the meat dish has been on the rich side)

Remember also, if you are "running the show" alone, try to find at least one or two things that can be prepared the day before so that you will be able to enjoy yourself and your guests.

If you entertain, it would be a good idea to keep a record of what you have served to your guests. Note the date, the guests' names, and the menu of that day. In this way you do not run the risk of repeating the same meal for the same guests.

ABOUT WINES

For a special occasion or a meal served for special guests wines are the perfect accompaniment, as they enhance the food and also provide visual enjoyment. There are some simple rules to follow in serving wines. The first basic rule is to start the meal with the lightest wine and end it with the most "generous" or full-bodied—except for the dessert wine which should be light.

Next, a dish prepared with a wine sauce is accompanied by a similar wine.

When you serve wines, do not shake the bottle—treat it gently.

White and rosé wines should be chilled (not iced) to 40 - 50°F. This brings out the refreshing bouquet. Keep it in the refrigerator two hours before serving. *Never* put the bottle in the freezing unit to speed chilling; you will ruin the wine!

Red wines should be served at room temperature (60-70°F), and they should be opened at least an hour before serving so that they will have time to react with the air and release their full bouquet.

---

*In France an *entrée* is a dish served before the main course or between courses; in America it is generally understood as the main course itself.

Champagnes and sparkling wines should be placed in a bucket of ice one hour before serving time. This process is called *frappé*.

When buying wines, you will hear or read special terms. Do not let them frighten you. Ask your wine merchant; he will help you. Meanwhile, here is an explanation of a few of the most used French and English terms:

Appellation refers to the specific location of the vineyard from which the wine was made. When *controllée* follows, it means the wine has been awarded the "best of region . . . highest of its category."

Balance, or correctness, of a wine is the harmonious blend of acidity and sweetness.

Body is the richness, the density of the wine—its content in alcohol and tannin.

Bouquet is the flavor of the aged wine after its elements have fully developed.

Brut means a very dry wine.

Château means castle (the name of the castle will follow).

Cru is the locale from which the wine was produced and also the vintage.

Domaine is the estate from which the wine comes (name of estate follows).

Mis en bouteille means bottled.

Mousseux means sparkling.

Sec, demi-sec — dry, semi-dry (wine).

The following list will provide some guidelines for the serving of wines:

Potages and soups	Madeira
Hors d'oeuvres	Light white dry wines
Shellfish	Light white dry wines
Crustaceans or fish	Light white dry wines, or some light red wines
Entrées	Dry white wines or dry rosé wines
White meats, poultry	Light red wines or champagne
Red meat, game, pâtés	Full-bodied red wines
Cold meats, vegetables	Dry white wines
Salad	Nothing but water
Fruits	Champagnes, *sec*
Desserts	Champagnes, *demi-sec*; sparkling or sweet wines

When serving wines with cheeses, follow the same rules as for other food:

Light cheeses	Light dry wines, white or rosé
Soft-ripened cheeses	Light dry red wines
Robust cheeses	Full-bodied red wines
Fondues	Dry white or rosé wines

And now . . . I hope you will spend many happy hours exploring the wonders of our cuisine and preparing and sharing some of my recipes with your family and friends.

A FEW VARIED MENUS

For a regular dinner

Crudités
Poulet au fromage (chicken in cream and cheese sauce)
Carottes persillées (parsley carrots)
Cream cheese

———

Cucumbers vinaigrette
Tarte amphitrite (seafood pie)
Ratatouille
Fresh fruits

———

Soupe à la poële (frying pan soup)
Omelette campagnarde (country omelet)
Salade verte (green salad)
Cheese

———

For a Sunday dinner

Slices of pâté campagnard (country-style pâté)
Poussins en fricassée (Cornish hen fricassee)
Salade d'asperges mimosa (asparagus salad)
Pêches grenadine (peaches with grenadine)

———

Oeufs farcis en tapenade (eggs stuffed with tapenade)
Filet de porc aux navets (pork roast, turnips)
Pommes de terre persillées (potatoes with parsley)
Salade verte (green salad)
Mousse d'abricot (apricot mousse)

———

For a reasonably priced gourmet meal

Caviar d'aubergines (eggplant caviar)
Poussins au vinaigre (Cornish hen, vinegar sauce)
Coeurs de laitues (hearts of lettuce)
Poires framboisées au Porto (raspberry-flavored pears with port)

———

Hors d'oeuvres or crudités
Rillettes provençales (pork meat spread on French bread slices)
Le caneton aux olives (duckling with olives)
Petits pois au lard (small peas and bacon)
Salade verte (green salad)
Tartelettes or barquettes de fruits (tartlets of fruit)

———

Brandade (codfish purée in patty shells)
Risotto à la Toulonnaise (chicken and rice Toulon)
Haricots verts maître d'hôtel (green beans with herb sauce)
Granité aux framboises (raspberry ice)

———

Between friends

Escargots table du roy (king's table snails)
Paupiettes de veau provençales (stuffed veal scallops)
Ratatouille or bohémienne (vegetable stews)
Macédoine d'oranges (macédoine of orange)

———

For brunch

Champignons farcis au fromage (mushrooms stuffed with cheese)
Tarte de tomates provençale (tomato pie, Provençal-style)
Salade de haricots verts (green bean salad)
Oranges au sabayon (orange sabayon)

———

Light luncheon

Velouté d'asperges au fromage (cream of asparagus, cheese)
Champignons surprise (mushroom surprise)
Tarte aux pommes (apple tart)

———

A summer or picnic meal

Macédoine de melon et fraises (melon-strawberry macédoine)
Pâté campagnard (country-style pâté)
Mayonnaise au chocolat (chocolate mousse)

———

KITCHEN TOOLS AND COOKING UTENSILS

What is more pleasurable for a cook than to enter a beautiful kitchen with a large expanse of counter-top, gleaming pots and pans hanging neatly, and handsome gadgets here and there! Unfortunately not everyone can own such a kitchen. But the secret of successful cooking does not lie in the amount spent on decor, or the expanse of space, or the expensive gadgetry. It is possible to produce delightful dishes with a minimum of equipment. I have done it for years.

The secret is to limit your repertory to what you can cook with at the moment, and to progressively add to that. Plan and buy carefully. If you are on a tight budget, avoid "gourmet supply stores" for the time being. Many items on the list given below can be found in budget stores or even secondhand places. For the more expensive items a good idea would be to check your local directory for "restaurant equipment supply stores"; you will find their prices often more reasonable than those of regular kitchen shops.

When looking for cooking pots or saucepans, remember that the most efficient ones are those with the heavier gauge; they spread the heat evenly through their surface.

At least one excellent knife is essential, even if you have to spend some money. It will be the best investment you can make. If you can afford only one knife, get a nine- or ten-inch professional carbon-steel or "chef's" knife. Another good investment would be a French "walking knife" (*hachoir* in French).* It has a curved stainless steel blade with two wooden handles, a wonderful tool for chopping and mincing. I could not do without one!

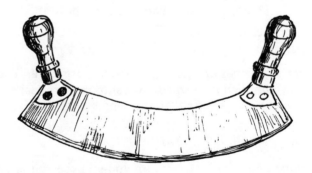

---

*Sometimes also called by the Italian name of *mezzaluna*, half-moon.

HELPFUL AND PRACTICAL IDEAS

The following ideas, gathered and used through years of cooking and experimenting, have successfully passed the test of practicality. I hope you will find them useful, too. They can help make your cooking easier.

For vegetables

To *peel a tomato,* drop it in boiling water and let it stay 15 seconds. Remove with slotted spoon. The skin will wrinkle and peel off easily.

If you want to *keep tomato paste* or purée for quite a while, put it in a sterilized jar, pour a thin film of oil over it, cover tightly, and keep it in the refrigerator.

If you have some doubt about the sanitary conditions in which your *lettuce* was grown and you want to make sure it is safe to use, rinse it in a large bowl filled with cold water and a tablespoon of vinegar.

Keep unpeeled *garlic* in a thoroughly dry, small plastic box or jar with a tight-fitting lid; dry the moisture from the box often. Or peel each clove and place in a glass jar filled with oil, and cover. Use the oil later in salad; it will carry the garlic flavor.

When cooking *cauliflower,* add a slice of lemon to the pan; it will keep the vegetable white and will eliminate the strong odor.

Green vegetables will stay green if you cook them in a quantity of rapidly boiling water and do not cover the pan.

To eliminate the pungent *odor of garlic* from your fingers, rub them with a piece of lemon skin.

To improve the *tenderness of peas or beans* when they have passed the small, tender stage, soak them for an hour in a bowl of lukewarm (almost cold) water with 2 tablespoons of flour in it.

To prepare thicker *asparagus* (not the finger sizes) for cooking, do not cut the stem bluntly across but peel it with a potato parer or sharp knife, then cut the tough end off. The asparagus will cook more evenly.

If you want to avoid tears when *peeling onions,* place them, unpeeled, in boiling water, for one minute, drain, and then peel.

To keep *fresh herbs or parsley* fresh after they have been picked, place them in a glass of cold water or small vase; place in the refrigerator or other cool place in your kitchen. Change water daily and snip small pieces from the stems as you would with flowers.

For fruits

Do not wash *fruits or berries* before storing. If you do not intend to use them right away, refrigerate as soon as possible after purchase. When ready to use, wash them briefly with the stems on, drain well, and then remove the stems. (It would be better not to wash them, but we can no longer be sure that they are free of toxic chemicals.)

To obtain the *zeste of an orange or lemon*, peel with a potato parer in order to get the thin, colored part of the skin which contains the sweet oil. Dry thoroughly and hang on a wire or place on a piece of paper toweling in a well-ventilated spot. Store in jars in a dry, cool place. You can use the *zeste* to flavor desserts or stews; it may also be reduced to powder in a blender or food processor.

If you want to get more *juice from a lemon*, place it in hot water one or two minutes before you squeeze it.

If you do not have pitted *green olives* to add to your dish, but do have a can or jar of regular olives, with a small sharp knife cut the flesh of the olive starting from one end and cutting in a spiral around the pit, trying not to break the olive. The flesh will coil back upon itself to form the shape of the original olive.

To peel *fresh peaches, apricots, and nectarines* easily, drop them in boiling water and let them stay one minute; drain and plunge them immediately in cold water; peel.

To prevent the *darkening of freshly cut fruits* (such as apples, peaches, pears, or nectarines), after peeling and slicing them, add one teaspoon of lemon or orange juice to a cup of fruit.

For eggs

To *separate the yolk from the white* of an egg neatly and efficiently, break the egg over a funnel; the white goes through, the yolk will stay in the funnel.

To prevent *eggs from cracking while boiling*, rub the entire surface of the shell with vinegar or lemon juice before cooking. Also avoid moving the eggs directly from the refrigerator to hot water; rather start with very cold water and bring it slowly to the boiling point.

If you are making *a mayonnaise or an aioli* and the mixture curdles, do not panic! Rinse a clean bowl with warm water and dry it thoroughly. Place a fresh egg yolk in the warm bowl; with a wooden spoon beat it briefly, then add the curdled mixture, a small amount at a time, to the beaten egg yolk, beating rapidly with a rotary beater or electric mixer (the beater being at room temperature).

When *poaching* an egg, do not salt the water; instead, add one teaspoon of vinegar to the water. Your egg will poach better and faster.

When beating egg whites for *meringues*, be sure the bowl and beaters are thoroughly clean and at room temperature. The egg whites should be free of any specks of yolk and at room temperature. A stainless steel or copper bowl is better than a glass bowl.

If you want *eggs at room temperature* and have forgotten to get them out of the refrigerator ahead of time, place them in a bowl, add warm water to cover and let them stay in it two minutes.

To *peel hard-boiled eggs* easily, plunge them as soon as they are cooked in a bowl of cold water to which ice cubes have been added. Let them stay two or three minutes, drain water and ice, tap the eggs against a hard surface, and the shell will come off easily.

For dairy products

If you need *unsalted butter* and all you have on hand is salted, cut it into small pieces and place in a small bowl with one cup of cold water to cover; with a fork mash and work the butter in the water two or three minutes. Drain the water; replace with clean, cold water; repeat the procedure of working the butter; rinse. Repeat. After three changes the butter should be sweet. Drain well, squeezing out the moisture; form butter into a ball; refrigerate until ready to use.

If *butter* has become *rancid*, place it in a small bowl with one cup of cold water in which is dissolved one teaspoon of bicarbonate of soda. Work the butter as described in the preceding paragraph. Rinse and work twice with cold water. Drain and squeeze out the moisture; form into a ball and refrigerate.

When *whipping cream* use a chilled bowl and chilled beater. The cream should of course also be chilled. Do not whip too much cream in one operation and beat it rapidly; the cream should not have time to get warm.

If you have kept a piece of *Swiss or Gruyère cheese* too long and it is now dry, wrap it for a few hours in a piece of cloth moistened with white wine.

For meats, soups, and gravy

To facilitate the *trimming of fat* from a piece of meat, chill it first, then trim. The same rule applies to slicing meat, especially if it must be sliced very thin.

To remove the *fat from soup and broths*, if you have time, chill; the fat will float to the surface where it will be easy to remove. If you are in a hurry, take several layers of cheesecloth, rinse it in very cold water, line a colander with it, and strain the broth or bouillon through it; the fat will stay in the cheesecloth.

Miscellaneous

When *unexpected guests* arrive and you have *no dessert*, you are saved if you have a can of applesauce or some apples to make applesauce. Add to the applesauce one or two tablespoons of any fruit brandy or kirsch and two tablespoons of orange marmalade. Mix well and spoon into pretty dessert glasses. Top with whipped cream if you have some.

Another *quick dessert* is made by whipping some good vanilla or coffee ice cream with two tablespoons of good liqueur (any flavor), coffee, or brandy. Spoon into dessert glasses and top with whipped cream.

If you have a very creamy pie filling and don't want the bottom of the prebaked *pie shell* to get *soggy*, brush the shell with beaten egg white and return it to the oven for two or three minutes until the white forms a glaze. Remove from oven and cool thoroughly before adding the filling.

If the *cake sticks to the mold*, rinse a towel in very hot water (almost boiling); squeeze it — carefully! Place it immediately over the mold to cover, until the cake comes out easily.

If you need a *double boiler* but do not own one, improvise: use a bowl for the top part and place in a saucepan with a small amount of water in the bottom.

If you have used *too much vinegar in your dressing*, repair the damage by simply mixing one level tablespoon of milk and one level tablespoon of oil; stir into the dressing.

If the *frying pan smells of fish* after having been washed, cover the bottom with moist tea leaves from brewed tea and heat the pan over very low heat for a few minutes. Discard the leaves, wash and rinse the pan; the smell will be gone.

French bread which has hardened can be restored. Sprinkle it with water; wrap it tightly in a large sheet of foil; place it in a 400° oven for 5-8 minutes.

For *oversalted soup or stew*, drop in a large piece of raw potato and reheat slowly; the potato will absorb the salt.

Sauces

France has always been known for its sauces, and more than anything else they have contributed to making French cookery renowned. The repertory of French sauces is so rich that it encompasses a realm of two hundred different preparations. With its Latin roots, the South of France of course has added its own contributions to this great variety.

The word "sauce" is derived from the Latin *salsus* meaning salted. The Romans' sauces were heavily salted in order to cover up the lack of freshness of their meats or fish, for in warm climates it was difficult to keep food fresh. The Romans were using sauces as early as the first century B.C.; in 63 B.C. Apicius (see chapter on history) was making mayonnaise.

In the nineteenth century, Carême, the greatest chef of France at that time and the founder of the *Grande Cuisine*, made an art of the preparation of sauces and used a great variety of them to please the palates of kings and other famous people.

Because this book has been prepared with emphasis on simplicity, I have chosen the more traditional sauces and those most often used. Some are very southern, and all are fairly simple or very simple to prepare. Anyone with average kitchen equipment will be able to produce these delicious concoctions, which not only add flair to meals but stretch the budget as well.

Basically, French sauces can be divided into four groups:

The *emulsions* or sauces made of eggs combined with oil or butter, such as mayonnaise and its variations (aioli, etc.), Hollandaise, and Béarnaise.

The *roux*, consisting of flour and butter bound by the addition of a liquid — milk, broth, or stock. These include white sauces such as Béchamel and its variations, and brown sauces such as Madeira, Financière, etc.

The *tomato sauces* and *wine sauces*, containing wines or tomatoes, tomato concentrates, or reductions (tomato sauce, *coulis de tomate*) — Le Sauçon, Sauce Chasseur, etc.

The *regional* and *miscellaneous sauces* such as Pistou, Rouille, Beurre d'Ail, etc.

In addition to these four categories of sauces, there are the stocks or *fonds de cuisine blancs* (white) or *fonds de cuisine bruns* (brown), resulting from the slow cooking of meat, fish bones, or vegetables. These are in a class by themselves (see chapter on *Soups*), and are the culinary bases of *grande cuisine*. They take time and patience but are well worth the effort. Two steps are involved in their preparation: first the stock; second the reduction of the stock, called *demi-glace*—a sauce in itself which when reduced to extreme becomes *glace de viande* (meat glaze), a flavoring agent.

Because a sauce is an accompaniment, it should not overshadow the food it is served with. It is intended to enhance, not overpower!

EMULSIONS

Because of its versatility, mayonnaise has sometimes been called the "mother sauce." The word mayonnaise probably derives from *moyeu*, which in the Middle Ages meant egg yolk. Whatever its origin, mayonnaise is an emulsion based on egg yolks and oil, very sensitive to cold. It is therefore of the utmost importance that all the ingredients, the bowl, and the whisk be at room temperature. Do not add the oil too fast to start with; a thin thread will suffice. When the mixture starts to thicken, add the oil at a little faster pace.

Keep the sauce refrigerated if you are not going to use it right away. It will keep two or three days if you add two tablespoons of boiling white wine vinegar; the color will lighten but it will taste as good.

Sometimes due to unpredictable circumstances the mayonnaise separates. Do not panic but start with a clean bowl. Place one tablespoon of warm water in it, then whisk vigorously while adding the curdled mayonnaise little by little. When it starts to hold together, add at a faster pace; then continue with the oil if there is some left.

The principles which apply to mayonnaise apply to Hollandaise and Béarnaise sauces as well. The difference lies in the fact that the latter sauces are "cooked" emulsions, and the fat is butter instead of oil. In Béarnaise, herbs and vinegar are used. Both of these sauces are served *warm*.

Sauce Mayonnaise
Mayonnaise (Basic Recipe)

---

2 or 3 egg yolks (stringy white removed)
Dash of salt
Dash of white pepper
1 to 1½ cups vegetable oil
½ tablespoon lemon juice or vinegar

Have all ingredients and utensils at room temperature.

Place egg yolks, salt, and pepper in bowl. Beat eggs until they begin to thicken slightly; add oil, one drop at a time until the emulsion thickens. Continue adding oil in a thread-like continuous stream until you have enough mayonnaise or until the oil is used up.

MAYONNAISE VARIATIONS

L'aioli (as made by hand)
Garlic Mayonnaise

Aioli has been called the "butter of Provence." Using garlic unsparingly, it was inevitable for the people of Provence to add it to mayonnaise. The word itself is a combination of *ail* (garlic) and *oli* (oil).

This traditional pungent and delightfully creamy sauce is served on Friday all over the South, with boiled vegetables such as potatoes, carrots, artichokes, cauliflower, green beans; or cold chicken and fish, especially cod; or *escargots*. Sometimes a cooled mashed potato or a slice of bread soaked in milk and squeezed dry is added to the egg yolks in the first part of the process. This makes the *aioli* thicker and more delicious (see electric mixer mayonnaise).

As for mayonnaise, all the elements of this sauce must be at room temperature.

(Serves 4-6; makes 2½-3 cups)

*8 whole cloves garlic, peeled**
3 egg yolks
2 to 2½ cups olive oil (pure)
Pinch of salt
1 teaspoon water at room temperature

In mortar or glass mixing bowl, mash the garlic; add the egg yolks and salt. Gradually and drop by drop, add oil, stirring constantly with pestle or wooden spoon until the *aioli* is thick and shiny. Add the teaspoon water; stir once more to blend (this gives a smoother appearance to the sauce).

If it is not to be used immediately, refrigerate; but let it come back to room temperature before serving.

L'aioli (by electric mixer)
Garlic Mayonnaise

(Serves 4-6; makes about 2½ cups)

1 slice white bread
⅓ cup milk
4 garlic cloves, peeled and crushed
2 egg yolks
2 cups olive oil
Pinch of salt
1 teaspoon water at room temperature

Soak bread in milk; squeeze thoroughly and discard milk. Place bread in bowl of electric mixer; beat until smooth; add egg yolks and garlic. Start mixing at medium speed; add oil drop by drop and continue beating until mixture is thick. Add salt; taste; rectify seasoning. Add water; stir by hand to blend.

---

*As the taste for *aioli* is *acquired*, I recommend that you start with 1 clove garlic per person.

Sauce Ondine
Undine Sauce

Ondine, or undine in English, is a female water spirit, popularized in 1939 by the French writer Jean Giraudoux. What a charming name for this sauce, which is to be served with fish! The piquancy obtained from the blending of lemon, capers, and mustard goes beautifully with any cold fish such as sole, flounder, or cod.

(Makes a little less than 2 cups)

½ cup sour cream
¼ cup whipped cream
¾ cup real mayonnaise (not salad dressing)
1 heaping tablespoon Dijon mustard
1 shallot, finely minced
1 garlic clove, finely minced
1 tablespoon lemon juice
2 tablespoons finely chopped capers
Salt and pepper

Combine all the ingredients in a bowl until thoroughly blended. Cover and refrigerate at least 4 hours before using.

Sauce rémoulade
Rémoulade Sauce

(Makes about 1 cup)

1 cup mayonnaise
2 shallots, chopped fine
1 clove garlic, minced fine
5 cornichons or baby dill pickles, chopped fine
1 tablespoon parsley, minced fine
1 tablespoon capers, chopped fine
1 tablespoon fresh dill, chopped fine, or ½ teaspoon dried dill, crushed

Blend all ingredients. Refrigerate 1 hour before using. Serve with fish.

Sauce rémoulade aux anchois
Rémoulade Sauce with Anchovies

(Makes a little over 1 cup)

1 cup mayonnaise (homemade or commercial)
2 shallots, chopped fine
2 anchovy fillets, chopped
1 tablespoon capers, chopped
5 cornichons or baby dill pickles, finely chopped
1 tablespoon minced parsley
A few drops lemon juice, to taste

Blend all ingredients. Refrigerate 1 hour before using. Serve with fish.

Sauce jaune Roussillon
Yellow Sauce

(Enough for 4 servings)

Appropriately named "yellow," this sauce is not only easy to make but tastes delicious. Serve it with mousse of fish, shellfish, or vegetables. It brings the taste of fish to a new height.

¾ cup mayonnaise
½ cup whipped cream
Enough saffron to color it a rich yellow
½ teaspoon Dijon mustard
Pepper

Combine all ingredients into a bowl until blended. Cover and refrigerate until serving time.

Sauce mayonnaise à la tomate
Tomato Mayonnaise

---

1 cup mayonnaise
⅓ cup chilled tomato purée
1 teaspoon minced fresh tarragon or ¼ teaspoon dried

Combine all ingredients in a bowl until well blended. Cover and refrigerate. Serve with fish or meats.

Sauce tartare
Tartar Sauce

1½ cups mayonnaise
1 egg yolk (hard-boiled), chopped fine
1 tablespoon finely minced parsley
1 tablespoon finely minced chives or scallions
1 teaspoon finely minced fresh chervil or ¼ teaspoon dried
1 teaspoon finely minced fresh tarragon or ¼ teaspoon dried

Blend all ingredients in a bowl. Cover and refrigerate. Serve with *Fondue bourguignonne*, cold slices of leftover meats, fish, or escargots.

Mayonnaise à la moutarde
Mustard Mayonnaise

---

1 cup mayonnaise
1 teaspoon lemon juice
1½ teaspoons Dijon or De Meaux mustard

Blend all ingredients in bowl; cover and refrigerate. If sweet pimientos are added, the sauce is called *sauce andalouse*. Whipped cream may also be added to give it lightness.

Serve with cold meats, in sandwiches, or as decoration for canapés.

Sauce corail
Coral Sauce

---

1 cup mayonnaise lightened with:
   ⅓ cup whipped cream
   2 teaspoons sweet paprika
   2 teaspoons cognac
   Dash of salt and white pepper

Use with cold fish or poultry, cooled vegetable such as asparagus, or chicken salad.

Sauce verte
Green Sauce

---

1 cup mayonnaise
1 teaspoon finely minced parsley leaves (watercress may be used)
1 tablespoon finely minced fresh chives
½ tablespoon finely minced fresh tarragon, or ¼ teaspoon dried

Blend all ingredients in bowl; cover and refrigerate. Uses are the same as for *Sauce corail*.

Mayonnaise au curry
Curry Mayonnaise

---

1 cup mayonnaise
1 garlic clove, mashed
1 tablespoon olive oil
1 teaspoon curry powder
1 teaspoon Dijon mustard

Warm curry gently in oil to remove the acrid taste of the raw spice, then blend with other ingredients.

Sauce de Collioure (Roussillon)
Collioure Sauce

---

1 cup mayonnaise
1 tablespoon anchovy paste
1 teaspoon grated garlic
1 tablespoon finely minced parsley

Blend all ingredients. A good accompaniment for cold fish.

Sauce aux oursins
Urchin Sauce

This is a sauce used in Marseille, where urchins are sold and widely used.

1 cup mayonnaise
Meat of 6 urchins
Salt and white pepper

Combine ingredients. Served with fish mousse, this makes a dish fit for a king!

* * * *

Sauce hollandaise

Sauce Hollandaise is made by whisking warm butter into thickened warm egg yolks. This is done over low heat. Adding lemon juice aids in the binding of the sauce. The classic Hollandaise is whisked by hand, but it is made very successfully in a blender, food processor, or hand electric mixer. It is used with eggs, fish, seafood, veal, or vegetables.

CLASSIC HOLLANDAISE
1¼ tablespoons lemon juice
¼ cup water
¼ teaspoon salt
¼ teaspoon white pepper
Dash of nutmeg
3 egg yolks
1 cup unsalted butter, melted and warm

Mix lemon juice, water, salt, and pepper in small saucepan. Bring to a boil; lower heat to simmer and reduce liquid to two tablespoons. Cool (to speed cooling, place the pan in a large bowl of cold water).

Meanwhile, beat yolks in the top part of a stainless steel double boiler until thick, to the consistency of cream. Water in bottom pan should be simmering and top pan should not be touching it. Add lemon reduction, slowly whisking until thickened but not dry. Remove pan from heat and add warm butter in a drizzle, whisking all the while until very thick. A small amount of hot water may be added to thin the sauce if too thick to pour.

If sauce curdles or separates, remove pan from heat; add one or two tablespoons of very hot water; beat vigorously. It will thicken and become smooth again.

BLENDER HOLLANDAISE
3 egg yolks (room temperature)
1 tablespoon fresh lemon juice
⅛ teaspoon salt
⅛ teaspoon cayenne or white pepper
Dash of nutmeg
1 stick (¼ pound) unsalted butter, melted (not browned but sizzling)

Combine egg yolks, lemon juice, salt, and pepper in blender; cover, removing the center section or knob on top. Whirl five seconds. With machine still running, pour the hot butter in a drizzle into the egg mixture; sauce will thicken as you pour, it will take about 15 seconds.

Sauce béarnaise

This sauce was invented by a Parisian chef, who named it after the Béarn region in honor of Henry IV, a connoisseur of good food.

½ cup tarragon vinegar
2 shallots, chopped fine
1 tablespoon dried tarragon leaves

Reduce in small saucepan until one tablespoon is left. Cool slightly. Use this reduction in place of lemon juice in the making of your basic Hollandaise.

BÉARNAISE VARIATIONS

Sauce paloise

Fresh mint is used in place of tarragon.

Sauce arlésienne

Tomato paste and anchovy paste are added.

Sauce charon

Chopped tomatoes are added.

All of the preceding sauces—*béarnaise, paloise, arlésienne,* and *charon*—are served with grilled or sautéed fish or meat. *Paloise* is especially good on lamb.

ROUX
Sauce béchamel

This is one of the most basic of the classic French sauces, and one of great versatility also. Its discovery is attributed to Louis de Béchameil, Lord Steward of the Household of Louis XIV.

(Makes 1½ cups)

2 level tablespoons butter or 3 level tablespoons margarine
2 level tablespoons flour*
2 cups milk heated to the boiling point*
Salt (very little), white pepper

Melt butter in enamel or stainless steel pan (iron gives a bad taste) over medium heat. Stir in flour and cook, whisking, for 2 minutes. Add milk a few drops at a time, whisking vigorously, off the fire if sauce thickens too fast. Keep on stirring until sauce starts to boil. Reduce to simmer; cover and cook 10 to 12 minutes, or until thickened.

If it is not to be used immediately keep covered with a buttered round of wax paper. It keeps well in a covered jar for a day or two. Always keep refrigerated. A good base for soufflés, au gratin potatoes, *oeufs à la tripe,* etc.

BÉCHAMEL VARIATIONS
Rich sauce Mornay (for chicken, eggs, or vegetables)

---

1 egg yolk, slightly beaten
3 tablespoons heavy cream
½ cup hot Béchamel
1 tablespoon grated Swiss or Gruyère cheese
1 tablespoon grated Parmesan

---

*Proportions are for medium consistency. For thicker sauce, either decrease milk or increase flour.

Mix egg and cream; blend with hot Béchamel; cook over very low heat or in double boiler over simmering water until sauce reaches the simmering point (do not boil). Add grated cheeses and blend.

Simple sauce Mornay (for eggs and vegetables)

To 1½ cups Béchamel add:
  2 tablespoons grated Gruyère
  1 tablespoon grated Parmesan
  Dash of cayenne and nutmeg
  Few drops of lemon juice

Sauce bâtarde (for boiled meat or fish, or vegetables)

To 1½ cups Béchamel add:
  1 large egg yolk, slightly beaten
  3 tablespoons heavy cream
  1 tablespoon lemon juice
  Salt and pepper

When hot, swirl in ¼ cup unsalted butter a few pieces at a time until blended. A sprinkling of capers will add zest.

Sauce aux anchois (anchovy sauce, for fish)

Add 1 to 2 tablespoons anchovy paste to a cup of Béchamel (no salt or pepper).

Sauce poulette (for leftover chicken or veal)

Cook 6 to 8 minced mushrooms in 1 tablespoon butter; add 2 minced shallots; reduce by half. Add to ½ cup Béchamel. Add 2 egg yolks beaten with 2 tablespoons cream. Bring to boiling point. Squeeze in the juice of ½ lemon plus ½ teaspoon chopped parsley.

Sauce velouté (for leftover chicken, veal, or vegetables)

Instead of milk, use veal, chicken, or white fish stock to make
Béchamel. Add a touch of nutmeg and lemon juice.

TOMATO AND WINE SAUCES

Le coulis de tomates
Tomato Sauce

The word *coulis*, alone, evokes the sweetness of the exceptional
climate of my native land. It brings visions of tomatoes ripening on
the vines under a brilliant sun and gathering of family and friends
under the grape arbor. The beautiful aroma drifts from the busy
kitchen, announcing a large dish of *pâtes* (pasta) smothered under
this delightful sauce.

In the back country where the olive trees grow, the virgin oil
extracted from the olives gives this sauce a special flavor and
smooth texture. It would seem that tomatoes have a natural affin-
ity for olive oil; their marriage makes this a remarkable savory
sauce.

Coulis is the traditional tomato sauce of the South. It is very often
made in quantity and canned to be used in the winter months with
almost everything—pasta, meat, fish, vegetables.

(Makes 2 cups light tomato sauce or 1 cup very thick)

5 tablespoons olive oil
1½ pounds well-ripened tomatoes, skinned and quartered (do not
    seed)
3 garlic cloves, peeled
2 large fresh basil leaves or 1 teaspoon dried
1 bay leaf
2 sprigs fresh thyme or 1 teaspoon dried thyme leaves
1 sprig fresh oregano (optional) or ½ teaspoon dried oregano
    leaves (optional)
1 sprig fresh summer savory or ½ teaspoon dried summer savory
    leaves
3 sprigs parsley
Pepper, salt

Heat oil over medium-high heat in heavy saucepan; add tomatoes, garlic, basil, bay leaf, thyme, oregano, summer savory, and parsley. Bring to light boil; reduce heat; cover and simmer for 15 minutes. Remove bay leaf (save it at this point); add very little salt. Put through a food mill or a sieve; pass all juice through sieve; return to pan with bay leaf.

If you want a *light sauce*, cook 5 more minutes over medium-low heat; then remove bay leaf and discard.

If you want a very *thick sauce*, cook 35-40 minutes longer or until sauce is as thick as you want; discard bay leaf.

If sauce is not to be used immediately, cool thoroughly, place in sterilized glass jars, and cover with ¼ inch oil; keep in refrigerator (will keep well for a few days).

Le sauçon (sauce tomate au poivre de cayenne)
Quick Tomato Sauce

This recipe was given to me by an old friend of the family who came from the Roussillon region. The addition of tarragon and cayenne, odd as it may seem, gives the sauce an unusual twist and a very pleasant flavor. Use it on pasta, zucchini, or eggplant; it is not only delicious but colorful.

The Roussillon region leans toward the Catalan cuisine. Olive oil, tomatoes, red pimentos, saffron, and cayenne pepper are commonly used, but because of its location Roussillon has retained its ties with Provence and the rest of the South of France.

This sauce is not to be mistaken for a Provençal spread, the *saus-soun*, made with anchovies, fennel, almonds, mint, and olive oil.

3 large tomatoes, well-ripened, skinned, seeded, and finely chopped, or 1-pound can whole tomatoes, drained and chopped
4 tablespoons olive oil
1 garlic clove, minced fine
½ teaspoon dried tarragon leaves, crushed

1 tablespoon minced parsley
1 light pinch cayenne pepper
Salt and pepper

Heat oil over medium heat in saucepan; add tomatoes, garlic, tarragon, parsley, and cayenne pepper; cover and cook over low heat for 20 minutes. Add salt 5 minutes before end of cooking time.

Sauce ravigote chaude
Warm Pickle Sauce

Ravigoter means to revive. This sauce is deserving of its colorful name in that it brings to life any leftover pieces of meat. It is also excellent on pork chops.

(Makes about ¾ cup)

½ cup red wine vinegar
2 shallots, finely minced
A bouquet garni *(thyme, bay leaf, tarragon; see chapter on herbs)*
1 tablespoon all-purpose flour
2 tablespoons butter
¾ cup chicken or veal stock
2 egg yolks
2 cornichons (small dill pickles), chopped very fine
1 tablespoon capers, chopped very fine

Reduce the vinegar and shallots and *bouquet garni* in a stainless steel pan over medium heat, until half the liquid is left. Remove *bouquet garni* and discard. Proceed as for Béchamel: add 1 tablespoon butter and let it melt; blend in flour rapidly and whisk. Add stock slowly but beat mixture rapidly to incorporate all the elements.

Away from the heat add the egg yolks to a small amount of the sauce; return mixture to the sauce in the pan; add the leftover tablespoon of butter and cook slowly until thick. Do not let it boil. Remove from heat. Add pickles and capers immediately and serve.

Sauce chasseur
Hunter's Style Sauce

This sauce is so named because of the beautiful way it marries with game meat.

1 tablespoon butter
2 shallots, minced
¾ cup chopped mushrooms
½ cup dry white wine
2 cups coulis *sauce or tomato sauce with 1 garlic clove, mashed, 1*
*   bay leaf, and 1 teaspoon dried thyme leaves*
Salt and pepper

Melt butter in saucepan over medium heat; add shallots and mushrooms; sauté for 5 minutes until transparent. Do not let shallots brown. Add wine; cook for 10 more minutes, fairly rapidly, on medium-high heat. Add *coulis*, salt, and pepper; continue cooking over medium-low heat for 10 more minutes. Sauce should be fairly thick.

If your *coulis* sauce is too thick, add a few tablespoons of consommé or stock. And if you do not want to go to the trouble of making your own *coulis*, use a fairly thick tomato sauce with the addition of 1 garlic clove, mashed, 1 bay leaf, and 1 teaspoon dried thyme leaves.

With rabbit or hare dry red wine is often used instead of white. Sometimes vinegar is used instead of wine.

This sauce can be served over leftover roast beef or veal.

MISCELLANEOUS SAUCES

Le beurre d'ail
Garlic Butter

Garlic—the wonderful magical bulb! What would the people of the South do without it? And for that matter, what would cooking as we know it today be without its captivating flavor?

Cultivated as far back as six thousand years ago in China, it then infiltrated with its lovely aroma the world of Egyptians and the countries bordering the Mediterranean Sea.

In Rome it was a symbol of strength; in Egypt, people took oath by it. Later in France and Italy garlic was used in the belief that it would ward off the plague and leprosy. In 1720 the Marseillais, during a terrible epidemic of the plague, wore garlic necklaces to protect themselves from the disease. Unfortunately it did not seem to help the 40,000 who died. Nevertheless, modern medicine recognizes some of its therapeutic qualities, such as those which reduce high blood pressure by dilating the blood vessels, lower the serum cholesterol levels in the blood, and prevent the building of fat deposits in the arteries. What better reasons for us to enjoy the bulb of this wonderful herb!

For grilled meat, hors d'oeuvres, or French bread.

2-3 garlic cloves unpeeled
4 ounces butter at room temperature
Salt and pepper

Place enough water in small saucepan to submerge garlic completely; bring to light boil and cook for 2 minutes; drain, dry, and peel garlic.

Place garlic in mortar or bowl; mash thoroughly; add butter, salt, and pepper; mix well.

Herbs such as basil or tarragon may be added. If anchovies are added it is called *beurre d'anchois* (anchovy butter) and is used for canapés; in this case, keep refrigerated before using.

For grilled meat, simply place a pat of this butter on the hot grilled meat just before serving. For hors d'oeuvre, spread on thinly sliced bread.

Pistou
Basil Sauce

This sauce was borrowed from our neighbors the Genovese, who call it *pesto*. We in Provence call it *pistou*. Basil is the principle ingredient. This fragrant herb grows in all the gardens of Provence, and often the city housewife will grow it in a pot on her windowsill. Otherwise she can always find it fresh at the marketplace, in a place of honor among the vegetables and herbs which enter into the Provençal cuisine. Fresh basil is a "must" for the preparation of *pistou*; if you are able to grow it or find some during the summer season, this sauce can be stored for several weeks in the refrigerator or even frozen. Freeze the paste in ice-cube trays first; then remove the cubes and place them in plastic bags to keep them frozen until time to use.

This versatile sauce, redolent of summer, is used in Provence mainly as the last addition to a thick vegetable soup. It is also served on spaghetti and other pasta, *gnocchi*, and steamed vegetables. Shaved zucchini is superb with it.

2 cloves garlic, peeled
6 large leaves fresh basil
¼ cup olive oil
2 tablespoons grated Parmesan cheese
Pinch of salt

Mash garlic with pestle or fork in mortar or glass bowl. Add basil; mash again. If you do not have a pestle, use wooden spoon this time; add olive oil a small amount at a time until used up. Add cheese and salt; blend well.

La rouille
Hot Sauce

This sauce gets its name from its rusty color; *rouille* means rust. *La rouille* originated in Martigues, a small fishermen's village near Marseille. This small port has been called the "Venice of Provence" because of its location on the Mediterranean and the many canals crisscrossing it, lined with pastel-colored houses.

It was natural for the wives of the fishermen to come up with a sauce which would relieve the monotony of the daily catch of fish, and probably when they served it with *bouillabaisse* it was so perfect that a trend was born! It is always served with *bouillabaisse*.

½ *dried red pepper (or, if you are brave, a whole pepper!)*
2 *garlic cloves, peeled*
1 *slice white bread (white part only), moistened with water and squeezed out*
1 *boiled potato, mashed and cooled (from the* bouillabaisse*)*
4-5 *tablespoons olive oil*

Crush red pepper, garlic, and bread in mortar or bowl; work it until well blended. Stir in slowly, a few drops at a time, 2 tablespoons olive oil; add mashed potatoes and the remainder of the oil, drop by drop, stirring all the while, until the mixture is creamy. You may wish to lighten the sauce by adding 2 or 3 tablespoons of the bouillon from the *bouillabaisse*.

Crème fraîche
Fresh Cream

Crème fraîche is a thick and delicately sour cream, widely used in France and found in every *alimentation*, dairy-food, or grocery store. It is used in sauces, on fresh fruits, on cooked vegetables, or as a base for a vinaigrette and on tarts and pies.

The following recipe gives the best result and is a very good substitute for this delicious cream.

½ *cup sour cream at room temperature*
1 *cup heavy cream*

Warm sour cream and cream gradually to 90°F in heavy saucepan. Place in bowl warmed to room temperature. Leave in warm place (75°) overnight or until thickened (it may take two days for the cream to thicken). When thick, keep refrigerated in warmer part of refrigerator.

Sauce au citron
Lemon Sauce

Fresh lemon and its enchanting flavor work magic in this very simple sauce. Slow cooking tames its piquancy somewhat; the fennel adds an unusual touch of sweetness which blends beautifully with the lemon flavor. A perfect accompaniment for fish!

2 lemons, peeled and sliced
1 tablespoon butter
1 sprig fresh fennel, or 1 teaspoon fennel tied in 1 layer cheesecloth
Salt and pepper

Melt butter in saucepan; add lemon slices, fennel, salt and pepper. Cook, covered, over low heat for 15 minutes; remove fennel. Serve over baked fish.

Beurre maître d'hôtel
Herb Butter

This butter provides a quick way to enhance any kind of broiled meats, chops, or even boiled vegetables. Make enough of it to freeze and you will always have a supply on hand when you do not have time to prepare for an elaborate meal. As soon as your meat is broiled, place a cube or ball on the meat and let it melt; serve. If the balls or cubes are frozen, remove from wrapper, let thaw while you cook the meat or vegetable; by the time you are ready to serve, the butter will be at the right consistency.

1 cube unsalted butter at room temperature
1 tablespoon finely chopped parsley
1 tablespoon finely chopped scallion or green onion
1 teaspoon dried basil, crushed
1 teaspoon dried summer savory, crushed
¼ teaspoon lemon juice
Salt

Soften butter by working with a wooden spoon in a bowl. Add remaining ingredients; mix well. Form into balls or cubes and store in glass container; keep refrigerated or freeze wrapped in plastic.

Sauce gribiche
Gribiche Sauce

(Makes about 1½ cups)

3 yolks from hard-boiled eggs
1 tablespoon wine vinegar
1 tablespoon lemon juice
½ cup olive or vegetable oil
2 teaspoons Dijon or regular mustard
1 tablespoon finely chopped parsley
1 tablespoon finely chopped fresh tarragon, or 1½ teaspoons dried
     tarragon leaves, crushed
1 tablespoon dried chervil, crushed
1 tablespoon finely chopped capers
Salt and pepper
1 tablespoon boiling water
3 whites from hard-boiled eggs, diced small

Mash or sieve egg yolks; blend in vinegar and lemon juice. Add oil,
mustard, parsley, tarragon, chervil, capers, salt and pepper; mix
well. Add boiling water to bind the mixture; add the diced egg
whites.

Use with hot or cold fish, sautéed veal liver, veal tongue, or a
vegetable such as cauliflower or broccoli.

Crudités and Hors d'Oeuvres

In the South of France, no meal worthy of its name is started without *crudités* and *hors d'oeuvres*. These works of art appease the hungry guest or traveler and excite the appetite for the feast to come. Furthermore, it is the clever way the French furnish needed vitamins and minerals which might be bypassed if the meat or fish were served first. When one enters the home or the *auberge* there is always a thrill of anticipation when the host or hostess brings those colorful and beautifully displayed raw vegetables, arranged in compartmented dishes or small rectangular white dishes.

I will not provide the recipes for *crudités*, as the list is too long and they are as varied as the cooks who prepare them are different. I will however mention a few to give the reader an idea of what is usually served:

Red or green raw cabbage *en vinaigrette*
Grated carrots *en vinaigrette*
Cucumbers with *crème frâiche*
Tender green peppers sliced thin and served with shallots
Beets with olives *en vinaigrette*
Sweet tomatoes with basil
Vegetables blanched rapidly in boiling salted water for a few minutes, drained and refreshed under cold water and served with a vinaigrette. (Such vegetables would be cauliflower flowerets, broccoli flowerets, snow peas.)

So the list goes on and on. With the accompaniment of a meat *pâté en gelée* or a fish hors d'oeuvre, they are the prelude to a good meal.

Anchoïade pour légumes et crudités   1
Anchovy Dip for Vegetables

1 2-ounce can anchovies with or without capers
1 clove garlic, mashed
2 tablespoons lemon juice or vinegar
1 cup mayonnaise (preferably homemade)
¼ cup capers, chopped fine
Pepper

Combine all the ingredients in glass or procelain bowl. Chill and serve with crudités.

Confit de fromages   1
A Cheese Spread

In the Var region and on the farms of Haute Provence the thrifty farm wives have devised a great way to use their leftover cheeses. They grate leftover pieces as they accumulate, and mix them in a crock with Calvados or cognac, and let the mixture mellow for a week or more in the crock in a cool place.* Reduced to a purée, the spicy creamy mixture is spread on dark bread and served with vin du terroir (wine of the region). It works well with our cheeses, and will take care of the small odd pieces left in the refrigerator. A good mixture could be:

2 ounces goat cheese**
2 ounces Roquefort, blue, or Gorgonzola
2-4 ounces Gruyère, Swiss, Gouda, or a combination of these
      semi-soft cheeses
¼ cup good cognac or Calvados
Pepper (no salt)
3-4 ounces cream cheese

Grate all the cheeses except the cream cheese; add brandy and pepper. Refrigerate 2-3 days. Add cream cheese; whirl in blender. Pack in crockery jars and keep refrigerated. (It will keep for days or even weeks.) Serve on rye bread, toast, or crackers.

---

*It improves with age.
**Soft goat cheeses such as Banon, St. Marcelin, Pyramide, or Montrachet, found in specialty cheese shops and some supermarkets.

Sandwiches chauds au thon   1
Hot Tuna Canapés

---

1 can tuna drained and mashed*
¾ cup shaved Gruyère or Swiss cheese
Slices French or Italian bread

Mix tuna and cheese; blend well. Spread over bread slices and broil until golden and bubbly.

L'anchoïade   1
Anchovy Hors d'Oeuvre

L'anchoïade is also called *la bagnaroto* in Provence. It is served either spread on slices of French country bread or as a dip with *crudités.*

(Serves 4)

8 slices French bread lightly toasted in oven, on one side only
2 garlic cloves, unpeeled
Water
2 2-ounce cans anchovy fillets
¼ cup olive oil
1 teaspoon red wine vinegar or lemon juice
Freshly ground pepper

Place garlic cloves in small saucepan with cold water to barely cover; bring to boil. Remove immediately; peel and mash the pulp in mortar or bowl with pestle or wooden spoon. Drain the anchovies of their oil and rinse under cold water; pat them dry with paper towel; add them to garlic and mash to a purée. Add vinegar or lemon juice, then, slowly, the oil, mashing and turning with pestle until the mixture is homogenous.

Spread the untoasted side of bread with purée, making sure to press it into the bread. Broil for 3-5 minutes. Serve immediately.

---

*Tuna packed in water could be used.

Beurre de crustacés   1
Crab Butter (for spread)

I have sometimes used tuna meat with good results; if you do this, choose tuna packed in distilled water and adjust the salt accordingly.

1 cup crab meat, mashed
1 tablespoon capers, drained and chopped
1 tablespoon finely chopped parsley
¼ teaspoon lemon juice
4 ounces butter at room temperature
Salt and pepper

Place the first four ingredients in mortar or glass bowl, mix thoroughly; add salt, pepper, and butter; blend well until smooth.

For canapés or toast or as hors d'oeuvres. Keep refrigerated before serving.

Champignons farcis au fromage   1
Mushrooms Stuffed with Cheese

(Makes 24 hors d'oeuvres)

24 medium size mushrooms and 2 tablespoons lemon juice
1 8-ounce package cream cheese, softened
2 tablespoons vinaigrette sauce
2 teaspoons finely chopped chives or the white part of green
    onions
Capers (optional)

Wash mushrooms rapidly under cold water; wipe with soft cloth. Remove stems and reserve for other uses. Place mushroom heads in a bowl with lemon juice; toss well to coat; set aside.

Mix cream cheese, vinaigrette, chives; combine thoroughly to a smooth paste. Spoon cheese paste into mushrooms or, for more decorative effect, pipe cheese through pastry bag. Garnish with capers.

Diablotins au Roquefort   **1**
Little Devils (Roquefort Canapés)

This is one of my favorite canapés. Serve it with a Sauternes or a St. Emilion.

(Serves 3-4)

½ *cup Roquefort or blue cheese at room temperature*
½ *cup sweet butter or margarine at room temperature*
½ *cup walnut meats chopped fairly fine*
Pinch of cayenne (a light one)
Thin slices of French bread or toasted sourdough triangles

Preheat oven to 450°.

Place bread in preheated oven and crisp the bread a few minutes; remove and cool.

Combine cheese and butter in a glass or ceramic bowl; work with fork until well blended and soft. Add walnut meats and cayenne; blend again. Spread the mixture over bread slices. Serve immediately.

Hors d'oeuvre de tomates   **1**
Stuffed Tomato Hors d'Oeuvre

This is a very easy hors d'oeuvre which requires little time and effort.

4-6 firm tomatoes
Macédoine *of vegetables: carrots, peas, green beans, asparagus,*
    cauliflower, or a combination
Thick mayonnaise (commercial or homemade)
Salt

Slice top off tomatoes; gently seed them and scoop out some of the meat to make a shell. (The meat can be used later in different dishes or soups.)

Mix mayonnaise and vegetables. Fill the shells. Replace the sliced tops. Chill until serving time.

La tapenade   **2**
Caper Spread

The word *tapenade* comes from *tapeno* in Provençal, or *câpre* in French. The caper is the flower bud of a bush growing all along the Mediterranean coast, including the South of France. The best capers are usually grown in the area between Marseille and St. Tropez; the caper plants produced there bear a large bud, far superior to the small ones of other parts of the Mediterranaan coast.

The predecessor of the flavorful spread below was brought to France by the ancient Greeks, the Phocaeans, when they came to establish their bases around Massilia (now Marseille).

Very versatile, this mixture can be used as a spread on slices of rye bread, as canapés, or as a filling for tomatoes, eggs, or sliced cucumbers.

½ cup oil-cured black olives, pitted and washed, or canned black
    olives, chopped fine
½ cup well-freshened anchovies, mashed to a paste
¼ cup well-freshened capers, chopped fine
½ cup regular canned tuna, or tuna packed in water, thoroughly
    drained and mashed
1 clove garlic, mashed
1 teaspoon Dijon mustard
1-2 teaspoons olive oil (enough to moisten)

Mix all ingredients except oil in bowl; pound until mixture is homogenous (food processor may be used if given only 2 or 3 off-and-on turns). Add enough oil to moisten.

There is no need to salt this mixture; black pepper may be used.

Champignons surprise   **2**
Mushroom Surprise

Serve this pretty dish at a luncheon or as an hors d'oeuvre at the beginning of a meal. I like to use chicory leaves because of their decorative effect.

(Serves 6)

6 eggs, hard-boiled and peeled
3 small tomatoes
½ cup mayonnaise
White pepper
⅛ teaspoon salt
⅛ teaspoon paprika
Chicory lettuce leaves, coarsely chopped
Oil

Slice about 1 inch off the tapered top of the eggs; remove egg yolks carefully, without breaking the whites. Reserve one egg yolk; mash the remaining 5 and blend with mayonnaise, pepper, salt, and paprika.

Slice a little of the bottom of the egg whites to enable them to stand upright. Fill them with egg yolk mixture.

Cut tomatoes in half and gently squeeze seeds out; take a little of the meat out so that each half-tomato fits over an egg to look like the cap of a mushroom. Rub a little oil over the "caps" to give them a gloss.

Arrange chicory leaves on a serving platter; stand "mushrooms" among the lettuce leaves. Sprinkle sieved egg yolk over oiled caps. Chill until serving time. May be filled with *tapenade* mixed with a little mayonnaise to moisten.

Les artichauts à la greque   2
Artichokes Grecian Style

Coriander, one of the oldest spices on earth, is the seed of a Mediterranean plant, *cilantro*, which belongs to the parsley family. It was said to have been grown in the hanging gardens of Babylon; the Egyptians used it for medicinal purposes. Now imported mostly from France, Morocco, and Yugoslavia, it is used, whole or ground, for seasoning, by itself or combined with other herbs and spices such as in curry powder and pickling spices. The hors d'oeuvre below shows the definite influence of our neighbors the Greeks.

(Serves 4)

12 very small artichokes
Boiling salted water
Vinegar or lemon juice
1½ cups water
¼ cup olive oil
½ lemon, sliced
¼ teaspoon coriander seeds, crushed
⅛ teaspoon fennel seeds, crushed
⅛ teaspoon dried thyme leaves
1 bay leaf
Salt and pepper
1 tablespoon olive oil

Wash artichokes, remove and discard the hard outside leaves; snip off the tips of the artichokes, quarter them. Place them in an enameled saucepan filled with boiling water to which a few drops of vinegar or lemon juice has been added. Parboil for 5 minutes. Drain well and cool.

Mix water, oil, lemon slices, coriander, fennel seeds, thyme, bay leaf, salt and pepper in enameled saucepan. Bring to a boil; add artichokes; cover and simmer for ½ hour or until the artichokes are tender but not too soft. (Watch closely; the artichokes should be firm.) The sauce should be fairly thick. Spoon into a serving dish. Sprinkle olive oil over it and refrigerate. Serve chilled as hors d'oeuvre.

Caviar d'aubergines   **2**
Eggplant Caviar

This is also called poor man's caviar, but as far as I am concerned, it is better than the original!

(Serves 4-6)

4 medium-sized eggplants, unpeeled, cut in half lengthwise
2 teaspoons lemon juice
2 large fresh basil leaves, chopped fine, or ½ teaspoon dried basil
*   leaves, crumbled*
⅛ teaspoon dried thyme leaves, crumbled
3 tablespoons olive oil
Salt and pepper
Toasted French or Italian bread slices (toasted in oven)

Preheat oven to 400°.

Bake eggplants cut-side-down for 20 minutes or until tender. Be sure to watch for tenderness by pricking through the skin with a toothpick. Remove from oven and peel. Mash the meat or purée in blender. Add lemon juice, basil, thyme, olive oil, salt, and pepper. Serve on toasted bread slices or in small tomatoes hollowed out (use tomato meat for soups or sauces).

Oeufs en gelée   **3**
Jellied Eggs

(Makes 12 hors d'oeuvres)

6 hard-boiled eggs, shelled
¾ cup mayonnaise, homemade or commercial
Pinch cayenne pepper
1 tablespoon Dijon mustard
Salt
1 envelope unflavored gelatin
2 tablespoons cold water
2 tablespoons dry white wine or wine vinegar

Capers
Pitted black olives
Rye Melba toast rounds

Halve hard-boiled eggs lengthwise; scoop out yolks (reserve white); mash or press through a sieve in glass or porcelain bowl. Blend in half of mayonnaise, cayenne pepper, mustard, and salt to taste.

Fill whites of eggs with yolk mixture; chill.

Meanwhile prepare *gelée*: sprinkle gelatin over cold water in small saucepan; heat slowly over low heat until gelatin is dissolved. Add wine and blend. Remove from heat; cool slightly and blend in remaining mayonnaise.

Place egg halves on cookie sheets and spread mayonnaise-gelatin mixture over eggs. Be sure to coat eggs evenly. Garnish top with olives or capers. Chill at least 6 hours. Before serving, trim gelatin around eggs; place on toast.

Petits choux au Gruyère   3
Small Cheese Puffs

(Makes about 30 hors d'oeuvres or canapés)

½ *cup water*
⅛ *teaspoon salt*
¼ *cup butter or margarine*
½ *cup all-purpose flour*
⅓ *cup finely grated Gruyère or Swiss cheese*
3 *whole eggs*

Preheat oven to 400°.

In medium-sized saucepan bring water, salt, and butter or margarine to a boil; add flour all at once and beat vigorously with wooden spoon until the dough leaves the sides of the pan. Rapidly blend in cheese; remove from heat.

Add eggs, one at a time, beating vigorously after each addition and until mixture is smooth. Let dough cool, then refrigerate 20 minutes.

Spoon small amount into mounds, about ¾-inch around onto buttered cookie sheets, about 2 inches apart. Bake 15-20 minutes at 400°; then reduce heat to 350° and bake 5 minutes longer or until golden brown and almost crisp, not soft. Remove with spatula to wax paper or foil. Cool.

To serve, cut slit in side and fill with *brandade, tapenade*, crab butter, cream cheese with chopped walnuts, *boursin*, or your favorite canapé spread.

Les rillettes provençales   **3**
Pork Meat Spread

This French specialty is in fact a potted meat. Each region has its own recipe for it, the best known being the *Rillettes de Tour* in the Loire region of Touraine. In Languedoc it is sometimes made of goose meat. *Rillettes* made with rabbit meat can be found all over the South. The following example is based on pork and savory herbs. It makes a wonderful spread or is equally delicious in sandwiches.

(Enough for 4 small crocks)

3 pounds lean pork (shoulder, loin, or butt)
3 pounds leaf lard (pork kidney fat), cut in small pieces
1 bay leaf
½ teaspoon dried sage, crushed
½ teaspoon dried summer savory leaves, crushed
½ teaspoon dried thyme leaves, crushed
1 garlic clove, mashed
½ teaspoon salt
½ teaspoon pepper
1 cup water
4 bay leaves

Cut meat in small pieces, about 1-inch cubes; marinate overnight with herbs and garlic. Next day, add fat, salt, and pepper; place in heavy enameled pan or Dutch oven. Add water and cook covered over low heat or in 250° oven in baking casserole for 4½-5 hours or until meat is very tender. Discard bay leaf.

Drain fat and reserve. Shred meat with fork. Pack in small earthen crocks or glass cups, leaving a little space on top for the protective layer of fat. Place a bay leaf on top of meat in each crock. Reheat reserved fat and pour over meat to fill jars.

Let cool until fat is set, then cover with foil or wax paper; store in refrigerator. (*Rillettes* keep for weeks refrigerated.)

May be served on toast or crackers decorated with pitted black olives or cornichons, or (if you can afford them) chopped truffles.

The same recipe can be used for *Rillettes d'oie*—Goose *Rillettes*.

Soups

Way back in the Middle Ages, meats, domestic or wild, were boiled in a cauldron over an open fire, and the bouillon was discarded. In all probability a discerning cook found this bouillon tasty and ventured to add some herbs or vegetables or both, and the result was soup, on its way to fame and fortune. Soup soon became the main element of the meal as served in roadside country inns to appease the hunger of the weary traveler and restore his energy. These rich and healthful concoctions cooked over a wood fire were eaten accompanied by huge slices of wholesome bread.

Through times of crisis—of which France has had her share and more—soups have often been the salvation of the people. Everything available went into the soup pot. Flavored with herbs when meat was scarce or unavailable, a good thick soup was filling as well as pleasing to the palate.

In France soups still play a prominent role, especially in the evening meals. Furthermore, they offer a great way for the creative and thrifty cook or housewife to make use of leftovers. On a cold wintry day, what better way to welcome the family than to place in front of them a beautiful, fragrant, steamy bowl of soup!

On the other hand, chilled creamy *potages* or soups in the summer months are very refreshing. They require little or no cooking, and now that we are blessed with such gadgets as the blender, cooking time can be minimized, conserving not only energy but precious vitamins and flavor as well. Even with a simple food mill one can turn out smooth, wonderful soups.

Soups' versatility lends them to many uses. They can be the main course of a meal: such soups are *pot-au-feu* and *bouillabaisses*. They can be served at the beginning of the meal to replace hors d'oeuvres, or at the end as a dessert—fruit soups enter into this category.

Meat stocks such as beef, veal, chicken, or a blend of these three make excellent bases for most soups; however, delicious soups are also made without these, a fact which appeals to vegetarians.

It is appropriate in this chapter to differentiate among the words soup, *potage*, and bisque:

Soups are liquid preparations using a liquid such as broth, milk, or water as a base and in which various ingredients such as vegetables, fish, meat, pasta, or cereals are cooked. In this category we should include bouillons and consommés.

Potages are soups based on purées or creamed preparations (*veloutés*).

Bisques are soups made of shellfish purées. (However, before the nineteenth century poultry and game entered into the preparation of bisques; these were very spicy and considered to be therapeutic and, given to invalids, had a reputation comparable to our famed chicken soup.)

The Provençal people say, "Good lodging, good bread, good soups, heady wines, warm friendship—what more do you want to make life beautiful!" This epitomizes the philosophy of the South.

An excellent soup can be made without stock, as you will see in this chapter. However, an *outstanding* soup starts with a good stock. When you make a stock, it is a good idea to make plenty and freeze it for later use.

The leek is an essential vegetable of the Provençal housewife; it gives a special rich flavor to the broth. When she goes to the marketplace she finds small packages ready to use for her stock, consisting not only of leeks but also of celery stalks, carrots, and parsley.

Rinsing the meat, bones, or chicken before you place it in the pot helps reduce the amount of skimming you will need to do later.

BASIC STOCKS

Bouillon de base au boeuf ou au veau
Beef or Veal Stock or Broth

---

4 pounds beef or veal bones, veal knuckles, skin of beef, marrow bones—one or a combination of several (a pig's foot added to the pot gives a very special and delicious flavor, if you are fortunate enough to find one)
Hot water to cover by 2 inches
2 cloves garlic, peeled
2 bay leaves
½ teaspoon dried thyme leaves

10 peppercorns
2 large onions (skin left on)
3 whole cloves
2 large carrots, pared and quartered
1 large turnip, pared and quartered
1 leek, if possible—white part and some of the light green leaves,
 thoroughly cleaned
2 stalks celery, with leaves

Preheat oven to 400°.

For more versatility when used with other recipes, do not salt or salt only very lightly.

Rinse bones under cold water; pat them dry; place them on a large lightly oiled baking sheet and bake for 40 minutes at 400°, turning once or twice.

Place bones in a large soup pot or heavy kettle; add water. Discard melted fat from the baking sheet but add the brown bits clinging to the bottom by scraping lightly and washing them down with a little hot water. Bring to a boil over medium-high heat; add ¼ cup cold water to bring the scummy matter to the surface. Skim thoroughly. Add the rest of the vegetables and herbs. Bring to just the boiling point; cover kettle loosely to permit steam to escape; reduce to a simmer and cook for 6 hours at least.

Strain through several layers of cheesecloth over a colander placed in a large bowl. Refrigerate, then skim the fat from the surface. Stock may be left in the refrigerator 4-5 days; frozen, it keeps up to 5 months.

The further reducing of the stock over a period of several more hours will produce a syrupy stock called *demi-glace*. If reduced longer (to about ⅓ the volume of the *demi-glace*), it becomes *glace de viande*.

Bouillon de base au poulet
Chicken Stock or Broth (using the whole chicken)

---

3 large carrots, cleaned but not peeled

3 onions (yellow or white) or 2 onions and the white of 1 leek
1 garlic clove, peeled
1 stalk celery with leaves
3 large sprigs parsley
1 large bay leaf
1 teaspoon dried thyme leaves
8 peppercorns
1 4-pound chicken, trussed (tied) and rinsed under cold water
½ teaspoon salt *
Enough water to cover

Place chicken in large kettle; place herbs and condiments in a piece of muslin and tie securely; add to the chicken with vegetables; add salt and water. Bring to a hard boil. Immediately add ¼ cup cold water (this brings the scummy matter to the surface); skim thoroughly. Reduce heat to low; cover loosely and cook for 2½ hours.

Remove chicken and use it later for a meal. Strain the stock; remove fat with paper toweling or paper napkin; or store in refrigerator and when fat has hardened, skim. Reduce stock by boiling another 10 minutes.

Soupe à l'oignon   1
Onion Soup (traditional French)

(Serves 4-6)

6 large onions, sliced thin
4 tablespoons butter or margarine
5 cups beef stock or broth
1 cup warm milk or cream
Salt and pepper
1 cup Gruyère or Swiss cheese, grated
4-6 slices French or Italian bread

---

* Stock can also be made with leftover chicken bones for a base to use in all sorts of soups. In this case do not add salt to the pot.

Sauté onion in fat over medium heat in large saucepan until deep golden in color, about 20-25 minutes. Add stock. Bring to light boil; reduce heat to simmer; cover and cook for 30 minutes. Add warm milk or cream; bring back slowly to medium-high heat. Remove from heat when steaming hot. Pour into individual oven-proof soup casseroles or bowls. Place bread slices on top; sprinkle with cheese and broil until cheese starts to melt and bubble. Serve immediately.

Crème de tomate   1
Cream of Tomato (hot or chilled)

Because it is so difficult, especially in the winter, to find fully ripened tomatoes, I use cherry tomatoes and find that they impart a better flavor. With the cherry type, instead of whirling the soup in a blender, purée it through a food mill; this leaves the skin behind.

(Serves 4)

1 tablespoon butter or margarine
1 medium-sized onion, chopped coarsely
1 pound cherry tomatoes, washed and stemmed, or regular to-
    matoes skinned and cut up
2 cups celery stalks and leaves, chopped coarsely
2 large sprigs fresh tarragon, snipped, or 1 tablespoon dry tarra-
    gon leaves, crushed
2 cups chicken broth or stock
Pepper
Salt if needed
4 lemon slices sprinkled with finely chopped parsley

Melt butter in large saucepan, add onion; sauté over medium heat until soft and golden. Add tomatoes, celery, tarragon, broth, and pepper to taste. Bring to light boil; cover; reduce heat to simmer and cook 15-20 minutes or until celery is tender. Whirl in blender or purée through food mill; return to saucepan to reheat if it is to be served hot; rectify seasoning. Ladle into individual bowls; float parsleyed lemon slices on top.

If it is to be served chilled, place in refrigerator at least 4 hours.

Aigo-boulido (eau bouillie)   **1**
Herb Bouillon

"L'aigo-boulido sauvo la vido" (*"aigo-boulido* saves life") is an old saying in Provence, referring to this delicious bouillon. This very old recipe was said to be therapeutic for fragile stomachs. It has an unusual and refreshing flavor. You will find it just right on cold days or when recovering from a cold.

(Serves 4)

6 cups water
3 garlic cloves, mashed
2 bay leaves
2 sprigs fresh sage or 1 teaspoon dried sage leaves
2 sprigs fresh fennel or 1 teaspoon dried fennel
2 pieces orange peel 1½ inches in length
3 cloves
Salt and pepper
3 tablespoons olive oil
2 cups shaved Gruyère or Swiss, or grated Parmesan cheese
8 slices day-old French or sourdough bread

Bring water to light boil in a saucepan or soup kettle; add next 6 ingredients. Bring back to light boil and continue cooking for 8 minutes. Remove from fire, cover and let stand 3 more minutes. Strain; add salt and pepper. Reheat; add olive oil. Ladle onto slices of bread smothered with cheese.

Aigo-boulido aux oeufs pochés   **1**
Aigo-Boulido *with Poached Eggs*

Poach 4 eggs in hot strained bouillon before serving. Remove eggs with slotted spoon and place them on bread slices. Add olive oil to bouillon; ladle over eggs and serve with cheese.

Crème de courgettes   1
Cream of Zucchini Soup (hot or chilled)

If you serve this cream soup without the rice, it can be served at the beginning of an elegant meal.

(Serves 4-6)

1 large onion, skinned and coarsely chopped
1½ tablespoons butter or margarine
3-4 medium-sized zucchini (about 1½ pounds), cubed; do not peel
2 large fresh basil leaves, or 1 teaspoon dried basil leaves
1 clove garlic, peeled
½ teaspoon curry powder
Pepper
1¾ cups chicken broth or bouillon
1 cup cooked rice (optional)
½ cup light cream or milk
Salt
1 tablespoon butter or margarine

Sauté onion in butter or margarine in soup kettle or large saucepan over medium heat until soft and transparent, about 5 minutes. Add zucchini and give it a few turns; add basil, garlic, curry, pepper, and broth. Bring to light boil; reduce to simmer; cover and cook 12 to 15 minutes or until tender.

Pour into blender container and purée or sieve through food mill. Return to pan. Add cooked rice and salt. Or if you want a more elegant *potage*, omit rice but add cream and salt to taste. Reheat slowly; add butter and serve.

To serve chilled, omit rice and butter; chill in refrigerator until ready to serve.

Crème de navet   1
Cream of Turnip Soup

This soup is so good you will want to make it often.

(Serves 4-5)

1 medium-sized onion, coarsely chopped
2 tablespoons butter or margarine
1½ pounds turnips, pared and diced
1 large carrot, cleaned and diced
2 scant cups chicken broth or beef broth
1 bay leaf
¼ teaspoon dry thyme leaves
⅛ teaspoon paprika
Salt and pepper
½ cup light cream or milk

Sauté onion in butter in soup kettle or saucepan over medium heat until transparent. Add turnips, carrot, broth, bay leaf, thyme, paprika, salt, and pepper to taste. Bring to light boil, reduce heat to low and cook covered 20-25 minutes or until vegetables are tender. Discard bay leaf.

Whirl soup in blender until smooth, or purée through a food mill. Add cream or milk gradually. Reheat and serve.

Soupe aux pois chiches   1
Chickpea Soup

The *pois chiche*, as it is called in France, garbanzo bean or chickpea as it is known here, is used extensively in the cuisine of the South. It has always been a favorite of the Latin countries of Europe and South America. From the leguminous family, the round bean is very nourishing because like all other beans it is rich in protein, iron, and B vitamins, but low in fat.

One of its many uses is in soups, and a favorite of mine is this *Soupe aux pois chiches*. However, if you make it often, as I do, it is quite a job to start it from scratch. I would advise you to keep a can or two on hand for use when you are in a hurry. If you prefer to make it from scratch by cooking the dry chickpeas, refer to the recipe for *Soupe de pois chiche et d'épinards*.

(Serves 4)

1 leek top (the white part), cleaned and chopped
1 tablespoon butter or margarine
1 can (1¼ pounds) chickpeas drained of liquid and refreshed
    under cold water
2½ cups warm water
1 teaspoon dry marjoram leaves, crushed
Salt and pepper
1 tablespoon butter (optional)
Fried croutons

Sauté leek in butter or margarine in large saucepan over medium heat until soft and transparent. Add chickpeas, warm water, marjoram, salt and pepper to taste. Bring to a light boil; reduce heat to medium-low; cook loosely covered until beans are soft, about 10-15 minutes. Sieve through food mill or whirl in blender. Return to saucepan; heat again; just before serving add butter (optional) and blend. Serve with fried croutons.

Soupe de potiron   1
Pumpkin Soup (hot or chilled)

Le potiron is the French name for pumpkin. This recipe represents a perfect soup for using up the Halloween pumpkin.

(Serves 4-6)

3 leeks (white only), chopped
2 tablespoons butter or margarine
4 cups pumpkin, pared, seeded, and cubed
1 medium-sized potato, pared and cubed
1 stalk celery, sliced
2 whole cloves, tied in a piece of muslin
3 cups hot water
Salt and pepper
½-¾ cup milk, cream, or half-and-half
1 tablespoon butter
Croutons (optional)

Sauté leeks in butter or margarine in a soup kettle or large saucepan over medium heat until soft and golden. Add pumpkin,
potatoes, cloves, celery, water, salt, and pepper. Bring to a light
boil; reduce heat to low; cover and cook 15-20 minutes. Remove
cloves and discard.

Sieve or whirl in blender to purée. Return to pan; add milk or
cream. Heat through; add butter and serve, sprinkled with
croutons if desired.

If served chilled, omit butter; chill until ready to serve — at least 4
hours. Serve topped with *crème fraîche* or sour cream.

Bouillon rafraîchissant   **2**
Refreshing Bouillon

The watercress gives this soup a slightly piquant flavor, which
makes it as the name indicates—very refreshing.

(Serves 4)

½ pound veal shanks
2 quarts water
1 leek, cleaned, trimmed, and cut up
1 small Bibb, Boston, or iceberg lettuce, cut up
1 bunch watercress, cleaned, trimmed
2 medium-sized carrots, scrubbed and sliced
2 small turnips, pared and cubed
½ cup fresh asparagus tips (in season)
Salt

Place veal shanks in a large saucepan or soup kettle; add water.
Bring to a boil, skim off scum; return to boil; add 1 tablespoon cold
water; skim off scum again. Cover loosely and simmer gently over
low heat for 1 hour. Add vegetables; salt lightly; return to simmer
and cook until vegetables are tender. Remove veal shanks and put
soup through a sieve or whirl in blender.

Remove meat from bones; cut up in small pieces and add to
bouillon.

Soupe de pois chiches et d'épinards   **3**
Spinach-Chickpea Soup

(Serves 4)

1 cup cooked chickpeas, canned or home-cooked ·
6 cups water (part of which may be water used to cook chickpeas)
1 cup fresh spinach, cooked, squeezed, and chopped, or 1 package
*   (10 ounces) frozen chopped spinach, squeezed*
4 tablespoons olive oil
2 egg yolks, slightly beaten
Salt and pepper
8 slices French or Italian bread

If canned peas are used, rinse under cold running water for a few seconds and place in large saucepan or soup kettle; add water and salt. Bring to a simmer and continue simmering for 10 minutes.

If dried peas are used, cook them according to directions below·; then add cooking liquid to enough water to make 6 cups. Do not add salt until the very last and only after testing soup. Add spinach to peas and simmer for 10 more minutes. Mash the chickpeas against the sides of the pan with a fork, or mash them in a large spoon or ladle. Add 2 tablespoons olive oil, pepper, and salt if necessary. Reheat to simmer; pour a small amount of the bouillon into the egg yolks, stir until blended, and return to kettle. Mix well; reheat and serve over slices of bread drizzled with remaining olive oil.

·To cook dried chickpeas: soak them overnight in lukewarm water to which 1 tablespoon salt has been added. Next day drain well, add fresh, cold water to cover by 1-1½ inches in which 2 tablespoons flour and ⅛ teaspoon salt have been added. Bring to boil, turn heat to medium-low and cook for 1 hour. Drain; add the same amount of rapidly boiling water and ⅛ teaspoon salt; continue cooking until tender. Do not discard this last water, as it will be used in the above recipe.

Soupe au sarrasin   1
Buckwheat Soup

High above my grandmother's village in the Provençal Alps is a fairly desolate region where few people used to live because of its isolation in the cold winter months. Those hardy men and women raised a few cows and some sheep and grew wheat and other grains in small patches of soil reclaimed from the rocky mountainsides. When the cols or passes were closed by snow and they could not get to the villages below, they had to survive for days at a time with the food they had been able to store.

They seem to have thrived on this diet, but the young, attracted by the cities, have now left the region and the little houses are silent. Nevertheless, some of the hearty cooking has been preserved, and here is one of the recipes.

This particular soup would make a good, substantial breakfast. Substitute butter for oil in the first part of the recipe, and serve with regular or brown sugar.

(Serves 4)

1 cup buckwheat
3 tablespoons oil or olive oil
2 cups hot water
Salt
1 tablespoon butter
4 cups warm milk or cream
Sugar or honey (optional)

Stir buckwheat and oil in heavy saucepan over medium-high heat until golden brown. Transfer to an ovenproof casserole; add water, salt, and butter. Bring to a boil, then cover tightly and bake at 400° for 1 hour. Remove lid (watch for steam); stir thoroughly, replace in oven and turn down to 250° until water is absorbed and grains are soft.

Serve with cream or milk.

Potage au cerfeuil 1
Chervil Soup

This soup can only be made with fresh chervil, but it is so deliciously different that I had to include it in this book. If you grow your own, you are in luck.

(Serves 3-4)

1 large shallot, chopped, or 2 tablespoons chopped green onion
    (white part only)
1 tablespoon butter or margarine
1 pound potatoes, peeled and cut into 1-inch cubes
⅔ cup tightly packed fresh chervil leaves
3 fresh basil leaves, or ½ teaspoon dry basil leaves
2¼ cups warm chicken bouillon or broth
Pepper
Salt if needed
1 tablespoon butter or margarine

Sauté shallot or green onion tops in butter or margarine in a large saucepan over medium heat until soft and transparent. Add potatoes, chervil, basil, bouillon or broth, and pepper. Bring to a boil; lower heat to simmer; cover and cook 15 minutes. Sieve through food mill or blend in electric blender (not too long—just 1 minute will be sufficient). Return to saucepan and heat slowly again.

Add salt if necessary. Just before serving blend in 1 tablespoon butter or margarine.

Soupe à la sartan 1
Frying Pan Soup

Sartan is the Provençal name for the frying pan. This soup is fragrant with herbs and can easily rival the famed onion soup. Very Provençal, it is also therapeutic: garlic is reputed to clear the blood of cholesterol; thyme is a stomachic, tonic, and stimulant; marjoram cleanses the system of impurities.

(Serves 4)

3 medium-sized onions, sliced
4 medium-sized ripe tomatoes, seeded and chopped coarsely
4 tablespoons olive oil
2-3 garlic cloves, mashed
1 bay leaf
1 teaspoon dried thyme, crumbled
¾ teaspoon dried leaf marjoram, crumbled
Salt and pepper
8 cups hot water
8 slices French or Italian bread, toasted in oven
¾ cup grated Gruyère, Swiss, or Parmesan cheese

Sauté onions in olive oil in a large skillet, saucepan, or soup kettle over low heat until deep golden; add tomatoes and cook five minutes longer. Add garlic, bay leaf, thyme, marjoram, salt and pepper, and water. Bring to light boil; reduce heat to medium-low and cook, covered, for 10-15 minutes. Put through a food mill or squeeze through a sieve. Reheat slowly to boiling point and pour over bread slices in individual serving bowls. Sprinkle with cheese.

Soupe de cébettes et de poireaux   1
Green Onion and Leek Soup

This soup provides a way to utilize the green part of green onions—the part which is usually discarded, but which is full of vitamins.

(Serves 4-5)

1 large leek top (white part) chopped coarsely
1 cup coarsely chopped green onion leaves or leaves and tops
2 pounds potatoes, peeled and cubed
1½ quarts water
Salt and pepper
2 tablespoons butter or margarine divided in as many pieces as
    there are persons to be served

Place leek, green onion, potatoes, water, salt and pepper to taste in a large saucepan. Bring to a boil; reduce heat to medium-low; cover loosely and cook 15-20 minutes or until potatoes are tender.

Rice through a food mill or whirl in a blender until smooth (do not whirl too long if you purée it in a blender). Ladle into individual soup bowls and place a piece of butter in each bowl of soup. Let each person blend his own butter with the soup.

Potage purée d'oseilles   1
Soup of Puréed Sorrel

Sorrel has long been a favorite of the chefs and housewives of Europe, especially in France, where it is used in soups, in sauces, and as an accompaniment for fish, meats, and the young leaves in salads. Rich in vitamins, this vegetable of the rhubarb family has a slightly sour taste which makes it an appetite stimulant. (The word for *oseille* in Provençal is *eigreto*—very descriptive as it is a derivative of *aigre*, sour.) In fact, in thirteenth century England sorrel was considered an herb.

Cook this vegetable in a stainless steel or enameled pan because, like spinach, it has a high oxalic-acid content.

If you are unable to find sorrel, substitute Swiss chard leaves or spinach.

(Serves 4)

2 tablespoons butter or margarine
1 leek top (white part), chopped coarsely
1 medium-sized onion, chopped coarsely
8 ounces or 4 cups tightly packed chopped sorrel or Swiss chard, washed and dried
1 medium-sized turnip, peeled and cubed
½ pound potatoes, peeled and cubed
4 cups hot water
1 teaspoon dry marjoram leaves, crushed
Salt and pepper
2 tablespoons butter or ½ cup sour cream
4 thick slices lemon

In a 3-quart saucepan melt butter or margarine over medium heat; add leek and onion; sauté until light brown. Add Swiss chard and stir about 2-3 minutes to wilt it; add turnip, potatoes, hot water, marjoram, salt and pepper to taste. Bring to a boil; reduce heat to simmer; cover and cook 15-20 minutes or until potatoes are tender. Sieve through food mill or whirl in blender (do not overwhirl).

In winter serve hot; add a chunk of butter to each individual soup bowl. In summer serve chilled; add a tablespoon sour cream to each individual soup bowl. Each guest should squeeze a few drops of lemon juice over soup.

Soupe à l'ail   3
Garlic Soup

(Serves 2-3)

6 tablespoons olive oil
1 head garlic (about 12 cloves, peeled)
3 cups meat broth or stock (beef or chicken), warmed
⅛ teaspoon nutmeg
Salt and pepper
3 egg yolks
4-6 slices toasted French or Italian bread

"Melt" the garlic by cooking it slowly over very low heat in 3 tablespoons of the oil in heavy saucepan; garlic should be soft but not brown (watch closely as garlic does brown easily).

Pour warmed meat broth over garlic; add nutmeg, salt, and pepper to taste; bring to gentle boil; reduce heat to simmer; cover and cook 20 minutes.

Pour into blender and whirl until smooth; return to pan.

Place egg yolks in a bowl and beat lightly. Beat a small amount of warm soup into egg yolks and blend.* Return the egg mixture slowly to the soup in the pan, stirring constantly; heat slowly.

---

*The egg whites may be poached in the soup at the end of cooking time.

When hot, pour over bread slices in soup tureen or individual bowls.

If the garlic as prescribed seems excessive, blanch it, with skin on, in boiling water to cover, 3 minutes; then peel and use as in above recipe.

Potage d'épinards florentine   2
Cream of Spinach Soup Florentine (hot or chilled)

When cooking vegetables high in acid, such as spinach, always use a stainless steel or enameled pan.

(Serves 6)

1¼ pounds fresh spinach or 2 10-ounce packages frozen spinach
2 tablespoons butter or margarine
1 medium-sized onion, chopped coarsely, or ½ cup chopped shallots
4 level tablespoons flour
2½ cups chicken broth or bouillon
¼ teaspoon nutmeg
Dash of mace
Salt and pepper
1 cup light cream or milk

If you use fresh spinach, cook in boiling water to cover for 5 minutes. Drain well. If you use frozen spinach, cook according to package directions, and drain.

Sauté onion or shallot in butter or margarine in a large saucepan over medium heat until soft and transparent. Blend in flour; add broth or bouillon slowly, stirring constantly. Add spinach, nutmeg, mace, salt, and pepper; cook 5 minutes or until soup thickens, stirring occasionally.

Pour into a blender and whirl until smooth, or sieve through a food mill. Return to saucepan; blend in cream or milk and reheat slowly.

If served chilled, place in refrigerator at least 3 hours.

Potage de cresson   1
Watercress Soup (hot or chilled)

Watercress is the best known of a variety of cresses, and is the one frequently used in cooking. It grows abundantly along streams and near ponds in North America and Europe. I remember being sent by my grandmother to pick it near her house where a pretty little slow stream ran and garlands of this peppery green would grow. The fresh, piquant flavor and the lovely leaves of watercress make any salad more interesting, and soups made from it are superb.

In ancient times many qualities were attributed to this aromatic herb, such as giving strength to men, promoting growth, and helping anemic children. Our ancestors with their well-developed instincts probably sensed that this herb had a high content of some element needed by the body; this element is iron.

Try this *potage*; it is not only good but good for you!

(Serves 4-5)

2 pounds potatoes, pared and cubed
1 onion, coarsely chopped
1 handful green Swiss chard or spinach, coarsely chopped
2 cups water
2 bunches watercress, washed and roughly cut up
Salt and white pepper
1 tablespoon butter
½ cup cream

Bring water, potatoes, onion, Swiss chard or spinach to a boil in a heavy saucepan. Reduce heat to medium and cook until potatoes are barely soft. Do not overcook. Add watercress, salt and pepper, and cook 5 minutes longer. Remove from fire. Put through a sieve (preferably) or whirl in blender. Return to pan and reheat slowly. Add butter, stir until melted; add cream. Add salt if needed. Serve.

To serve chilled, omit butter, add cream, and place in refrigerator until well chilled—at least 3 hours.

Pain cuit   **2**
Bread Crumb Soup

Another fine way to use leftover bread.

(Serves 3-4)

1½ cups fine dried bread crumbs
2 whole eggs, beaten
½ cup grated Parmesan cheese
4 cups hot beef broth
1 teaspoon olive oil
Pinch of nutmeg
Pepper and salt

Add bread crumbs to eggs; mix in Parmesan. Gradually pour hot beef broth into mixture. Add olive oil, nutmeg, and pepper. Cook on medium-low heat until thickened. Add salt if necessary.

Serve piping hot.

Crème de poireaux à l'ancienne   **2**
Old-Fashioned Cream of Leek Soup

My grandmother, being thrifty and creative, as were her contemporaries, refused to throw anything away. This is one way she used the leftover bread.

Do not let the simplicity of this recipe deceive you. This soup is one of the creamiest and most delicious you can make.

(Serves 4)

1 cup dry bread (French or Italian preferable) with crust, broken in
*   small pieces*
½ cup milk
3-4 leeks, white tops only, coarsely chopped (about 2 cups tightly
*   packed; save green part of leeks to add to vegetable soups)*
3 tablespoons butter or margarine

2½ cups hot water
Salt and pepper
2 egg yolks slightly beaten
½ cup light cream

Soak bread in milk until it has absorbed all the milk. Set aside.

Melt butter or margarine in large saucepan. Add leeks and sauté
over medium-low heat until soft and transparent. Do not let them
color. Add hot water and cook over medium-low for 5 minutes.
Add bread and milk mixture, salt and pepper to taste; bring to light
boil; turn heat down to simmer, cover and cook for 20 minutes.

Whirl soup in blender until smooth or purée through food mill.
Return to saucepan; reheat slowly over low heat.

Meanwhile blend eggs and cream; add slowly to the soup, stirring
constantly. Cook over medium heat, stirring often until thickened. Serve immediately.

Potage de laitue   2
Lettuce Soup

"Never throw anything away!" This motto, ingrained in us by the
mothers of my generation, has more significance than ever in these
days of high food costs. With this in mind, what better way to use
the coarse outer leaves of lettuce! This soup is not only economical but delicious. Your family and guests will not even recognize
the humble ingredient.

(Serves 4)

2 tablespoons butter or margarine
1 medium-sized onion, coarsely chopped
1 tablespoon flour
1 cup chicken stock or broth
6 cups tightly packed shredded lettuce (of one kind or mixed)
1 cup hot milk or light cream
1 egg yolk, lightly beaten
Salt and pepper

Sauté onion in fat in saucepan until soft and transparent. Stir in flour, then add broth gradually and cook over medium heat until slightly thickened, stirring constantly. Add lettuce, mix well with the liquid; cover and simmer for 5 minutes or until lettuce is wilted and limp. Add hot milk or cream. Whirl in blender until smooth, or purée through food mill. Return to saucepan.

Stir some of the soup into the egg yolk until smooth; return this to the soup. Blend well; add salt and pepper to taste. Reheat slowly on medium to medium-high heat, stirring until steaming hot and thickened, about 5 minutes. May be chilled, too.

Consommé   **2**
Consommé (hot or chilled)

This consommé makes a delicious base for soups.

2 pounds lean beef
2 large carrots, scrubbed
1 medium-sized onion, minced
1 clove
1 bay leaf
1 egg white
3½ quarts clarified beef stock
Salt and pepper

Combine meat, carrots, onion, bay leaf, clove, egg white, beef stock, and salt and pepper to taste in large kettle. Bring to light boil; watch carefully and stir often. Reduce heat to simmer and cook uncovered for 1½ hours.

Strain through cheesecloth in large bowl. Add salt and pepper to taste.

Serve hot, or chilled until firm.

This consommé can be made with chicken or veal. Use chicken or veal meat *and* stock instead of beef.

Soupe de choux-fleurs
Cauliflower Soup

2

The cauliflower, or *choux-fleur* (flowering cabbage) is a vegetable of oriental origin from the cabbage family. It is rich in vitamins (with more vitamin C than oranges) and mineral salts. The leaves are a particularly rich source of vitamins and minerals; for this reason I always add some of the most tender leaves left around the "curd" (flower) to my soup.

When buying a head of cauliflower, choose a compact head, white, firm and unspotted, with fresh green or light green leaves; this will mean a good quality product with the nutrients still there.

(Serves 4)

½ cup onion, coarsely chopped
1 tablespoon butter or margarine
2½ cups tightly packed and chopped cauliflower flowerets (include the very tender leaves surrounding flowerets)
3 cups warm milk
1 level tablespoon all-purpose flour
1 tablespoon butter or margarine
½ cup grated Swiss or Gruyère cheese
Salt and pepper

Sauté onion in butter or margarine in large saucepan over medium heat until soft and transparent. Add cauliflower flowerets and stir; add warm milk; bring to a very light boil (watch; milk has a tendency to boil over); reduce heat to low and let simmer gently, *partly covered*, 25-30 minutes or until cauliflower is tender. Keep warm.

Melt remaining tablespoon butter in small saucepan; blend in flour; pour in small amount of the hot soup mixture; stir to blend and return to soup in saucepan. Blend again and cook over medium heat, stirring constantly until soup thickens lightly, about 3-4 minutes.

Remove saucepan from heat; add cheese and stir until cheese is melted. Serve immediately.

Soupe fermière
Farmer's Soup
2

A healthful and nourishing soup is a welcome sight when it is cold outside. This one fits the bill.

(Serves 4)

1 small Swiss cabbage (preferable) or regular cabbage
8 cups chicken broth, homemade or canned
3 tablespoons butter or margarine
1 large onion studded with cloves
2 stalks celery with leaves, diced
1 cup turnip, pared and diced
1 cup carrot, scrubbed and diced
2 cups potatoes, pared and diced
1 cup fresh or frozen green beans, slightly thawed
Pepper
½ cup uncooked long-grain rice
Salt
¼ cup parsley, minced

Wash cabbage, remove coarse exterior leaves and stem. Cut in 4 wedges. Blanch for 5 minutes in boiling salted water. Freshen immediately in cold water. Squeeze out as much water as possible. Shred or chop coarsely and set aside.

Sauté celery, turnip, carrot and potatoes in butter. Add green beans, broth, onion, cabbage, and pepper. Bring to a light boil, then reduce to medium-high heat and cook for 20 minutes. Remove onion and clove. Add frozen green beans and bring back to light boil. Add rice, salt; cook 15-20 minutes covered on low heat or until rice is tender. Serve with parsley.

Soupe aux châtaignes
Chestnut Soup
2

The aroma of roasting chestnuts drifting through the cool autumn air is one of the many fond memories of my youth in Marseille. In October on the famous Canebiere, the main avenue of my hometown, the chestnut vendors and their small carts would suddenly appear, heralding the coming of winter.

The nut of the majestic tree immortalized by Longfellow grows all over Europe and on this side of the Atlantic as well. In Europe, the chestnut has long been used in a variety of ways. Its versatility and its high protein content make the beautiful mahogany-colored nut a great staple. In France, and especially in the South, it is used in purées, in soups, and is braised as a vegetable to accompany fowl such as turkey or goose. But it is perhaps at its most glorious when served in desserts or jams or when it is candied.

The following soup, which is my version of a soup prepared in the Dauphiné region, is indeed different, but so delicious you will agree it should be classified among the great soups!

(Serves 4-5)

1 15-ounce can whole chestnuts or the equivalent in fresh-cooked
    chestnuts *
1 medium-sized onion, chopped coarsely
2 tablespoons butter or margarine
1 garlic clove, minced
1 leek top (white part), minced
1 large carrot, scrubbed and cubed
Salt and pepper
3 cups hot water
⅔ cup light cream or whole milk

Drain chestnuts of their liquid; rinse under running cold water. Drain and set aside.

Sauté onion in butter or margarine in a large saucepan over medium heat until soft and transparent. Add garlic and leek; sauté 1 minute longer; add carrot, salt and pepper to taste, and hot water; bring to light boil; cover and turn heat down to low; cook 30 minutes.

Purée or sieve mixture through food mill or in blender. Return to saucepan; add cream or milk; reheat slowly. Serve as is or with croutons frits.

---

* To cook fresh chestnuts: shell and peel (as well as possible) 2 pounds chestnuts; place in heavy saucepan with 2 cups water and 1 cup milk; add small amount of salt. Bring slowly to light boil; cook, bubbling gently, for 1 hour or until soft. Drain, if any skin is left, peel again.

Soupe de haricots verts   **2**
Green Bean Soup

A wholesome soup, delicious in the fall when the nip is already in the air.

(Serves 4)

2 tablespoons olive oil
1 large onion or 2 medium onions, pared and chopped
2 cups green beans, strung and snapped in half
1 medium-sized tomato, skinned, seeded, and chopped
2 large potatoes, pared and diced in 1-inch cubes
6 cups water
Salt and pepper

Sauté onion in oil until transparent in saucepan or soup kettle. Add tomatoes and beans; stir over medium-high heat until the moisture from the tomatoes has evaporated.

Add potatoes and water, salt, and pepper. Bring to light boil; reduce heat, cover and cook on low heat for 1 hour or until potatoes are tender. Before serving, mash potatoes with fork, a small amount at a time in a soup ladle, returning potatoes to soup. Reheat and serve.

Soupe au lard   **2**
Bacon Soup

In the mountainous region of the Dauphiné, this soup is a favorite.

(Serves 3-4)

½ pound fat bacon, cut up in small pieces called lardons
3 medium-sized onions, sliced thin
3 cups hot water or meat stock (preferably)
Salt and pepper
¾ cup grated Swiss or Gruyère cheese
½ cup cream or half-and-half
8 slices French or Italian bread

Preheat oven to 350°.

Melt bacon over medium heat in heavy saucepan or soup kettle. Remove *lardons* when crisp and set aside. Add onions to fat and sauté over medium-low heat until light golden color. Add hot water or stock, salt, and pepper; simmer for 20 minutes.

Place a layer of bread, a layer of cheese, a layer of *lardons* in deep ovenproof casserole; repeat. Cover with bouillon; add cream; bake in 350° oven for 5-10 minutes or until very hot.

Soupe de lentilles au riz   2
Lentil Soup with Rice

The combination of lentils and rice provides the complete protein in this soup.

(Serves 4-6)

1 pound dried lentils
3 quarts water
1 large leek, white part only
1 large carrot, pared and diced
1 medium onion, studded with cloves
1 garlic clove, halved
½ cup cooked rice
Salt and pepper
1 tablespoon butter or margarine

Wash and sort lentils. Place them in large saucepan; add water, leek, carrot, onion, garlic, and salt to taste. Cover and bring to boil; turn down to simmer and cook 1½-2 hours or until lentils are very tender.

Purée through a sieve or food mill or in a blender. Add cooked rice, salt if needed, pepper; reheat slowly. Just before serving add butter, blend.

Soupe aux herbes   **2**
Vegetarian Soup

Barley is one of the oldest grains on earth; in prehistoric times it grew all over Europe and Asia. In fact, one type of this cereal can still be found growing in Russia just as it was thousands of years ago. Because of its ability to grow and survive anywhere, even in the poorest soil or in very harsh climates, it is the ideal grain to plant in the arid soil of the mountainous plateaus of Haute Provence. The people of this region use it in soups or combined with the meat of the lambs they raise.

This is my version of a soup made in that region. I have added watercress to perk up the flavor.

(Serves 4-5)

1 large onion, skinned and chopped fine
1 large leek top (white part), cleaned and chopped fine
2 tablespoons butter, margarine, or vegetable oil
5 cups hot water
Salt and pepper
½ cup hulled barley
1 sprig parsley, minced
1 cup finely chopped fresh spinach or sorrel
⅛ cup finely chopped watercress
1 small head lettuce—Bibb, Boston, or Escarolle—chopped fine
1 tablespoon butter or margarine

Sauté onion and leek in a saucepan in fat until soft and transparent; add hot water, salt and pepper to taste; bring to a boil; add barley; cover; reduce heat to low; cook 15 minutes; uncover; add parsley, spinach, watercress, and lettuce; bring back to boil; cover; reduce heat and cook 25-30 minutes or until vegetables and barley are tender. Before serving add the tablespoon butter or margarine and blend to dissolve. Serve with French or sourdough bread.

Soupe aux blettes   **2**
Swiss Chard Soup

Blette is the French word for Swiss chard, a vegetable of the beet family. This vegetable is fairly easy to find in our markets or supermarkets, especially in the spring and summer months. However, if you are unable to find it, you may substitute spinach or sorrel leaves and get an equally delicious soup. The sorrel will give it a more refreshing taste.

When you purchase Swiss chard, make sure the leaves are fresh and green, sometimes with a red tint; yellowish color means the chard is not fresh. The ribs or stalks should be dense and white, not hollow or rubbery.

Save the ribs from the Swiss chard to prepare *Cardons au gratin* (see vegetable chapter).

(Serves 2-3)

*3 cups tightly packed Swiss chard leaves which have been
    cleaned, dried, and coarsely cut*
2 medium-sized potatoes, pared and quartered
1 tablespoon butter or margarine
3 cups water
Salt and pepper
⅛ teaspoon nutmeg
1 egg yolk, lightly beaten
2 tablespoons milk
1 tablespoon butter

Melt butter in soup kettle; add chard; cook over medium-high heat for 3 minutes, stirring constantly. Add potatoes, water, salt, pepper, and nutmeg. Bring to light boil; reduce heat to medium-low and cook 20-25 minutes or until potatoes are soft. Take a large ladle and mash the potatoes with a fork, a small amount at a time in the ladle, until all the potato pieces have been mashed.

Mix egg yolk and milk, beat until smooth; add a small amount of hot soup to it; mix well and return to kettle; heat again; add butter and serve.

La gratinée provençale or soupe à l'oignon provençale

2

Provençal Onion Soup

This is another version of the traditional French onion soup. It is more pungent and very Provençal indeed, with the addition of garlic and spices.

(Serves 4-6)

6 *large* onions, sliced thin
4 *tablespoons butter or margarine*
1 *tablespoon all-purpose flour (try browning the flour first)*
6 *cups hot water or beef broth*
Salt and pepper
¼ *teaspoon nutmeg*
2 *garlic cloves, mashed to a paste*
1 *bay leaf*
1 *cup grated Gruyère or Swiss cheese*
4-6 *slices of French or Italian bread*

Sauté onion in fat over very low heat in saucepan until deep golden color, 10-15 minutes at most. Stir in flour and let it take color slightly; blend in hot water slowly, stirring all the while; add salt, pepper, nutmeg, garlic, and bay leaf. Bring to light boil and reduce heat to simmer; cook covered for 30 minutes. Remove bay leaf.

Pour soup into individual ovenproof casseroles or bowls. Place bread slices on top; sprinkle with cheese and place under broiler until cheese melts and bubbles. Serve immediately.

Velouté d'asperges au fromage

2

Cream of Asparagus and Cheese

The term *velouté* (velvety) is used when a thickening agent is added to a sauce or soup. In this case flour and cream are added to the soup to make it thicker. The addition of cheese gives it more substance and flavor.

(Serves 3-4)

2¼ cups boiling water
Salt
1 pound trimmed and cleaned asparagus
1 large onion, coarsely chopped
1 tablespoon butter or margarine
1 tablespoon all-purpose flour
1 cup light cream
Salt and white pepper
1 cup grated Edam or mild cheddar cheese

Add salt to boiling water in large saucepan; drop asparagus in; return to boiling and cook at a gentle rolling boil, uncovered, until just tender, 5-7 minutes. Drain liquid into a container and reserve. Cut off a few tips for garnish and keep asparagus warm.

Sauté onion in butter or margarine in same saucepan until soft and transparent; blend in flour; slowly add the cooking liquid, stirring to prevent lumps. Cook over medium heat until thickened. Return asparagus to this liquid and pour into blender, whirl until smooth. Return to saucepan; blend in cream slowly; add salt if needed, pepper, and cheese. Reheat slowly, stirring until cheese has melted. Ladle into serving bowl; garnish with asparagus tips.

Soupe du jardin 1
Garden Soup

I like to use the name "garden" because a variety of vegetables is used.

(Serves 4-6)

2 tablespoons olive oil
2 large carrots, scrubbed and finely diced
1 large onion, peeled and chopped fine
1 small head iceberg or Boston lettuce, shredded
2 large potatoes, pared and finely diced
6 cups hot water
Salt and pepper
1 box (10 ounces) frozen peas or 1½ cups fresh shelled peas
2 tablespoons olive oil

Heat oil over medium heat in a soup kettle; add carrots, onions, and lettuce. Sauté over medium-high heat, stirring frequently until onion and lettuce are limp; add potatoes and stir for 2 minutes; add water, salt and pepper. Bring to a light boil; cover and reduce heat to low; cook until potatoes are tender but firm (about 20 minutes). Add peas and olive oil and cook until peas are tender.

Épinards en bouillabaisse   2
Spinach in Bouillabaisse

This is another version of *Bouillabaisse borgne* (see next recipe) using spinach. In Provence it is prepared in an earthen casserole called a *poëllon*, which can be brought from the fire to the table.

(Serves 4-5)

2 pounds spinach, cleaned and washed
Salted boiling water
3 tablespoons olive oil
1 onion, chopped fine
5 potatoes, peeled and sliced ¼ inch thick
Pinch of saffron
Salt and pepper
5 cups boiling water
2 garlic cloves, minced
½ teaspoon dried fennel weed or dill weed, crushed
4 or 5 eggs
4 or 5 slices French or Italian bread, ½ inch thick

Blanch spinach 5 minutes in salted boiling water. Freshen under cold water, drain well, and squeeze as much moisture as possible by pressing with your hands. Chop spinach coarsely.

Sauté onion in olive oil in Dutch oven or soup kettle until transparent and soft. Add spinach and cook over low heat for 5 minutes, stirring often.

Add potatoes, salt, pepper, saffron, boiling water, garlic, fennel. Bring back to light boil; cover and reduce heat to low. Cook until potatoes are tender, about 15 minutes.

Break eggs carefully one at a time over liquid and poach for 4 minutes, not more. Bring to table. Ladle eggs and liquid over bread slices in individual soup bowls, being careful not to break the eggs.

La bouillabaisse borgne (aigou san-d'iòu) 3
One-Eyed Bouillabaisse

Borgne means one-eyed or blind in French, perhaps so named because of the one egg lying atop each serving. Whatever, this is a mock bouillabaisse. The fish has been replaced by eggs.

(Serves 4)

2 tablespoons olive oil
1 medium-sized leek (white only), minced
1 medium-sized onion, chopped fine
1 large tomato, peeled, seeded, and chopped, or 2 teaspoons to-
    mato paste
2 garlic cloves, mashed
1 sprig fresh fennel, or ⅛ teaspoon dried fennel, crushed
1 2-inch piece orange rind
¼ teaspoon dried thyme leaves, crushed
1 bay leaf
1 sprig parsley
5 cups hot water
⅛ teaspoon saffron
Salt and pepper
1 pound white potatoes, peeled and sliced ⅛ inch thick
4 whole eggs
4 slices day-old French or Italian bread
⅛ cup finely minced parsley

Sauté leek and onion in olive oil in large saucepan over medium heat until transparent. Add tomatoes, garlic, fennel, orange rind, thyme, bay leaf, parsley, and hot water. Bring to a rapid boil. Add saffron, salt, pepper, and potatoes. Continue cooking rapidly until potatoes are tender but not soft.

Break eggs one at a time in a saucer. Slide them into the hot liquid and poach until done. Remove with a slotted spoon and keep them warm. Remove potatoes to a warm platter, place eggs on top and sprinkle with parsley. Pour the golden liquid over the bread slices in a soup tureen or in individual bowls.

Soupo pistou (soupe au basilic)   **3**
Basil Soup

As nourishing as it is fragrant, this soup is a meal in itself when served with garlic bread and a salad. Basil and garlic are the essence of the delicious purée called *"pistou"* which is added at the very last. For this reason fresh basil is preferable to dried. (The Provençal housewife always has a pot of basil growing on her window sill. You can do the same and enjoy the luxury of being able to make this delicious *potage* year-round.)

(Serves 4-6)

*1 cup fresh shelling beans (in season), shelled, or fresh black-eyed
    peas (sold in plastic bags)
1½ cups fresh green beans, strings removed, or 1 10-ounce box
    frozen green beans
3 medium-sized potatoes, peeled, cubed in about 1-inch pieces
2 medium-sized zucchini, cubed or sliced
2 medium-sized tomatoes, skinned, seeded, and coarsely chopped
¾ cup elboroni, shelroni, or large vermicelli
Enough water to cover by 2 inches
Salt and pepper
½ cup grated Swiss, Gruyère, or Parmesan cheese*

"Pistou" (Basil-Garlic Purée):
*2 or 3 cloves garlic (depending on taste)
½ cup fresh basil leaves
¼ cup olive oil*

Place vegetables in large soup kettle with water to cover by 2 inches, salt and pepper. Bring to boil, then reduce to simmer and cook for 20-30 minutes or until vegetables are almost tender. Add pasta; increase heat to a gentle boil and continue cooking 15 minutes longer or until pasta is done.

While soup is cooking, prepare purée by crushing garlic and basil in a mortar or heavy bowl. Add oil slowly, mixing all the while as in making mayonnaise, until the mixture has a creamy consistency. Before serving add to the soup, mix well and serve immediately, sprinkled with cheese.

Soupe hivernale   **3**
Winter Soup

This *potage* was made in the depth of winter when vegetables were at their low point. Celery was kept fresh and crisp in the garden under burlap sacks covered by straw and snow. I have used leeks to give the soup a slightly different taste.

(Serves 4)

1 pound lean salt pork
3 cups boiling water
2 cups beef stock (canned or homemade)
2 large carrots, scrubbed and diced small
2 large turnips, pared and diced small
2 medium-sized onions, cleaned and diced small, or 2 large leeks
*   (white only), cleaned and diced small*
2 large stalks celery with leaves cleaned and diced small
1 pound potatoes, peeled and diced small
Salt
Pepper

Slice salt pork in 4 equal pieces. Blanch it in rapidly-boiling water to cover for 5 minutes. Drain water and discard; reserve salt pork.

Bring water and stock to a boil in soup pan or kettle; add blanched salt pork and return to light simmer; cover and cook 35 minutes; add vegetables and pepper, minus potatoes. Return to simmer and cook covered 30 minutes; add potatoes and salt; cook 20 minutes longer covered at simmer.

Serve the soup with the salt pork and slices of French or light rye bread.

Some barley or rice may be added to thicken the soup and make it richer.

Potage velouté à l'oignon
Velvety Onion Soup

3

This is a dish that my mother prepares for company.

(Serves 4)

3 cups coarsely chopped white onions
2 large shallots, chopped coarsely
1 leek (white only), or 4 green onions (white only)
2 tablespoons butter or margarine
2 level tablespoons flour
1¾ cups chicken broth, canned or homemade
1 teaspoon dry rosemary leaves, finely crumbled
Salt and white pepper
½ cup light cream at room temperature
1 egg yolk, lightly beaten

Combine onion, shallots, leek or green onions, and butter or margarine in heavy saucepan; heat over medium-low heat until butter is melted; continue cooking until onion is transparent and soft; cover and continue cooking 5 minutes. Uncover and blend in flour; add chicken broth slowly and stir until thoroughly blended.

Add rosemary, salt and pepper to taste; heat over medium heat until mixture starts to thicken; cook, stirring constantly 1 minute. Reduce to simmer, cover, and cook 30 minutes.

Whirl in electric blender until smooth, or sieve through food mill. Return to saucepan.

Add cream slowly to beaten egg yolk in a bowl. Beat in some of the hot soup; return mixture to the remaining soup in the saucepan. Blend well and reheat slowly until hot, stirring often. (Do not let it boil.) Check for seasoning again. Serve immediately.

Soupe de moules à la marseillaise
Mussel Soup Marseille Style

3

These delicious mollusks can now be served without fear of water contamination. Mussels entering the marketplace are farmed and

grown under controlled conditions: they are constantly checked
and monitored along the East Coast, and quarantined from June
through September on the West Coast.

(Serves 4)

4 dozen mussels if large, 5 dozen if small
3 cups water
1 cup dry white wine
1 onion, skinned and quartered
2 bay leaves
2 tablespoons olive oil
1 onion, skinned and sliced thin
5 garlic cloves, minced
1 bay leaf
1 fresh sprig thyme, or ¼ teaspoon dried thyme leaves
2 tomatoes, skinned and coarsely chopped
1 tablespoon coulis *(see page 31) or tomato paste*
Pepper
Pinch of saffron
⅓ cup vermicelli
Grated Gruyère or Swiss cheese (optional)
Rouille *(see page 36; optional)*

Make sure mussels come from unpolluted area; discard any that
are not tightly closed. Scrub them well in cold water; remove
beard. Soak them for several hours in cold water; drain and wash
again.

Place mussels in water in saucepan; add wine, onion, and bay
leaves. Bring to rapid boil and cook until all mussels are open.
Strain the bouillon through a fine sieve. Shell the mussels; discard
shells; keep mussels warm.

Cook onion and garlic in olive oil in another saucepan over
medium heat until lightly colored. Add bay leaf, thyme, tomatoes,
coulis, and pepper. Add broth from mussels, and additional water
to make 4 cups. Bring to light boil, cook 10 minutes. Strain; add
saffron. Return to boil; add vermicelli; cook until pasta is tender.
Return mussels to soup; add salt. Serve with cheese and/or *rouille.*

Bisque d'écrevisses   **3**
Shrimp Bisque (hot or chilled)

A shrimp bisque is worthy of a king's table. It is one of the most delicate and sophisticated of soups and yet few people realize they can prepare it at home without any touble. In my recipe I always add an unpeeled apple; it gives the final product a lovely sweet flavor and reinforces the pretty pink tint of the soup.

(Serves 4)

1 medium-sized onion, chopped coarsely
2 tablespoons butter or margarine
1 small red apple, cored and chopped coarsely (do not peel)
½ pound small cooked and frozen, deveined and shelled shrimp
    (reserve a few for garnish)
1 tablespoon + 1 teaspoon (all level) flour
1½ cups chicken broth
1 teaspoon lemon juice
1 piece lemon peel 2 inches in length
¼ teaspoon curry powder
¼ teaspoon dill weed, crushed
Salt
2 tablespoons dry white wine, warmed
1 cup light cream, warmed
White pepper
Thin lemon slices (optional)
Croutons fried in butter (optional)

Sauté onion in butter or margarine in saucepan over medium heat until soft. Add apple and continue cooking 3 minutes longer, stirring often. Add shrimp, blend in flour; add broth, lemon juice and peel, curry powder, dill weed, and salt. Bring to a light boil; turn down to simmer; cook covered 10 minutes.

Remove lemon peel; blend mixture in blender or purée through a food mill. Return to saucepan; add warm wine; reheat slowly. Add warm cream gradually; reheat; ladle into soup bowls. Garnish with shrimp. Serve with lemon slices and a few shrimp on each bowl of bisque. May be served with fried croutons.

If served chilled, omit fried croutons, pour into a large bowl and chill in refrigerator at least 4 hours.

Soupe de morue à la marseillaise   **2**
Codfish Soup Marseille Style

This soup compares favorably to the famous *Soupe de poissons* and offers the advantage of being easy to prepare; it is also inexpensive.

(Serves 4)

1 cup onion, chopped fine
¼ cup olive oil
2 large cloves garlic, minced fine
1 pound well-ripened tomatoes, skinned and chopped fine, or the
*   equivalent in canned tomatoes without their juice*
¼ cup finely minced parsley
1 large bay leaf
1 teaspoon dry fennel weed, crushed
1 teaspoon dry thyme leaves, crushed
Salt and pepper
5½ cups fish stock or water, heated
1 teaspoon grated lemon or orange peel
½ cup dry white wine, warmed
4 medium-sized potatoes, peeled and cut in 1½-inch cubes
3 pounds (approximately) fresh or frozen fish fillets, cut in 1½-
*   inch cubes*
Grated Parmesan cheese (optional)

If fish is frozen, thaw in refrigerator ahead of time.

Sauté onion in olive oil in kettle or heavy soup pot over medium heat until a light golden color; add garlic; stir 1 minute; add tomatoes; stir 1 minute more; add parsley, bay leaf, fennel, thyme, salt, and pepper; cook over medium heat for 8-10 minutes or until tomatoes are on the dry side. Add fish stock or water, wine, grated lemon or orange peel, and potatoes. Bring to a light boil; reduce heat to medium; cover and cook until potatoes are done but very firm (about 15 minutes).

Serve immediately in individual soup bowls; pass Parmesan (optional—it is good without it). Serve with slices of French bread.

Pot-au-feu de Provence et de Languedoc (Bouta-couire)
Provençal and Languedoc Pot-au-Feu

3

Years ago in the country, when the French housewife cooked on a wood or coal-burning stove, she would keep a pot of soup simmering on the back of the stove for the family to help themselves whenever they would return from working in the fields. She would constantly add meat and vegetables, never letting the pot get cold. This thick soup came to be called "pot on the fire," or *pot-au-feu* in French.

The *pot-au-feu* as we know it today provides not only a rich bouillon but also the meat and vegetables that make it a complete and nourishing meal.

The traditional *pot-au-feu* in France is always served with the noon meal and is made with beef or chicken or both. In Provence, veal and salt pork are added. In Languedoc it is made in essentially the same manner but the potato has been replaced by white beans and cabbage, and sausage is used instead of salt pork. Sometimes for certain occasions a stuffed chicken is added to the pot instead of meat or sausage.

(Serves 6)

5 pounds lean short ribs of beef or chuck filet
2 pounds veal shoulder
1 medium-sized marrow-filled beef bone*
¼ pound lean salt pork
Cold water
1 teaspoon salt
3 cloves garlic
1 large celery stalk cut in half
1 medium onion, studded with 3 cloves
1 bay leaf
2 juniper berries (optional), or 2 whole cloves
Pepper
8 small turnips, pared
12-14 small carrots or 6 medium, scrubbed and halved
12-14 small potatoes or 6 medium, pared and halved
*2 large or 4 medium leeks (white only), cleaned, trimmed, and
    halved*

2 large tomatoes, skinned, seeded
6-8 slices French bread, toasted
⅓ cup capers, chopped
⅓-½ cup port wine (optional) * *

Place bones in bottom of large soup kettle, add meat and salt pork. Add water to cover and salt. Bring to boil, skim, return to boil; add 2 tablespoons cold water to bring up more of the scum; skim again.

Add garlic, celery, onion, bay leaf, juniper berries or whole cloves, and pepper to taste. Cover and cook covered over low heat 2½ hours (it should bubble very gently).

Add turnips, carrots, potatoes, leeks, tomatoes. Return to a light boil; turn down to simmer; cover and cook 30-40 minutes longer or until vegetables and meat are tender.

Skim fat by dragging a piece of paper toweling over it or use special brush sold for that purpose. Lift vegetables with slotted spoon onto warm serving platter; keep warm. Lift out bones, remove marrow and spread it on toasted bread slices (this step may be omitted if one does not like marrow). Place bread in bottom of soup tureen or individual soup bowls.

Remove meat from bones and set aside; keep warm. Pour broth through sieve onto large saucepan; reheat; add port; pour over bread slices.

Place meat with vegetables on serving platter and serve sprinkled with capers.

---

*Marrow will not come out of bone if base is wrapped in cheesecloth.
* *Addition of port wine to the bouillon gives it a touch of elegance and a piquant flavor.

Hot Entrées and Egg Dishes

Hot entrées and egg dishes were invaluable in the gastronomic past of a basically Catholic France where meat was not to be eaten on Friday, and when it was a rather rare and expensive item, to be used sparingly.

The French cook was not dismayed, but rose to the occasion: with her ingenious and fertile mind she succeeded in conceiving nutritious as well as tasty dishes. Some of them were inspired by her neighbors the Swiss, the Italians, and the Spanish. These have been adapted to the French taste to give them a touch that is unique. With the egg and cheese providing the necessary protein, these delicious dishes are a tribute to the imaginative and versatile French.

ABOUT EGGS

Contrary to popular belief, brown eggs are no better than white ones — only prettier. The color of the shell just indicates the type of hens that laid them. As for the yolk, its color does not represent its nutritive value or freshness, but rather reflects the type of feed consumed by the hen.

To store and keep eggs fresh, three factors are to be considered:

1. Because the egg contains an air pocket which grows progressively larger as the egg gets older, and the quality of the egg is better maintained if the air pocket is in the narrow end, it is better to keep that end down.
2. The shell being very porous, it is essential to keep eggs in the carton or away from food with strong odors.
3. Light and heat are detrimental to the freshness of eggs; they should be kept in a cool, dark place.

Lucullus, a Roman general living around 60 B.C., a gourmet and gourmand, is said to have produced the first omelet after he retired from service in the Roman army and gave himself entirely to his hobby, cooking.

The Basics of Making an Omelet

An omelet is really easy to make if you respect a few simple rules, described as follows:

The eggs should be fresh—the fresher they are, the better the omelet.

Eggs should be at room temperature when you are ready to start. If too cold, the white will not be light and fluffy, because it can't get enough air bubbles.

Beat the eggs in a bowl of stainless steel, copper, or glass; beat with a fork or whisk with a good vigorous down-and-around stroke.

Now the fanatics say you must make your omelet in a special omelet pan, the kind you find in gourmet cook stores. But actually a good frying pan with non-stick surface and sloping sides will do nicely. A good average size is 8 inches in diameter. (For a one-person omelet use a 5½-inch pan.)

Following is a basic recipe for one or two persons, depending on your appetite.

Omelette simple   1
Plain Omelet

(Serves 1 or 2)

2 eggs
1 tablespoon water
Salt and pepper
1 tablespoon butter (increase butter to two tablespoons if you use
    three or four eggs)

Break eggs in bowl; start beating with a vigorous down-and-around stroke, counting twenty beats; add water and seasoning; beat ten more times.

Place omelet pan on high heat for 8-10 seconds or until very hot; add butter (it should sizzle when it hits the pan); move it around to coat the pan well, bottom and sides; pour in eggs quickly before butter turns brown; mixture should start bubbling immediately.

With the back of a fork or, if you are using a non-stick pan, a plastic spatula, draw eggs from edge toward center and at the same time tilt the pan so the eggs, yet liquid, flow into the space created and coagulate there, filling that space. Keep doing this until there are no uncooked eggs left and you have a uniform mass. Do not overcook; it is better to have your omelet on the moist side (*baveuse*).

With spatula lift the edge which is near you about halfway and fold it lightly over the other half. Then slide it all into a warm serving plate. A small amount of butter may be spread on the finished omelet to gild it.

In the South of France omelets are often made with the addition of vegetables to the eggs. This addition increases the volume, flavor, and nutritional value of the omelet. See the following recipes.

Omelette marseillaise   1
Marseille Omelet

This is really a summer omelet. It may be served cold in sandwiches for a picnic. If you have herbs in the garden, use all the herbs you wish. In winter use a little more fresh parsley to give the omelet the fresh flavor of spring.

(Serves 3-4)

2 medium-sized tomatoes, skinned, seeded, and chopped
1 tablespoon olive oil
3 sprigs parsley, chopped
2 garlic cloves, minced fine
3 large basil leaves, chopped, or 1 teaspoon dried basil leaves
1 sprig thyme, or ⅛ teaspoon dried thyme leaves
2 sprigs summer savory, or ¼ teaspoon dried summer savory
       leaves
3-4 tarragon leaves or a pinch dried tarragon

4 eggs
Salt and pepper
2 teaspoons cold water
2 tablespoons olive oil or vegetable oil

Cook tomatoes in skillet in 1 tablespoon olive oil for 3 minutes over medium heat. Add parsley, garlic, and herbs; cook, covered, over low heat for 5-8 minutes or until fairly thick. If too thin uncover and cook until thick. Cool; reserve (do not salt).

Beat eggs lightly in bowl; add salt and pepper and 2 teaspoons cold water; beat again until blended. Add tomato purée to the eggs and beat just enough to blend the purée with the eggs.

Heat omelet pan over medium-high heat; add remaining oil; rotate pan to coat it well and heat for 2-3 minutes. Pour in egg mixture when oil is very hot; let it set for 5 seconds; lift around edges and tilt pan toward lifted edge to let the uncooked mixture from the center run into the space and fill it. Repeat all around until all the mixture is set. Watch the heat; if it gets too hot, turn down to medium. Omelet should set quickly. Fold omelet and slide onto warm serving platter.

Keep refrigerated if it is to be used later for a picnic.

Omelette d'aubergines (Roussillon)   1
Eggplant Omelet

(Serves 4)

2 cups peeled and cubed eggplant
1 teaspoon salt
1 medium-sized onion, peeled and sliced
3 tablespoons olive oil or vegetable oil
1 small garlic clove, minced fine
1 teaspoon dried thyme leaves
½ cup chicken or beef broth
4 eggs, slightly beaten
Salt and pepper
2 tablespoons oil

Salt eggplant in glass dish; let stand for 30 minutes; rinse well; pat dry.

Sauté onion in 1 tablespoon oil in heavy skillet over medium heat for 8 minutes or until golden. Transfer onion to a dish and reserve.

Add 2 tablespoons oil to same skillet. Add eggplant, garlic, and thyme; stir over medium heat for 2-3 minutes. Add broth and bring to light boil; reduce to simmer and cook, covered, for 10 minutes, or until eggplant is tender. Add onion and cook, uncovered, over medium heat for 10 more minutes or until thick. Cool thoroughly.

Add eggplant mixture, salt, and pepper to eggs; beat gently to mix and pour into hot oil in omelet pan. Proceed as for *Omelette marseillaise.*

Omelette à l'oseille et aux épinards   2
Sorrel and Spinach Omelet

This omelet is eaten at Eastertime in the region of Arles and the Camargue. Swiss chard may be substituted for sorrel, which is sometimes hard to find.

(Serves 6-8)

¾ *cup diced bacon or salt pork blanched in boiling water for 8*
    minutes
1 *cup cooked, squeezed-dry, chopped spinach*
1 *cup cooked, squeezed-dry, chopped sorrel or Swiss chard*
1 *tablespoon butter or margarine or bacon grease*
4 *eggs*
4 *tablespoons olive oil or vegetable oil*
½ *cup cooked rice*
1 *garlic clove, minced*
Salt and pepper

Cook rice according to package instructions; drain. Cook bacon or salt pork in heavy skillet over medium-low heat until crisp. Remove to paper towel to drain; reserve. Reserve 1 tablespoon bacon grease.

Heat reserved bacon grease or butter in same skillet and sauté spinach and Swiss chard over medium heat for 5 minutes; set aside. Add rice, spinach, bacon crisps, garlic, salt, and pepper to eggs.

Heat 4 tablespoons olive oil or vegetable oil in large skillet until hot; pour in mixture and cook over medium-high heat until set. Turn omelet by inverting a dish over it and giving it a quick turn so that it ends up in the dish; slide it back in the pan and cook the other side for 3 more minutes. Slide on serving dish and serve.

Omelette campagnarde   2
Country Omelet

A deliciously nutritious omelet made in the regions of Haute Provence and the Var.

(Serves 3-4)

4 slices bacon cut up into pieces 1 inch wide
1 medium-sized onion, diced fine
1 cup potatoes, peeled and diced fairly small
4 eggs, slightly beaten
½ cup shredded Gruyère or Swiss cheese
2 tablespoons butter or margarine
Salt and pepper

Cook bacon in medium-sized skillet over medium-low heat until it has rendered its fat and is almost crisp. Remove with slotted spoon to drain on paper towel; drain almost all the bacon grease except 3 tablespoons. Add onion and potatoes to fat in skillet; cook over medium-low heat, stirring often until potatoes are soft and golden brown, 8-10 minutes. (Cover the last few minutes if potatoes take too long to cook, then uncover to crisp.) Remove from heat, transfer to bowl; set aside and keep warm.

Beat eggs lightly; add bacon, potato-onion mixture, Gruyère or Swiss, salt, and pepper, and blend lightly.

Melt butter or margarine in omelet pan or clean skillet until hot but not brown; pour in egg mixture. Proceed as in basic recipe. Keep omelet on the moist side. Serve immediately.

Omelette de famille   1
Family Omelet

My mother, being thrifty, never discards the outer leaves of the curly endive. This is one way she utilizes them. The green leaves go into this omelet, while the heart is mixed with any other kind of lettuce in a salad.

(Serves 4)

4 eggs
1 tablespoon water
Green leaves from 1 head curly endive lettuce, chopped
2 tablespoons olive oil or vegetable oil
1 garlic clove, finely minced
2 tablespoons minced parsley
Salt and pepper
2 tablespoons olive or vegetable oil

Sauté lettuce in 2 tablespoons olive oil in skillet over medium-low heat for 1 or 2 minutes. Add garlic and parsley; stir over medium heat for 2 additional minutes to blend. Reserve.

Add lettuce mixture, salt, and pepper to beaten eggs. Beat gently to blend.

Add two tablespoons oil to omelet pan; heat until oil is hot; pour in egg mixture; and proceed as in basic omelet.

Omelette à l'ancienne   2
Old-Fashioned Omelet

This omelet, prepared on the farms of Haute Provence, is as delicious as it is nourishing.

(Serves 4)

1 medium-sized onion, sliced thin
½ cup cooked ham, cut in ¾-inch cubes
2 medium-sized potatoes, peeled and cut in ¾-inch cubes

3 tablespoons butter or margarine
4 eggs, slightly beaten
Salt and pepper
2 tablespoons oil

Melt 1 tablespoon butter in large skillet over medium heat; add onion; sauté until golden and soft. Add ham and stir; cook for 3 more minutes to heat ham through. Remove from skillet and keep warm.

Add 2 tablespoons butter or margarine to same skillet; add potatoes and reduce heat to low; cook, covered, for 15-20 minutes or until potatoes are tender; uncover and cook 3 more minutes to crisp them. Return onion and ham to potatoes; mix well and remove from heat; keep warm.

Add salt and pepper to eggs; beat lightly; add onion, potato, and ham mixture; beat gently to blend. Heat a 10-inch omelet pan over high heat, add 2 tablespoons oil, rotate pan to coat, and heat for 2-3 minutes. When oil is very hot, pour egg mixture in and proceed as for basic omelet. Serve immediately.

Oeufs brouillés aux écrevisses   1
Scrambled Eggs with Shrimp

A nice luncheon or brunch dish.

(Serves 6)

1 cup small shrimp, shelled
3 tablespoons butter or margarine
Pinch paprika (⅛ teaspoon)
6 large eggs, beaten slightly
Salt and pepper
⅓ cup light cream
6 slices white bread, toasted

Sauté shrimp in saucepan over medium-high heat in butter or margarine until heated through, stirring constantly; add paprika.

Blend eggs, salt, pepper, and cream in a bowl; beat slightly again.

Pour over shrimp, stirring gently to mix egg and shrimp; cook over medium-low heat, stirring gently until eggs begin to set but are still moist.

Serve immediately over toasted bread.

La piperade au basilic   **2**
Basil Piperade *(an egg-vegetable dish)*

Imported from our neighbors the Basques of the French Pyrenees into Languedoc and Roussillon, this robust dish makes a complete meal if served with a salad of greens and crusty bread.

(Serves 3-4)

1 medium-sized onion, skinned and sliced very thin
1 green pepper, seeded and sliced thin
1 red pepper, seeded and sliced thin
4 tablespoons olive oil
3 large tomatoes, skinned, seeded, and chopped, or 1 1-pound can
*   whole tomatoes, drained thoroughly, chopped*
2 large cloves garlic, minced
Salt and plenty of pepper
6 eggs beaten as for an omelet
2 teaspoons olive oil
4 large basil leaves, chopped, or 1 teaspoon dry basil leaves,
*   crushed*
½ cup diced cooked ham (optional)

Heat 3 tablespoons olive oil over medium heat in large skillet; add onion and cook until transparent and golden, about 10 minutes; add green pepper, continue cooking 10 more minutes or until green pepper is tender. Add tomatoes, garlic, salt, and pepper; bring to a light boil; reduce heat to very low; cook uncovered until liquid has evaporated. Mixture should be thick.

Add remaining oil and basil to mixture. Pour in eggs and gently stir as for scrambled eggs. Remove from heat when top has just set. *Piperade* should be creamy. Serve immediately.

Croque-monsieur   2
Hot Ham and Egg Sandwich

The word *croquer* means to crunch; hence the name *croque-monsieur*—a crunchy, munchy sandwich for Monsieur.

There is also a *croque-madame* that is basically the same as *croque-monsieur* except that the eggs have been replaced by slices of Gruyère cheese.

In the *croque-grandmère* (grandmother), the eggs are combined with mashed cream cheese and cooked as in *croque-monsieur*.

Serve any of these sandwiches with a salad of mixed greens such as romaine, Bibb, watercress, or *salade provençale*, and you will have a very nutritious lunch.

(Serves 4)

2-3 tablespoons butter or margarine
8 slices white bread, crust removed
8 thin slices cooked ham
4 large whole eggs, slightly beaten
2 tablespoons butter
4 tablespoons light cream
Salt and pepper

Melt 2 tablespoons butter or margarine in heavy skillet. Place bread slices two at a time in skillet and fry lightly on both sides. Add more butter if needed. Keep warm.

Melt 2 tablespoons butter in saucepan. Combine eggs and cream, salt, and pepper; carefully pour into saucepan, stirring all the while with wooden spoon; cook over low heat, stirring constantly until the mixture starts to set but is still soft, about 8 minutes. Remove immediately and place away from heat. Prepare the bread slices by placing 4 slices on serving dish and arranging 1 slice of ham on top of each slice.

Divide egg mixture equally on top of ham; cover with leftover bread slices to make 4 sandwiches. Serve immediately with tomato salad or tomato slices.

Oeufs à la provençale   **2**
Provençal Eggs

(Serves 4)

2 large, firm tomatoes, cut in half and seeded
Salt (light)
2 tablespoons olive oil
1 large clove garlic, minced fine
3 tablespoons minced parsley
1 large basil leaf, minced, or ¼ teaspoon dried basil leaves
Pepper
2 tablespoons dried bread crumbs
4 eggs
2 tablespoons butter, margarine, or oil

Salt tomatoes lightly and cook in skillet with 2 tablespoons oil over medium heat for 3 minutes on both sides. Remove carefully to a plate; keep warm.

Add garlic, parsley, basil, and pepper to same skillet. Stir over medium-low heat for 2 minutes; watch carefully. Add bread crumbs; stir again for 1 minute and sprinkle over the cut sides of the tomato halves.

Fry eggs in another skillet in butter or oil the way you like them. Place on tomato halves and serve hot.

Oeufs à la chasseur   **2**
Eggs Hunter-Style

(Serves 4)

8 hard-boiled eggs, peeled and cut in half lengthwise
1½ cups Hunter-style sauce (see index)

Preheat oven to 350°.

Arrange hard-boiled eggs in shallow serving-baking dish, cut-sides-up. Pour sauce over and warm for 15 minutes in 350° oven.

Champignons en croûtes
Mushrooms in Pastry Shells

This is the Southern way of preparing mushrooms for a fancy entrée.

6-8 pastry shells or bread shells (see recipe below)
½ pound fresh mushrooms, cleaned and sliced
1 tablespoon lemon juice
2 tablespoons butter or margarine
1 large clove garlic, minced fine
3 tablespoons fine bread crumbs
1 tablespoon finely minced parsley
1 teaspoon anchovy paste
⅓ cup (approximately) light cream
1 egg yolk, slightly beaten
Salt and pepper

Mix mushrooms with lemon juice; set aside. Melt butter or margarine over medium heat in large skillet; add mushrooms and sauté, stirring often, until soft, about 1-2 minutes. Add garlic, stir and cook 1 minute longer; blend in bread crumbs, parsley, anchovy paste; stir for another minute.

Combine cream, egg yolk, salt and pepper. Add slowly to mushroom mixture in skillet; stir until thickened. Fill warmed pastry shells with cooked mushroom mixture.

Bread shells:

6-8 sandwich-style white bread slices
2 tablespoons butter or margarine, softened at room temperature

Preheat oven to 350°

Trim crust from bread slices with sharp knife; spread one side of bread slices with softened butter or margarine. Press slices, buttered-side-up, into ungreased muffin pans, being careful not to tear bread; bake in preheated oven for 15-20 minutes or until bread is toasted. Keep warm until ready to serve.

Oeufs maritchu   3
Eggs Pyrenees

This delicious dish comes from Languedoc and Roussillon.

(Serves 4)

2 tablespoons olive oil or vegetable oil
1 small onion, chopped
1 pound tomatoes, chopped (canned tomatoes may be used, but
    strain the juice and use it in soup)
2 cloves garlic, mashed
Salt and pepper
1 package frozen artichoke hearts, cooked according to package
    directions and drained thoroughly of liquid
2 tablespoons butter or margarine
6 eggs, slightly beaten
2 tablespoons minced parsley
Salt and pepper

Sauté onion in olive oil over medium heat in saucepan until transparent; add tomatoes, garlic, salt, and pepper; simmer covered 15-20 minutes or until thickened. If it takes too long to thicken, cook uncovered for 5 more minutes. Sieve through food mill or purée in blender; set aside; keep drained and warm.

Sauté cooked artichokes in butter or margarine in frying pan over medium heat for 5 minutes until heated through; keep warm.

Prepare scrambled eggs by melting 1 tablespoon butter or margarine over medium-low heat in frying pan. When butter is hot, add eggs, parsley, salt, and pepper; stir with spatula until eggs start to thicken. Remove from heat and stir in the leftover tablespoon of butter until mixture is creamy.

Arrange artichokes in serving dish; pour sauce around and over it. Place scrambled eggs on top of artichokes and sauce and serve immediately with toasted bread slices.

Les petits chapeaux (capeletti)   **3**
Little Hats

These ravioli-type pasta are called "little hats" (*capeletti* in Provençal) because of their resemblance to hats of the Napoleonic era.

(Makes about 1½ dozen)

Filling:

1 cup cooked, squeezed-dry finely-chopped fresh spinach or Swiss
*   chard (frozen spinach may be used)*
⅓ cup freshly grated Parmesan
¼ teaspoon nutmeg
Salt and pepper
1 cup finely chopped cooked chicken or beef (leftover meat is
*   perfect for this filling)*
1 egg yolk, slightly beaten

Combine all these ingredients well; chill for 2½-3 hours.

Pasta:

2 cups sifted all-purpose flour
1 whole egg, lightly beaten
1 egg yolk, lightly beaten
1 tablespoon olive oil, or 1 tablespoon butter, melted
⅔ cup freshly grated Parmesan
2 tablespoons butter or margarine, melted

Mound the flour in a large bowl and make a well in the center. Combine eggs, olive oil or butter; pour in the well. With your fingers, incorporate flour, a small amount at a time, with the egg mixture, until all flour is blended; add 1 tablespoon water if dough is too stiff.

Place dough on floured work table and knead until smooth and elastic. Let dough rest covered with towel for 20 minutes. Knead again for a few minutes and let dough rest again another 30 minutes. Uncover and roll out dough with rolling pin to get a very thin sheet, about ⅛ inch thick. With a glass 2½ inches in diameter, cut circles from dough.

Place a very small amount of filling on each circle. Wet edges of dough lightly, fold circles in half, press firmly to seal. Turn both corners up to resemble small hats. Let them rest, covered, for 1 hour on a floured cloth. When ready to cook, poach in 5 quarts boiling salted water, dropping one at a time into the water, but never cooking more than 12 at a time. Poach 8-10 minutes or until they float to surface; remove with slotted spoon and let drain in colander.

Place in a well-buttered baking dish, drizzle with melted butter or margarine; sprinkle with Parmesan; place under broiler until golden brown.

Tarte aux épinards   3
Spinach Pie

Persian in origin, spinach was introduced into Europe via Spain when the Moors, who knew and ate the vegetable, invaded the continent during the Medieval era. This versatile vegetable is low in calories and contains a fair amount of iron, vitamins A and C, and potassium oxalate (known as oxalic acid, a *mild* diuretic). The following "pie" makes a good luncheon dish.

(Serves 4-5)

1 partly-baked 9-inch pâte brisée *shell* (see index) *rolled out in a*
    1-inch-deep pie, quiche, or flan pan
1 pound spinach, cleaned
1 medium-sized onion, chopped fine
3 tablespoons butter or margarine
¼ teaspoon each, nutmeg and mace
Pepper
6 ounces Neufchatel or cream cheese
¼ cup heavy cream
3 egg yolks
Salt
3 egg whites
1 heaping tablespoon grated Parmesan
2 hard-boiled eggs, shelled and sliced

Preheat oven to 375°.

Place cleaned spinach in 2 quarts of salted boiling water and cook in lightly boiling water for 4-5 minutes. Drain well, squeeze the water out; chop fine. Set aside.

Melt 2 tablespoons butter or margarine in a skillet over medium heat and sauté onion in it until soft and transparent; add chopped spinach, nutmeg, mace, and pepper; cook on medium-low heat, stirring often, for 5 minutes.

Mash the Neufchatel or cream cheese in a bowl, blend in the spinach mixture, cream, egg yolks, and salt. Cool thoroughly as the spinach will still be warm.

Beat egg whites until they stand in stiff peaks when beater is held up. Fold in spinach and cream cheese mixture with an up-and-over motion until the whites are blended. Do not overmix.

Pour into shell; sprinkle with grated Parmesan, dot with butter cut up in small pieces; bake in preheated oven for 25-30 minutes. Remove from oven; decorate with egg slices.

Tarte aux poireaux   3
Leek Pie

A good entrée or luncheon dish.

(Serves 6)

1 9-inch pie pan lined with pâte brisée shell
8 slices bacon cut into small pieces about 1 inch wide
2 cups chopped leeks (white part only)
Water to cover by 1 inch
2 cups grated Swiss or Gruyère cheese
1 cup milk
½ cup cream or light cream
3 whole eggs, lightly beaten
⅛ teaspoon nutmeg
Salt and pepper

Preheat oven to 400°.

Cook bacon in skillet over medium-low heat until barely brown. Drain on paper towel and reserve.

Drop leeks into boiling water in saucepan and blanch 6-8 minutes or until barely soft; drain thoroughly.

Combine bacon, leeks, cheese, milk, cream, nutmeg, salt, and pepper; blend by beating slightly.

Pour into pastry shell and bake in preheated 400° oven for 10 minutes; reduce to 350° and continue to bake until knife inserted slightly off-center comes out clean (about 30-35 minutes).

Tarte de tomates provençale   3
Tomato Pie Provençal Style

(Serves 6)

1 9-inch lightly-baked pâte brisée shell
1 pound onions, peeled and sliced thin
1 garlic clove, minced
6 tablespoons olive oil
Salt and pepper
2 pounds well-ripened tomatoes, peeled, seeded, and chopped
3 tablespoons olive oil
2 garlic cloves, minced fine
3 large fresh basil leaves, minced fine, or 2 teaspoons dried basil
      leaves, crushed
⅛ teaspoon dried thyme leaves, crushed
Pinch of salt and pepper
⅔ cup pitted black olives, sliced
6 anchovy fillets, freshened

Preheat oven to 350°.

Place onions, garlic, and olive oil in large skillet and cook 20 minutes over low heat, stirring from time to time until they are soft and transparent; add salt and pepper.

Heat the remaining 2 tablespoons olive oil in another skillet; add tomatoes, garlic, basil, thyme, salt, and pepper; cook over medium-low heat 10-20 minutes or until liquid is evaporated, stirring occasionally. Cool.

Spread the onion mixture in the bottom of the baked shell; spread the tomatoes over the onions; sprinkle with olives; arrange anchovy fillets like the spokes of a wheel over the olives.

Place in preheated oven for 15-20 minutes. If edge browns too fast, cover with strips of foil. Serve either hot or cold.

Tourtière de légumes   3
Vegetable Pie

Contents of this pie vary with the region and the cook; for example, peas may be used instead of lima beans, squash or eggplant instead of zucchini.

(Serves 6-8)

Pastry dough for a 2-crust 10-inch pie (see index for Swiss Chard
*   Pie—*Tourte aux blettes)
¾ pound spinach, cleaned
1 pound green zucchini, cleaned and coarsely grated
1 pound yellow zucchini, cleaned and coarsely grated
1 cup fresh or frozen baby lima beans
2 cloves garlic, minced fine
1 tablespoon butter or margarine
¼ cup chopped onion
¼ cup chopped leek (white part only)
1 cup grated Gruyère or Swiss cheese
2 eggs slightly beaten
¼ cup light cream
2 tablespoons olive oil
1 teaspoon dried summer savory leaves, crushed
⅛ teaspoon dried oregano leaves, crushed
Good pinch of freshly-ground pepper
Salt
1 egg yolk slightly beaten

Preheat oven to 400°.

Make pastry dough according to directions; divide dough into two balls. Roll out one ball to fit 10-inch pie or *flan* pan, leaving 1 inch of dough hanging over the edge; set aside. Finely chop leaves of spinach and place in large bowl with green and yellow grated zucchini, baby lima beans, and garlic. Set aside.

Melt butter in skillet and add onion and leek; sauté over medium heat until soft and golden; add to vegetables in bowl with cheese, eggs, cream, olive oil, summer savory, oregano, pepper, and salt to taste. Blend together and fill the crust with this mixture.

Roll out second ball of dough for the top crust; place over filling; trim edge; pinch together and flute to seal.

Beat egg yolk with 2 teaspoons water and brush the edges and top of pie with this mixture. Make slits in the top crust with sharp knife so that steam can escape during cooking. Place in preheated oven and bake 1 hour. (Watch toward end of baking time; if crust edge browns too fast, cover edge with strips of foil.) Serve pie warm or cold.

Pan bagnat   3
Picnic Sandwich

Originally this sandwich was intended to be used as a vehicle for tasting the newly-pressed olive oil. The farmers of the region of Nice, where the oil is produced, would freely rub slices of country bread with garlic, dip the slices in the new oil and place them at the end of a long fork; then they would toast them over an open fire. This procedure was called *la briscanda* or *pan bagnat* (*pain mouillé* in French means wet bread). The tradition is still maintained in some sections of Provence. *Pan bagnat* has now evolved into the delicious picnic sandwich described below. It keeps well refrigerated, in foil.

(Serves 4-6)

1 large (1-pound) loaf or 2 8-ounce loaves French or Italian sour-
      dough bread
4 teaspoons olive oil, or more
Salt and pepper
Pissalat* *or sardines*
2 basil leaves, chopped, or ½ teaspoon dried basil leaves, crum-
      bled
1 garlic clove, mashed or minced fine
1 large tomato, thinly sliced
1 medium-sized green pepper, thinly sliced
2 tablespoons chopped capers

Slice bread in half lengthwise; remove some of the interior to form
a boat; soak both exposed inside surfaces with 2 tablespoons olive
oil; salt and pepper lightly. Mix *pissalat* with the 2 remaining
tablespoons olive oil; add garlic; stir to incorporate the garlic in the
paste. Spread paste inside bread. Cover with tomatoes and green
pepper. Sprinkle capers over. Add more oil if necessary. Press both
sides of bread together, slice, and serve.

*Pissalat (Fish Paste):

This purée is the specialty of the fishermen of the Mediterranean
coast, around Cannes and Menton. The original is made with tiny
sardines called *poutines.* They are placed in a barrel with salt and
anchovies and marinated for eight days, reduced to purée, and
blended with cloves and nutmeg.

6 anchovy fillets, freshened, dried, and mashed
1 3¾-ounce can sardines in oil, drained
Pepper, salt (light)
Pinch of nutmeg
1 clove, crumbled

Mix all ingredients in mortar or glass bowl and blend well, using
pestle or wooden spoon to make paste.

Les gnocchi à la provençale   **3**
Provençal Gnocchi (dumplings)

Gnocchi has been around since the Roman empire, and it is rather natural to assume that Italy would be the only place where this dish might be found. But Germany, Austria, Hungary, and France also have their own versions of *gnocchi*. In the South of France it is prepared in several different ways. Following are two recipes from the regions of Provence and the Var.

(Serves 4)

1 cup milk
¼ cup butter or margarine
⅛ teaspoon nutmeg
Salt (a little) and pepper
1 heaping cup sifted all-purpose flour
3 tablespoons grated Parmesan cheese
4 whole eggs, medium-sized
1 tablespoon olive oil
Salted water
½ cup grated Parmesan cheese
Coulis or béchamel *sauce or the juice from a* daube

Place milk, butter, salt, pepper, and nutmeg in medium-sized saucepan. Bring to boil. Combine flour and Parmesan; drop mixture into the boiling water all at once, stirring rapidly; remove from heat and continue stirring for 1 minute or until mixture comes away from sides of pan and forms a ball. Add eggs one at a time, beating vigorously after each addition. The dough will be smooth. Cool.

Bring salted water to a boil in large saucepan; add the olive oil. Drop the *gnocchi* into the water, a dozen at a time, and poach for 5 minutes or until they float to the surface. Remove with a slotted spoon and drain in colander. Add more boiling water until all the *gnocchi* are poached.

Place *gnocchi* in shallow baking dish; cover with *coulis* or *béchamel* sauce and sprinkle with Parmesan; place under broiler for a few minutes, until lightly browned. Or cover *gnocchi* with *daube* sauce and broil.

Gnocchi aux noix   3
Gnocchi with Walnuts

This surprising and delicious recipe comes to us from the Var and
Haute Provence, where walnut trees grow in abundance, especially
in the Haut-Var.

1 cup all-purpose flour
2 eggs, medium-sized
¼ teaspoon salt
Boiling salted water
½ cup finely chopped walnuts
Butter

Preheat oven to 375°.

Sift flour and salt together in a bowl. Make a well and put eggs in it.
Mix thoroughly with fingers until smooth.

Flatten dough to a sheet ½ inch thick on floured work table or
board. Cut in small squares 1"x1".

Poach in boiling, salted water for 5 minutes or until they float to
the surface. Remove with slotted spoon to colander to drain.

Place in well-buttered shallow baking dish. Sprinkle with walnuts, dot with butter. Bake in preheated oven for 10 minutes or
broil until golden. I like to sprinkle brown or white sugar over
nuts.

La pissaladière   3
Onion Pizza

The name comes from *pissalat*, a mixture of anchovies, sardines,
and herbs (more fully described on page 111 in the recipe for
Pan bagnat). It is the Provençal version of the Italian pizza. In the
region of Nice it is made only with onions; in and around Marseille
it is prepared with anchovies and herbs. The recipe below comes
from an old *Marseillaise* friend of the family.

(Makes 2 12-inch pizzas)

Crusts:
1 package active dry yeast
⅔ cup warm water (110°-115°)
2 to 2¼ cups all-purpose flour
½ teaspoon salt
1 egg slightly beaten
2 tablespoons olive oil

Soften yeast in warm water. Blend 1 cup flour and salt in large bowl. Beat in softened yeast, egg, and oil. Stir in enough of the remaining flour to make a fairly stiff dough.

Turn out on lightly floured working surface. Knead 5 minutes or until dough is smooth and elastic. Place in greased bowl; turn once to grease the entire surface of the dough. Cover and let rise in warm place about 1-1½ hours or until doubled. Punch down; divide in half to form 2 balls. Cover again and let rest 10 minutes.

Preheat oven to 350°.

Filling:
4 large yellow onions, skinned and sliced thin
4 garlic cloves, minced
1 teaspoon dried thyme leaves, crushed
2 boxes cherry tomatoes or small Italian tomatoes, cut in half
8 anchovy fillets cut in half lengthwise
6 ounces black olives, pitted and halved
½ cup olive oil
Salt and pepper
4 tablespoons olive oil

Pour ¼ cup olive oil into heavy skillet; add onions and cook slowly on low heat until onions are very tender; stir often. Onions should not brown. Add salt and pepper. Set aside.

Pour the remaining ¼ cup olive oil in another skillet; add tomatoes, garlic, and thyme. Cook over medium-high heat until tomatoes wilt. Add a pinch of salt. Remove from heat. Set aside. Roll out balls of dough on floured surface to make 2 12-inch circles. Fit them into 2 well-oiled pie dishes or pizza pans. Spread cooked onions over the bottom; spread tomato mixture on top; arrange olives and anchovy fillets over pizza. Sprinkle with olive oil and place in preheated oven for 1 hour. Remove from oven and sprinkle about ⅛ teaspoon black pepper over.

Vegetables

The sun-drenched land of the South of France, hugging the warm Mediterranean sea and sheltered by the Alps, has always been graced by a favorable climate for the growing of vegetables and fruits. The open markets which abound in all the cities, towns, and villages are a feast for the eyes; they are a tapestry of colors with their rows of vegetables, fruits, and scented herbs.

The housewife goes early in the morning to make her selection of the seasonal vegetables when they are at the peak of quality and their price at the lowest. This bounty of nature probably explains why vegetables are so important in the French diet.

Now with the new health awareness in America, vegetable cookery is the perfect answer to low-calorie cooking. Furthermore, the use of herbs will help diminish the need for salt. To further improve the flavor of some vegetables, cooking them in chicken broth or stock is sometimes recommended. Vegetables that lend themselves to this method are zucchini, Brussels sprouts, broccoli, carrots, and green beans.

Our word vegetable is derived from the Latin *vegetabilis*—enlivening, animating; and indeed, our dinner table can be enlivened and animated by the presence of succulent vegetables, cooked the right length of time at the right temperature and perhaps enhanced by a delicate sauce.

Especially with our own vegetables grown in suburban gardens or city plots, we have the opportunity now to give fresh vegetables and herbs the glorious place they deserve in a well-planned and healthful menu.

Now may I add a word or two of caution about the way vegetables should be treated in order to preserve their freshness and their nutritive value. Not every vegetable responds to the same treatment. Most respond well to refrigeration and should be placed as soon as possible after purchase in plastic bags or closed containers in the vegetable compartment. This will limit loss of moisture and loss of vitamins.

However, tomatoes and avocados fare better at room temperature if possible; therefore buy these vegetables in small quantity. Tomatoes should be fully ripe, very red, for immediate use. If pink, leave them to ripen in a warm, open place out of the direct sun with the stem end up.

If you find your slicing tomatoes too bland, slice them first, then sprinkle them very lightly with sugar and let them stand a few minutes before serving.

Avocados which are not ripe enough can be made to ripen quickly by burying them in flour for several hours.

Potatoes, sweet potatoes, and squash such as acorn or pumpkin should not be refrigerated, or their starch will convert into sugar. Keep them in a dark, cool place — especially potatoes, which lose their vitamins easily. Our ancestors knew this; instinctively they stored these vegetables in root cellars where they were kept in the dark at an even, cool temperature.

Finally, it is a good idea to buy vegetables in reasonable quantities in order to maximize freshness and minimize spoilage.

POMMES DE TERRE—POTATOES

The history of the potato is one of the most interesting in the vegetable kingdom. Originating in Peru, it is cultivated to this day by the successors to the Incas on the high plateau of the Andes. In 1540 the Spaniards brought it back to Spain, and it was introduced into France in 1616 when it was served for the first time to Louis XIII. After a long period of neglect, owing to suspicions as to its edibility, the potato was reinstated and popularized as a valuable vegetable by Parmentier in about 1771. Since then Europe, going from war to famine to war, has always depended on the lowly root, for it grew easily even in poor soil, and, being underground, it was safe from the marching armies devastating the fields.

New potatoes are very rich in vitamin C. Immediately after being dug, they contain 100 mg. of the vitamin for 4 ounces of potato. They are also rich in potassium, iron, and phosphorus.

On Potato Cookery

Bouillie (Boiling Method)

Scrub potatoes, remove decayed or green spots. Peel thinly with vegetable parer or sharp knife. Cover with cold water until ready for use, but keep the soaking short to prevent the loss of vitamins. When ready to cook, cut potatoes in chunks if you wish to purée them or leave them whole if they are to be sliced; in the latter case, try to use small potatoes.

Place 1 inch of water in heavy saucepan; bring to boil; add potatoes; return to boiling; cover tightly and reduce heat to medium (gentle simmering); cook until tender when pierced with a fork (about 30-35 minutes for larger potatoes, 20-25 minutes for small potatoes or chunks).

À l'étouffée or à l'étuvée (Steaming Method)

Use thin-skinned potatoes such as new white or small red, unpeeled or peeled or sliced. Place 1 inch water in large saucepan, then place a steamer basket or wire basket set on a rack over the water so that the bottom of the basket does not touch the water.

Place potatoes in basket; bring water to boil; cover tightly; reduce heat to medium or medium-high (water must steam steadily); steam until tender, about 20-30 minutes for larger potatoes, 10-15 minutes for very small or sliced potatoes. Never throw away the water; use it for soups as it contains valuable mineral salts.

Purée de pommes de terre (Mashed Potatoes)

Very often when tasting *purée de pommes de terre* the foreign visitor in France marvels at the fluffy and light texture. The secret is simply in the "ricing" of the boiled potatoes through a ricer or food mill; then the melted butter, salt, and pepper are added.

Carrotes persillées   1
Parsleyed Carrots

I remember my grandmother bringing carrots in from the garden to the cellar in the fall to be buried in a thick layer of sand. However, she would always leave some buried in the ground, covered by a layer of straw and gunny sacks where they would be protected from snow and frost until dug up later, to be eaten raw, crisp and crunchy. What a treat it was for us children visiting her house in the mountain of Provence at Christmastime! We would fight over the privilege of digging for them. Wrapped in warm clothing, we would troop into the garden and one of us, under Grandmother's direction, would brush away the snow and lift the gunny sack, stiff from the cold; there under the straw they would be, with their bleached tops, ready to be dug. Triumphant and pink-cheeked with cold, we would return to the house with our bounty.

(Serves 4)

1 pound carrots, scrubbed, sliced on the diagonal
3 cups chicken bouillon
Salt
2 cloves garlic, minced fine
¼ cup finely chopped parsley
2 tablespoons butter or margarine
Salt and pepper
½ teaspoon lemon juice

Bring carrots, chicken bouillon, and salt (very little and only if needed) to a boil in a saucepan; reduce heat to medium and cook carrots until tender but firm, about 5 minutes. Drain well; reserve carrots and keep bouillon for a soup base.

Melt butter or margarine in skillet; add carrots, parsley, and garlic; sauté 5 minutes over medium heat; add salt, pepper, and lemon juice. Serve.

Concombres au persil
1
Parsleyed Cucumbers

When you have a wealth of cucumbers from your garden, prepare them this way; it will help relieve the monotony of the usual cucumber salad.

(Serves 6-8)

3-4 medium-sized cucumbers, pared and seeded
Salt
Boiling water to barely cover
½ cube sweet butter
1 tablespoon finely chopped parsley
½ teaspoon dry dill leaves, crushed, or 1 tablespoon fresh dill,
    minced
Salt and white pepper

Cut cucumbers into 1-inch chunks (crosswise); drop into salted boiling water; cook uncovered in boiling water about 5-6 minutes; they should be tender but firm. Drain and refresh immediately under cold running water; set aside.

Melt butter in skillet slowly over medium heat; add cucumbers, parsley, dill, salt, and pepper; return to medium heat and sauté for 5 minutes until heated through. Serve immediately.

Beignets de courgettes 1
Zucchini Fritters

Les courgettes, or *coucourdes* as they are tenderly referred to in Provence, are an important part of the diet of the people of the South. It seems they came a long way from their place of origin, the Americas. This soft-skinned wonder is a member of the squash family. The South American Indians were growing squash thousands of years before the Spaniards landed on their shores. When the cultivation of this vegetable spread to North America, it was called *kass-na-squash*. The conquistadors brought squash back to Spain from where it spread all over the Mediterranean basin and eventually the world.

The fact that squash contains a wealth of vitamin A should be enough to encourage one to serve it often. Following is a quick and delicious way to prepare it.

(Serves 3-4)

2 medium-sized zucchini or 3 small ones
2 tablespoons olive oil or vegetable oil
1 garlic clove, finely minced
⅓ cup grated Parmesan or Swiss cheese
¼ teaspoon dried marjoram or basil leaves

Shave zucchini on coarse side of grater, then squeeze the liquid out through layers of cheesecloth or press through a strainer.

Place zucchini in mixing bowl; mix in olive oil, garlic, cheese, and herbs. Form patties 3 inches in diameter and fry on hot greased griddle.

Riz au safran

Saffron Rice

1

Rice is a relative newcomer to the Camargue region of Provence, but it adapted beautifully as the climatic conditions are quite favorable to its growth.

(Serves 6)

1 medium-sized onion, minced fine
2 tablespoons butter or margarine
2 cups long-grain rice
3 cups chicken broth, canned or homemade
⅛ teaspoon saffron
Salt
2 teaspoons grated lemon peel

Sauté onion in large heavy skillet in melted butter or margarine over medium-high heat until golden brown. Add rice; mix well; stir for 1 or 2 minutes; remove from heat.

Bring stock to a light boil in saucepan; add saffron and salt lightly. Add rice and mix well; bring to boil; reduce heat to simmer; cover and cook for 20 minutes or until all liquid is absorbed.

Just before serving, add lemon peel and fluff.

Tian de courgettes

Zucchini Casserole

1

In the region of Nice zucchini are served in this manner.

(Serves 3-4)

2 medium-sized zucchini, sliced thin with skin on
½ cup water or chicken broth or bouillon
1 cup cooked rice
1 whole egg, lightly beaten
2 tablespoons butter or margarine, melted
3 tablespoons milk or half-and-half
Salt and pepper
⅓ cup grated Gruyère, Swiss, or Parmesan cheese

Preheat oven to 350°.

Place zucchini in heavy saucepan or skillet with water or broth, and a pinch of salt. Cook over medium heat until water is completely evaporated. Shake frequently. Mix zucchini with rice, egg, butter, milk, salt, and pepper.

Turn this mixture into a greased or buttered baking dish, sprinkle with cheese and bake for 15-20 minutes or until set.

Poireaux à la vinaigrette   1
Leeks Vinaigrette

The leek, a vegetable of the onion family and a native of North America, long ago crossed the Mediterranean and was introduced into French and Italian cuisine. It was the Romans who helped propagate it during the invasion of England. The English word leek is the descendant of the Old English *lēac*, as *poireau* (or *porreau*) is of the Latin *porrum*.

Uncooked, the leek contains a large amount of vitamin C, some B vitamins, and traces of iron. It is also rich in potassium, a fact which should be good news for those lacking in this mineral.

(Serves 4)

8 large leeks, cleaned thoroughly
Boiling water
Salt
Vinaigrette sauce

Trim leeks, leaving 1 inch of green tops. Cook in salted boiling water to barely cover for 30 minutes or until tender. Drain; reserve water for use in a soup base.

Arrange leeks in serving dish; sprinkle vinaigrette over it. Two tablespoons mayonnaise and 1 tablespoon finely minced sweet onion may be added to the vinaigrette for a slightly different taste.

Courgettes gratinées   1
Zucchini au Gratin

This recipe made converts of some of our friends who professed to dislike zucchini.

(Serves 4)

5-6 medium-sized zucchini, sliced ⅛-inch thick lengthwise
Pinch of salt
⅓ cup water
2 tablespoons coarsely grated onion
⅓ cup fine bread crumbs
⅓ cup grated Parmesan cheese
1 teaspoon dried oregano leaves, crumbled
Salt and pepper
3 tablespoons olive oil

Put zucchini slices in lightly salted water in large heavy skillet. Cook over medium heat until tender but firm, about 5 minutes; drain thoroughly.

Arrange zucchini in one layer in large buttered baking dish. Mix onion, bread crumbs, Parmesan, oregano, and salt and pepper to taste. Sprinkle over zucchini; drizzle with oil and place under broiler (6 inches from heat source) until golden brown.

Daube de topinambours   1
Jerusalem Artichoke Stew

The Jerusalem artichoke was unknown in France until the end of the sixteenth century. It originated in North America. Its flavor resembles the flavor of the artichoke, but there the resemblance stops, for it is a member of the sunflower family; the part we use is the root.

The term *daube* is usually applied to a dish consisting of braised meat, but here it is a vegetable braised in wine.

To prepare the Jerusalem artichokes, scrub under cold water to prevent discoloration, and cut them in pieces into a bowl of water to which a few drops of lemon juice have been added.

(Serves 4)

2 tablespoons good vegetable oil or olive oil
1 medium-sized onion, peeled and chopped fine
1 pound Jerusalem artichokes, peeled and cut in 1-inch pieces
2 garlic cloves, minced fine
⅛ teaspoon nutmeg
1 bay leaf
1 tablespoon minced parsley
½ cup dry white wine
½ cup water

Sauté onion in oil in heavy skillet over medium-high heat until golden brown. Add Jerusalem artichokes, garlic, nutmeg, bay leaf, parsley, salt, and pepper; cover pan and simmer for 15 minutes, stirring once or twice. Add wine and water; increase heat to medium-high and let the mixture boil lightly for 3 minutes. Reduce heat and simmer partly covered until artichokes are tender and the sauce is reduced by half.

Croustade aux champignons   **1**
Mushroom Casserole

The marvelous fungi called mushrooms in all their varieties have been on earth for thousands of years. The Egyptians believed mushrooms were scattered on earth by thunderbolts, and called them "food of the gods." But it was not until the seventeenth century in France that the cultivated mushroom made its appearance. This special type was called *champignon de Paris* because it was in the capital that the cultivation was started in order to supply the table of Louis XIV, who greatly appreciated the fungus.

The meatiness and earthy flavor of mushrooms make them a favorite for meatless meals. Furthermore they are low in calories (a cup contains about 20 calories) but high in protein, niacin, vitamins B, C, and K, and minerals such as iron and potassium. We should serve them often, with or without meat.

(Serves 4)

8 ounces fresh mushrooms, cleaned and sliced
1 tablespoon butter or margarine
1 large shallot, chopped
1 tablespoon dry vermouth
2 tablespoons cream (half-and-half or whipping)
Salt and pepper
¼ cup grated Emmenthal or Swiss cheese

Preheat oven to 350°.

Melt butter or margarine in medium-sized frying pan; add mush-rooms; sauté over medium heat about 2-3 minutes or until mois-ture has evaporated and mushrooms are fairly tender but still firm. Add shallot, stir and cook 1 minute longer; add vermouth and stir until thoroughly heated; add cream, blend and heat 1 minute longer.

Butter a shallow baking dish; transfer mushroom mixture to it; sprinkle with grated cheese and place in preheated oven for 15 minutes or until top is golden brown. Serve immediately with white wine (Anjou, for example) or a good sparkling cider.

La truffade   2
Sautéed Potatoes and Cheese

This dish originated in Auvergne, but is also prepared in Haute Provence with a cheese called *tomme.* It was originally cooked by the shepherds over a wood fire which gave the dish a delicious flavor. A very satisfactory facsimile may be prepared with *ricotta salata*, an Italian cheese found in specialty cheese shops. This cheese, with its white, moist, grainy appearance and sweet taste, lends itself well to the dish.

(Serves 4)

¼ pound salt pork, diced and blanched
2-3 tablespoons oil or olive oil
6 potatoes, pared and sliced thin
Salt and pepper
6-8 ounces **ricotta salata** *cheese, sliced in thin strips or diced*

Sauté salt pork in heavy skillet until it has rendered its fat and only crisp *lardons* are left; remove *lardons* (they may be used in soups).

Add oil to fat in skillet; add potatoes, salt, and pepper and raise heat to medium-high; toss potatoes for 2-3 minutes; cover; reduce heat to simmer and cook for 20 minutes.

Add *ricotta* cheese, mix gently with potatoes; continue cooking, covered, for 5 minutes, stirring once. Uncover; raise heat to medium and cook 3 more minutes. Serve immediately.

Champignons farcis à la provençale   2
Stuffed Mushrooms Provençal Style

A great-looking accompaniment to any meat dish. Place one on each plate alongside the portion of meat and a vegetable of your choice.

(Serves 4)

3 tablespoons oil
5 large fresh mushrooms 2½-3 inches in diameter
3 tablespoons minced parsley
1 large clove garlic, minced fine
1 tablespoon butter or margarine
2 tablespoons fine bread crumbs
Salt and pepper
1 tablespoon grated Parmesan cheese
1 tablespoon butter or margarine

Preheat oven to 350°.

Wash mushrooms quickly and wipe with soft cloth. Remove stems and chop fine, adding 1 whole mushroom and chopping it also. Oil the 4 remaining caps and place in a well-buttered or oiled shallow baking pan. Set aside.

Sauté chopped mushroom and stems in skillet in 1 tablespoon butter or margarine over medium heat for 2 minutes; add parsley and garlic; continue cooking 2 minutes longer, stirring once or twice. Blend in bread crumbs, salt, and pepper; stir and remove from heat. Fill mushroom caps with mixture; sprinkle with grated Parmesan; dot each cap with ¼ tablespoon butter or margarine.

Bake in preheated oven 10-12 minutes. Serve immediately.

Haricots verts maître d'hôtel   1
Green Beans with Herb Butter

A nice accompaniment for roast lamb, veal, or pork. Of course, fresh beans are almost a must for this recipe. If it is impossible for you to obtain fresh green beans, I recommend a good name brand of canned beans rather than the frozen type. Drain the packing liquid; rinse the beans briefly under cold water.

(Serves 4-5)

1 ½ cups water
Salt
1 pound green beans, picked and cleaned
1 tablespoon finely minced parsley
½ tablespoon finely minced fresh tarragon leaves, or 1 teaspoon
*   dry tarragon leaves, crushed*
4 tablespoons butter or margarine
2 teaspoons lemon juice
¼ teaspoon nutmeg
Salt and pepper

Place water and salt to taste in medium-sized saucepan; bring to boil; add beans; bring back to light boil; cover; turn down to medium heat and cook until beans are tender but firm (8-10 minutes). Drain liquid and keep to add to soups. Freshen beans under running cold water for 1 or 2 minutes if you want to keep them bright green. Drain well. (If you are afraid of losing some vitamins, do not freshen.) Set aside.

Place parsley, tarragon, and butter in small bowl. Work mixture to blend all ingredients together.

Return beans to saucepan; add herb butter, lemon juice, nutmeg, and salt and pepper to taste; warm slowly until butter is melted and beans are hot. Serve.

Courgettes farcies   **3**
Stuffed Zucchini

Serve this dish as a hot entrée or for a lunch with *Salade provençale*.

(Serves 4)

1 slice bread
¼ cup milk
4 medium-sized zucchini
16 ounces cooked ham or beef, chopped fine
1 onion, chopped fine
1 clove garlic, minced fine
⅓ cup minced parsley
Salt and pepper
2 tablespoons oil
1 egg yolk, lightly beaten
½ cup grated Parmesan
1 tablespoon olive oil

Preheat oven to 375°.

Tear bread into chunks and soak in milk; set aside. Cut zucchini
lengthwise; drop into boiling salted water and parboil for 5 minutes; drain. Hollow out the inside by scooping out pulp, leaving a
shell resembling a small boat; set aside. Arrange the shells in a
shallow greased ovenproof casserole.

Squeeze milk from bread; discard milk; mash bread. Mix bread,
zucchini, meat, onion, garlic, parsley, salt, and pepper in a bowl.

Heat 2 tablespoons oil in heavy skillet over medium-high heat; add
vegetable mixture; cook, stirring often, for 3-4 minutes; add egg
yolk, stirring rapidly until well blended; continue cooking for 3
more minutes. The mixture should be thick.

Fill shells with this mixture; sprinkle with Parmesan cheese and
drizzle with olive oil. Bake at 375° for 15-20 minutes.

Endives gratinées   2
Broiled Endive

This smooth, slender lettuce, sometimes called French or Belgian endive, should not be confused with the curly-headed lettuce of the same name. Endive appears on the market during the winter months. It is about 4 inches in length, very compact, and has white leaves with a tinge of yellow or light green at the tips. The light colors are due to the endive's being taken from the field to cellars and buried in dirt during the winter. It is rather expensive but worth the try.

(Serves 6)

6 Belgian or French endive, cleaned
1 quart water with 1 teaspoon salt
2 tablespoons lemon juice
4 tablespoons butter or margarine
¼ cup grated Swiss or Gruyère cheese

Preheat oven to 450°.

Bring water, salt, and lemon juice to rolling boil in saucepan. Add endive and bring back to light boil; continue boiling 15 minutes. Drain well; reserve endive.

Melt 2 tablespoons butter or margarine in large skillet; add endive and sauté over medium heat until lightly colored; remove from heat.

Butter a shallow ovenproof pan. Arrange endive in bottom; sprinkle cheese over; dot with 2 remaining tablespoons butter; place in preheated oven. Bake 15 minutes; brown lightly under broiler, 2-3 minutes. Serve immediately.

Fèves à la ménagère
Housewife's Lima Beans

2

So many vegetables have become popular in the cooking repertory that one has to wonder why the fava has not become one of them here in the United States. It is a delightful treat to eat them very young and fresh out of their velvety pods, with a touch of salt and accompanied by French bread. This is the way we eat them at home as an hors d'oeuvre we call *à la croque-sel.*

The fava is a broad bean from the legume family and as such is an excellent source of protein, iron, vitamin B and fiber. The fat of the bean is polyunsaturated, making this legume a great nutritional addition to the diet.

(Serves 3)

1 10-ounce package frozen baby lima beans or the equivalent in fresh baby lima beans or fava beans (if you are fortunate enough to find very young ones or if you grow your own)
1 small onion, skinned and chopped fine
1 tablespoon olive oil or vegetable oil
1 large sprig summer savory, leaves only, chopped, or ⅛ teaspoon dried summer savory, crumbled
¼ cup cooking liquid
Salt and pepper
1 egg yolk lightly beaten
2 tablespoons cooking liquid

Cook frozen baby lima beans according to package directions as far as water is concerned, but reduce cooking time to 5 minutes. Drain water completely; save water; set beans aside.

Sauté onions in olive oil or oil in saucepan until soft and golden color. Add lima beans, ¼ cup cooking liquid, summer savory, salt and pepper. Bring to simmer and cook, covered, 15 minutes or until beans are tender.

Blend egg yolk and 2 tablespoons liquid and stir slowly into beans. Heat until slightly thickened. Serve immediately.

Poireaux gratinés   2
Leeks au Gratin

For this recipe choose medium-sized leeks; trim them, leaving the white part and the very light green part. Use the leftover green leaves for soups or stocks. This dish is very good served as a hot entrée. It is also excellent with baked ham. I would serve a nice Chablis, Pinot Chardonnay, Chenin Blanc, or Pinot de Loire with it.

8 medium-sized leeks
Boiling water
Salt
Béchamel sauce (see index)
Grated Gruyère or Swiss cheese

Trim leeks, leaving 1 inch of green tops. Cook in salted boiling water to barely cover for 30 minutes or until tender. Drain; reserve water for a soup base.

Arrange leeks in shallow buttered baking dish. Cover with Béchamel sauce, sprinkle with grated Gruyére or Swiss cheese; broil until golden brown.

Ragoût de carottes et petits pois   2
Medley of Peas and Carrots

Ragout as we know it usually contains meat and vegetables. Sometimes however the name is applied to vegetable dishes cooked and bound with a liaison of eggs or a white or brown sauce. It is a nice accompaniment to any kind of meat.

(Serves 3-4)

8 ounces young carrots, scrubbed
⅔ cup water
½ cup shelled peas
1 tablespoon butter or margarine
⅛ teaspoon nutmeg
Salt and pepper
1 large egg yolk, slightly beaten
6 tablespoons cream

Slice carrots about ⅛-inch thick; set aside; bring water to boil in medium-sized heavy saucepan; add carrots; bring back to light boil; cover and cook over medium-low heat 5-8 minutes or until tender but firm. Drain; reserve liquid for soups.

Place carrots, shelled peas, butter or margarine, nutmeg, and salt and pepper to taste in same saucepan; cover and cook over medium heat until peas are tender, about 5-8 minutes.

While vegetables are cooking blend egg yolk and cream; when vegetables are ready, add egg and cream mixture; reheat slowly until hot and sauce has thickened. Serve immediately.

Poivrons aux capres   1
Green Peppers with Capers

In Provence the green pepper is a non-bell type, long and sweet, known in the United States as Italian sweet pepper or sweet pimiento. Its thin flesh is less watery than the bell pepper, but this dish can be prepared very successfully with bell pepper. It is very good as an accompaniment to fish.

It is interesting to note that both the green and red pepper contain more vitamin C than oranges.

(Serves 6)

4 green bell peppers or 4 large Italian sweet peppers, seeded and sliced
2 tablespoons olive oil
3 medium-sized tomatoes, skinned, seeded, and chopped
2 tablespoons capers
2 large fresh basil leaves, minced, or 1 teaspoon dried basil leaves, crushed
Salt and pepper

Heat olive oil in deep, heavy skillet over medium heat; add green peppers and sauté, stirring until they lose their color and start to become limp. Add tomatoes, capers, basil, salt, and pepper; cook, covered, over medium-low heat about 20 minutes.

Pommes de terre persillées   2
Potatoes with Parsley

The best potatoes for this dish are small new potatoes. If not available, carve out your own from red thin-skinned or long white potatoes. (Use large end of a melon-baller. The leftover potato carvings may be used in soups.) Serve around a leg of lamb or any type of roast.

(Serves 4)

1 pound new potatoes, scrubbed, or equivalent in carved-out
    potatoes
2 tablespoons butter or margarine
¼ cup finely minced parsley
Salt and pepper

Drop potatoes in cold water after peeling. When ready to cook, drain water; steam them according to directions on page 117; drain thoroughly in colander.

Melt butter or margarine over medium heat in heavy skillet or saucepan until it starts to foam; add potatoes, parsley, and salt and pepper to taste; shake pan carefully to coat potatoes with butter and parsley. Cover for a few minutes until thoroughly hot, shaking once or twice.

Pommes de terre au gratin à la dauphinoise   2
Potatoes au Gratin in the Dauphiné Style

The Dauphiné is a southern region, bordered by Provence on the south, Languedoc to the west, Savoie to the north, and Italy to the east. A mountainous region, its cuisine is a mountain cuisine. It has nevertheless absorbed some of the cooking of Provence and the other surrounding regions. Like inhabitants, its cuisine is of a more hearty and rugged nature.

One of the main crops of the Dauphiné is potatoes of a good quality; another product is its cheese. The combination of these two has contributed to making the following dish famous.

(Serves 4)

2 pounds potatoes, pared and sliced ¼-inch thick and patted dry
1 garlic clove, mashed
1 tablespoon butter or margarine
½ cup grated Gruyère or Swiss cheese
Salt and pepper
1½ cups milk or light cream
¼ cup grated Gruyère or Swiss cheese
2 tablespoons butter, melted
2 eggs, lightly beaten
½ cup milk

Preheat oven to 350°.

Rub a baking dish with garlic, then with butter or margarine. Mix potatoes, salt, and pepper to taste, ½ cup cheese, and the 1½ cups milk in a bowl; place in baking dish; sprinkle with ¼ cup remaining cheese and melted butter. Bake for 1½ hours.

Combine eggs and ½ cup milk, pour over potatoes; continue baking for another ½ hour. The top should be golden brown; if not, place under broiler for a few minutes.

Laitues braisées au jus   2
Braised Lettuce

Few people know that lettuce goes back to the Roman era. The word *salade*, also used in French to refer to lettuce, comes from the Latin *salata*—salty, descriptive of the seasoning of the greens. At that time cultivated lettuce was still unknown, but meadows abounded in wild greens which the Romans served with a salty vinaigrette.

It was not until the 1600s, during the reign of Louis XIV of France, that the great chef LaVarenne used salads as an accompaniment to the meals served to the king. As the story goes, Louis ate them in quantity. Today a meal is not a meal without a salad. But all over France, the South included, lettuce is served cooked in many ways. The taste is entirely different.

(Serves 4-6)

4 medium or 6-8 small Bibb or Boston lettuce heads, rinsed and
   trimmed
3½ quarts (approximately) salted water
3 tablespoons butter or margarine
1 medium-sized onion, chopped fine
½ teaspoon grated nutmeg
¾ cup canned beef broth or beef stock (homemade)
Salt and pepper

Bring salted water in large kettle to boil; drop lettuce heads in boiling water and boil 3-4 minutes; drain thoroughly. If heads are small, leave whole; if too large, cut in half lengthwise.

Melt butter over medium heat in large heavy skillet; add onion and sauté until transparent and soft.

Arrange lettuce heads or halves, cut-side down, over onion; sprinkle nutmeg over lettuce; add broth. Bring to light boil; reduce heat to simmer; cover pan with a round piece of buttered waxed paper, butter side down. Put lid on top of waxed paper and cook, simmering, for 25-30 minutes or until tender. Remove cover and increase heat to very light boil until liquid is reduced to fairly thick consistency. Add salt and pepper; baste with juice; serve.

Cardons ou blettes au gratin   2
Swiss Chard au Gratin

The *cardon* in French, or cardoon in English, is the rib or midrib of a vegetable akin to the artichoke. In France it is considered a great delicacy, especially in the South and the Lyonnais region. Cardoons are even canned like asparagus and sold all over the world. The ribs of Swiss chard may be used in the same manner.

(Serves 4)

4 cups chard stalks or ribs cut into pieces 2-3 inches in length
¾ cup Béchamel Sauce (see index)
2 egg yolks, beaten lightly
3 tablespoons grated Parmesan or Gruyère cheese

Preheat oven to 375°.

Blanch chard ribs in salted boiling water; drain well; arrange in buttered shallow casserole or glass pie plate. Cover with Béchamel sauce into which the egg yolks have been thoroughly blended. Sprinkle with cheese; place in 375° oven for 10 minutes, then broil lightly until golden brown.

Tomates provençales   2
Provençal Tomatoes

The tomato, referred to in the South as *la pomme d'amour* (love apple) came to the Old World from Peru, Ecuador, and Bolivia. It was once a weed, with a fruit the size of a small prune, before hybridizing gave us the tomato as we know it today. The first plants were brought to Spain by the conquistadors more as a curiosity than as a food. In fact, it was thought to be poisonous, and it was not until the sixteenth century in Europe and the nineteenth in the United States that the tomato became indispensable.

In addition to its versalility, this beautiful fruit has the advantage of being low in calories, high in vitamins A and C and potassium. Serve the following dish with any kind of chops—lamb, veal, or pork—and a nice Claret, Zinfandel, or Cabernet Sauvignon.

(Serves 6)

6 medium-sized tomatoes, halved and seeded
6 tablespoons olive oil
6 tablespoons finely chopped parsley
1 tablespoon finely chopped fresh basil leaves, or 1 teaspoon dried
    basil leaves, crushed
3 garlic cloves, minced fine
2 tablespoons fine bread crumbs
Salt and pepper

Sprinkle tomatoes lightly with salt. Put 4 tablespoons oil in skillet and heat over medium-low heat; add tomatoes, cut-side down; cook until juices have evaporated, 1-2 minutes, being careful not to overcook, for the tomatoes must be firm. Turn carefully and cook the other side 1 minute longer. Remove to gratin dish, cut-sides up; sprinkle lightly with salt. Reserve oil.

Place the 2 remaining tablespoons oil in small, heavy skillet or saucepan; add parsley, garlic, basil, salt, and pepper; cook over medium heat for 2 minutes; remove from heat; add bread crumbs; mix well. Spoon over tomato halves; drizzle with reserved oil. Place under broiler for a few minutes until very light golden brown.

The filled tomatoes can also be baked entirely in a 400° oven: halve and seed the tomatoes, salt lightly, let them drain 15 minutes on paper towels. Divide parsley mixture among tomato halves. Place on oiled baking dish; drizzle with olive oil; bake, uncovered, at 375° for 10-12 minutes.

Gratin de navets de grandmaman 2
Turnips au Gratin, Grandma's Style

We seldom think of preparing turnips, and yet, like other root vegetables, they are rich in minerals which should be included in our diet. The unusual addition of an apple gives this dish a wonderfully different flavor.

(Serves 3-4)

2 cups water
Salt
1 pound white turnips, peeled and quartered
¼ cup green onion tops (white part), chopped
1 tablespoon butter or margarine
1 medium-sized red apple, peeled, seeded, and coarsely chopped
½ cup light cream, heated
⅛ teaspoon paprika
Salt and pepper
1 tablespoon fine bread crumbs
1 tablespoon butter

Preheat oven to 350°.

Bring turnips, water, and salt to boil in saucepan; continue cooking at fairly rapid boil until turnips are tender (15-20 minutes). Drain; keep turnips warm; set aside.

Sauté green onion tops in medium-sized skillet in butter or margarine over medium heat until transparent; add apples; stir over medium heat 1 more minute.

Add hot cream to turnips and whirl until fairly smooth in electric blender; add green onion-apple mixture; whirl just enough to blend.

Spoon into buttered shallow baking dish and bake 15 minutes in preheated oven; sprinkle with bread crumbs and dot with butter; place under broiler until golden brown. Serve.

La crique
Potato Pancake

2

La crique is a thick pancake, basically made of grated potatoes. It is cooked rather slowly, served golden and puffed. It makes a complete meal when served with a salad of greens or mixed vegetables and crusty French bread. I even leave the skin on the potatoes as it contains a lot of minerals. If you do this, scrub the potatoes thoroughly with a stiff brush and remove the eyes and green spots if any are present.

(Serves 2)

2 tablespoons olive oil
2 cups coarsely grated potatoes
1 clove garlic, minced fine
2 tablespoons parsley, chopped fine
2 eggs, slightly beaten
Salt and pepper
1 or 2 tablespoons olive or vegetable oil

Heat 2 tablespoons olive oil in a heavy skillet to the point where a drop of water sprinkled on the oil dances; add potatoes, garlic, and parsley; reduce heat to medium; cover and cook for 2 or 3 minutes, stirring once or twice. Cool slightly.

Heat 1 or 2 tablespoons oil in an omelet pan. Meanwhile add the potato mixture to the eggs; add salt and pepper and pour into hot oil. Cook over medium-high heat until set on the bottom. Place a dish or lid larger than the circumference of the pan over it; flip pan quickly to transfer pancake to dish or lid, then slide it back into skillet, cooked-side up, to cook other side for 3-5 more minutes. Serve hot.

La rapée   2
Mountain Potato Pancake

Come Friday, *le jour maigre* ("lean" day), *Grandmaman* would often serve *la rapée*. It was a substantial and satisfying lunch that would keep her family going until the evening meal. She would serve slices of her beautiful round mountain bread and an enormous salad with it. Cheese and fruits would follow. Truly a feast!

This dish resembles *la crique*, but the taste is different because the grated potatoes are not precooked, flour is added, and only nutmeg is used as flavoring.

(Number to be served depends on appetite!)

1 pound potatoes, pared
3 eggs, slightly beaten
1 tablespoon melted butter or margarine
2 level tablespoons all-purpose flour
Salt and pepper
⅛ tablespoon nutmeg (freshly grated or powdered)
2 tablespoons butter or margarine

Grate potatoes on coarse grater. Blend potatoes, eggs, melted butter, flour, salt, pepper, and nutmeg in a bowl.

Melt butter or margarine in medium-sized skillet over medium-high heat until it starts to foam; tilt pan to coat with butter. Add egg-potato mixture; cook over medium-low heat until set in the bottom, proceeding as with an omelet.

Loosen around the edges with spatula; place a platter or lid over skillet to cover entirely with some overlap; hold it with the hand.

Take skillet handle in other hand and flip skillet upside down to loosen omelet onto the platter or lid. (Do this operation over the sink until you are expert at it, as some of the hot butter could spill onto the stove.) Slide omelet back into skillet, and cook the other side 5 minutes longer or until potatoes are done. Pancake should be on the crisp side.

Tomates farcies
Stuffed Tomatoes
2

The same preparation as for *stuffed zucchini* (see index) is used, but do not parboil. Slice off top part of tomatoes; seed, then chop the top and pulp; add to meat and herbs. Stuff as for zucchini and bake in a 400° oven for 15 minutes.

Pommes de terre à la Robert
Potatoes Robert
3

A nice change from mashed potatoes.

(Serves 6)

1 clove garlic, mashed
1 tablespoon butter or margarine
8 good-sized potatoes, pared and quartered
Boiling water to cover, or milk
Salt
¼ cup butter or margarine
¼ teaspoon nutmeg
¼ cup milk, or half-and-half
Salt and pepper

Preheat oven to 375°.

Blend garlic and 1 tablespoon butter or margarine to make a paste;

rub the sides and bottom of a large, shallow baking dish with this paste; set aside.

Bring potatoes, water, and salt to a boil in saucepan; cover and keep at light boil until potatoes are tender; drain. Rice potatoes in ricer or mash in electric mixer. Add butter or margarine, nutmeg, milk, salt, and pepper; beat until fluffy.

Fill prepared baking dish with potato mixture and bake for 45 minutes or until hot. Place under broiler for 2 more minutes to brown top.

Ragoût de haricots à égrener   **3**
Shelling Bean Ragout

If you are lucky enough to have shelling beans at the end of the growing season, try this recipe and you will be in for a treat!

(Serves 4)

5 cups water
Salt
2 cups shelled fresh shelling beans
1 large bay leaf
2 sprigs parsley
2 sprigs fresh thyme, or 1 teaspoon dry thyme leaves
1 large garlic clove
2 tablespoons butter or margarine
1 medium-sized onion, chopped fine
2 teaspoons flour
½ cup dry white wine
½ cup chicken bouillon or broth
2 teaspoons tomato paste
Salt and pepper

Bring salted water to boil in large saucepan; add beans, bay leaf, thyme, and garlic. Bring back to light boil and cook 15-20 minutes, loosely covered, until beans are tender but firm. Discard herbs and garlic; drain liquid and reserve beans; keep them warm.

Melt butter or margarine in large heavy saucepan or skillet; add onion; sauté over medium heat until golden; blend in flour; add wine slowly; stir to blend flour; add bouillon, tomato paste, and salt and peppar to taste; cook over medium-low heat 5-10 minutes longer. The gravy should be fairly thick.

A purée of beans can be made by straining beans and gravy through a food mill (do not use blender). Add 1 tablespoon butter to the purée, reheat and serve.

La bohémienne   2
The Gypsy (a vegetable stew)

This dish was originally prepared by the Gypsies of Provence, who used to serve it with the meat of a hedgehog. Fortunately for the prickly, charming little beast, we use the dish without him now and serve it as a vegetable or a sauce for cooked pasta. It resembles ratatouille and could have been its precursor.

In the Camargue region a very similar dish is prepared using only tomatoes and eggplant; it is known there under the name of *guincho-clau*. In the Languedoc it is prepared with tomatoes, eggplant, parsley, garlic, and a mushroom called *cèpe* (an edible Boletus). If you want to try this delicious dish, Languedoc style, use our hothouse mushrooms; the large and slightly open ones are perfect for this. Do not bake, and omit the cheese. Delicious!

This recipe can be served as a vegetable dish or as a garniture for pasta.

(Serves 4)

3 large tomatoes, skinned, seeded, and chopped coarsely
2 large eggplants, peeled and cubed
1 large green pepper, seeded and cubed small
1 large garlic clove, minced fine
3 tablespoons olive oil
Salt and pepper
½ cup grated Parmesan or Gruyère cheese

Preheat oven to 400°.

Sprinkle eggplant with salt; set aside for 30 minutes. Drain, rinse under cold water; pat dry.

Combine tomatoes, eggplant and green peppers in heavy skillet; cook uncovered over medium heat until liquid has completely evaporated. Mash mixture with fork from time to time. Process will take 10-15 minutes.

Add garlic, olive oil, salt, and pepper; continue cooking until thickened, about 20 minutes. Transfer mixture to oven-proof shallow baking dish. Sprinkle with cheese; bake in 400° oven until cheese melts. Serve as vegetable dish to accompany chicken or fish.

For pasta, add to cooked pasta. Mix well and serve with Parmesan.

Pommes de terre en croquettes   3
Potato Croquettes

There are a great number of recipes for *croquettes de pommes de terre*. This one however is the most often-used in home cooking.

(Serves 6-8)

5-6 Idaho or russet potatoes (about 1 pound), peeled and quartered
      (leftover mashed potatoes may also be used)
¼ cup butter
1 whole egg, beaten lightly
1 egg yolk, beaten lightly
⅛ teaspoon nutmeg
Salt and pepper
1 egg white, lightly beaten
⅔ cup very fine bread crumbs
¼ cup grated Parmesan cheese
Oil or fat for deep-fat frying

Boil potatoes according to directions (on page 116) or in your own favorite manner. Cook until tender. Drain thoroughly and discard water. Rice them through a food mill into a large saucepan; add butter, whole egg, egg yolk, nutmeg, salt, and pepper to taste; blend well. Stir rapidly with wooden spoon over low heat until it becomes a firm and homogenous mass.

Transfer to a plate; pick up small amounts of mixture, the size of a walnut, and mold into oblong shapes. Dip in egg white, then bread crumbs and cheese; using a spoon drop them one at a time into hot fat ½-inch deep, heated to 375° in deep fryer or deep pan. When golden brown, remove with slotted spoon to drain on paper toweling. Serve around a roast or braised piece of meat as garniture.

*   *   *

Pommes de terre en boulettes

A *boulette* is a small ball. Follow preparation as above, but add about ½ cup flour to the mashed potatoes; shape into small balls the size of a large walnut. Poach them in salted boiling water for 3-4 minutes; drain in colander. Place in greased baking dish; sprinkle thoroughly with Parmesan and ¼ cup melted butter and place in 400° oven until golden brown.

Fonds d'artichauts farcis   **3**
Stuffed Artichoke Bottoms

This makes an excellent first course or a side dish to be served with meat.

(Serves 4)

4 medium-sized fresh artichokes
4 ounces fresh mushrooms, scrubbed and chopped fine
2 tablespoons finely minced parsley
2 large garlic cloves, minced fine
2 tablespoons olive oil
1 tablespoon fine bread crumbs
Salt and pepper
1 tablespoon grated Parmesan cheese
1 tablespoon butter or margarine

Cut off artichoke stems and the tough outer leaves with large sharp knife. Cut through artichokes about ¾ inch above the bottom. Discard leaves above the cut part; what is left are the bottoms. Cook bottoms in boiling salted water to cover for 20-30 minutes or until tender but not soft. Drain water and discard. Cool bottoms. When easy to handle, remove the chokes and discard. Set bottoms aside.

Preheat oven to 375°.

Mix chopped mushrooms, parsley, and garlic in bowl. Heat oil in medium-sized skillet over medium heat; add mushroom mixture and sauté for 3 minutes, stirring often; add bread crumbs; salt and pepper to taste; blend thoroughly by stirring; cook one more minute or until mixture comes together in a mass. Remove from heat.

Fill each artichoke bottom with some of the mixture; sprinkle with Parmesan; dot each with butter or margarine and place in a buttered shallow baking dish. Bake in preheated oven for 8-10 minutes; then place under broiler until light brown. Watch carefully.

Haricots blancs nouveaux   3
Fresh Podded Beans

This dish is a meal in itself. Toward the end of the growing season, it provides an excellent way to utilize the beans that have gone to seed. Sometimes the local markets or supermarkets offer shelling beans. If so, by all means buy them and try this dish. If you are unable to find them, substitute fresh black-eyed peas.

(Serves 4-6)

3 cups shelled fresh shelling beans or black-eyed peas
3½ cups water
Salt
1 onion, peeled
1 carrot, scrubbed and quartered
1 bay leaf
4 sprigs parsley
2 sprigs thyme or ½ teaspoon dried thyme
1 garlic clove, peeled

Bring salted water to boil in large saucepan; add beans, onion, carrot, bay leaf, parsley, thyme, and garlic clove. Bring back to light boil; reduce heat to medium and cook until half-done (about 15 minutes). Drain beans, reserving liquid; strain liquid through fine sieve; set aside.

2 tablespoons fat or oil
1 onion, chopped fine
⅛ teaspoon nutmeg
¼ teaspoon dried thyme leaves, crumbled
1 bay leaf
¼ cup chopped parsley
Salt and pepper
Enough country or German sausages for 4 or 6 people
¼ pound slab bacon, ¼-inch thick, blanched

Sauté onions in fat in large, heavy saucepan over medium heat until light brown; add half-cooked beans and just enough cooking liquid so that it can be seen through the top layer. Add salt, pepper, nutmeg, thyme, bay leaf, and parsley, the sausages and the bacon. Bring to light boil; reduce heat to very low; cover and cook until beans have absorbed the liquid.

Aubergines à la provençale   3
Eggplant Casserole

The South adopted the eggplant as wholeheartedly as it did the zucchini and the tomato. This purple fruit came to France from India at the end of the sixteenth century. The French *aubergines* are larger and thinner than ours, and the better-known in France are the Barbentane and the "long purple."

Eggplant is a great meat substitute because of its texture. Low in calories and carbohydrates, and rich in potassium, phosphorus, and calcium, it makes the ideal substitute for meat for vegetarians and calorie-watchers.

If you have a small amount of leftover meat, adding it to the eggplant provides all the protein you need. In this recipe leftover ham is indicated, but you could use pork or beef as well.

(Serves 4)

8 *small eggplants about 7 inches in length, peeled*
¾ *cup cooked ham, chopped fine*
⅓ *cup minced parsley*
2 *garlic cloves, minced fine*
Salt and pepper
3 *tablespoons olive oil*
⅓ *cup grated Parmesan cheese.*

Preheat oven to 375°.

Cut the peeled eggplants in half; scoop out some of the center to leave a shell; chop pulp fine and set aside. Salt inside of eggplant shells and let them drain for 30 minutes. Rinse; poach for 2 minutes in boiling salted water. Drain and freshen under cold water until cool; pat dry; set aside.

Mix chopped pulp, ham, parsley, garlic, salt, and pepper; fill eggplant cavities with this mixture. Place in ovenproof casserole. Sprinkle oil over it and bake, covered, for 20 minutes. Remove from heat, uncover; sprinkle Parmesan over eggplants and place under broiler until golden brown.

Aubergines gratinées à la catalane   **3**
Stuffed Eggplant, Catalan Style

The Roussillon is a very fertile region where all kinds of vegetables and fruits grow under a most favorable sky. One of the favorite vegetables there is eggplant. One way the housewife of the region serves it is stuffed and with the addition of hard-boiled eggs instead of meat. Following is the recipe for this delicious dish which can also be used as an hors d'oeuvres (entrée).

(Makes 4 servings as an entrée, 2 as a vegetable)

4 *small eggplants split in half lengthwise*
4-5 *tablespoons olive oil*
¼ *cup finely chopped onion*
2 *cloves garlic, minced fine*

¼ cup finely chopped parsley
1 hard-boiled egg, chopped fine
Salt and pepper
½ cup dried bread crumbs

Preheat oven to 350°.

Scoop out pulp from the halves of eggplants, leaving a shell ⅛-inch thick. Salt the inside and place them cut-side down on a piece of paper toweling to drain for 30 minutes.

Cube the pulp and sprinkle with salt; let it drain in a colander ½ hour.

Rinse shells, pat dry, brush inside and out with oil and place them in an oiled baking dish. Bake at 350° for 15-20 minutes or until softened but firm to the touch.

Meanwhile rinse pulp, pat dry, and chop fine; reserve. Place 3 tablespoons olive oil and chopped onion in heavy frying pan; sauté until transparent over medium-low heat. Add garlic, sauté 1 more minute; then add the pulp and parsley, salt and pepper, and sauté 2 minutes. Remove from heat; add chopped hard-boiled egg and blend. Divide this mixture among the prebaked shells; sprinkle with bread crumbs, drizzle with the leftover olive oil. Return to hot oven and bake for 20 minutes or until top is golden and crisp. If the top does not become crisp, place under broiler for a few minutes.

Épinards gratinés aux oeufs   **3**
Spinach and Hard-Boiled Eggs au Gratin

I have always loved spinach and my children love it also. I attribute this unusual fondness for the leafy vegetable to my way of preparing it, which was my mother's way. The finer it is chopped after cooking it in water and squeezing it dry, the better the texture will be. The *hachoir* knife or the chef's knife is best for this purpose. The blender has a tendency to make spinach "mushy," and the food processor gives it an uneven texture; with the *hachoir* you have perfect control.

(Serves 4-5)

4 hard-boiled eggs, peeled and quartered or sliced
1 pound fresh spinach, cleaned and washed, or 2 10-ounce pack-
    ages frozen spinach
2 tablespoons butter or margarine
2 tablespoons all-purpose flour
1 cup warm milk
¼ teaspoon grated nutmeg
Salt and pepper
⅓ cup bread crumbs
1 tablespoon melted butter or margarine

If fresh spinach is used, cook it in 6 cups rapidly-boiling salted
water for 4 minutes; drain thoroughly by squeezing every bit of
moisture out; chop fine.

If frozen spinach is used, cook according to package directions and
proceed as above; set aside.

Preheat oven to 400°.

Melt butter or margarine in medium-sized saucepan over
medium-low heat; blend in flour, breaking all lumps with wooden
spoon; blend in warm milk, stirring constantly. Add nutmeg and
salt and pepper to taste; cook over medium heat, stirring until
thickened and smooth.

Combine with spinach and place in buttered ovenproof casserole.
Arrange eggs in sections or slices over and around top; sprinkle
with breadcrumbs; drizzle with melted butter or margarine; bake
10-12 minutes in preheated oven. Place under broiler a few minutes to brown top lightly. (Watch carefully; it should be golden—
not dark brown.)

Fonds d'artichauts aux pommes de terre   3
Hearts of Artichoke with Potatoes

This dish is a meal in itself. I have prepared it hundreds of times,
but each time its aroma is the magic carpet which transports me
home to Maman's kitchen. It spells Provence and all its magic.

(Serves 4)

4 medium-sized fresh artichokes, or 2 10-ounce packages frozen
    artichoke hearts
3 cups water with 1 tablespoon lemon juice
1 pound round red or white potatoes, pared and sliced ¼ inch
    thick
¾ cup bacon or salt pork, diced small
1 tablespoon vegetable oil
1 medium-sized onion, chopped fine
1 large garlic clove, minced fine
2 tablespoons finely minced parsley
1 medium-sized ripe tomato, skinned, seeded, and chopped fine
1 teaspoon dried thyme leaves, crushed
1 bay leaf
⅔ cup hot water
Salt and pepper

If fresh artichokes are used, prepare hearts: wash; cut off stem at
base; snap off all the leaves with your fingers; remove the choke or
thistle part from center with knife or vegetable parer. This will
leave the crisp white bottom part called the hearts, or buttons, of
the artichoke.

Cut hearts in half; slice ¼-inch thick; drop in bowl of cold water
with lemon juice (to prevent discoloration). Drop pared potatoes in
same water and set aside.

Blanch the bacon or pork-fat pieces in small saucepan in rapidly
boiling water 2 minutes. Drain, pat dry, and reserve.

Place the vegetable oil in heavy saucepan or Dutch oven and
reserved bacon or salt-pork pieces; sauté over low heat until crisp.
Remove crisps to paper toweling; reserve.

Add onion to fat in same saucepan and sauté over medium heat
until soft and golden; add garlic and parsley, stir to blend; add
tomatoes, thyme, and bay leaf.

Drain artichoke and potato slices; add to onion mixture in saucepan.* Add hot water, salt and pepper, and reserved bacon crisps.

---

*If you are using frozen artichokes, add them at this point, with potato slices, to
onion mixture.

Bring to a boil; reduce heat to very low and cook, covered, for 20 minutes or until vegetables are tender. If too thick, add a little hot water during cooking. (It should be thick, not watery; but your potatoes have a great deal to do with the absorption of water; so watch once or twice during cooking for thickness.)

Lentilles au vin   3
Lentils in Wine

The history of the lentil is as old as the history of man himself. In fact, the seed of this legume was cultivated in Asia as far back as 10,000 B.C. It is a staple used almost daily in many Middle Eastern countries. Because of its wealth of protein (four times its equal weight in meat), it is an ideal food in those countries where meat is not consumed. The French have long included lentils in their cooking repertoire. Here is the way my mother prepares them.

(Serves 6)

1½ cups lentils (green or brown)
1 onion studded with whole cloves
1 bay leaf
1 garlic clove, peeled
1 medium-sized carrot, cleaned and quartered
1 teaspoon salt
Water to cover by 1 inch
1 medium-sized onion, chopped fine
2 tablespoons oil
1 level teaspoon tomato paste
1 level tablespoon all-purpose flour
¼ cup dry red wine
¾ cup cooking liquid
½ teaspoon dried thyme leaves, crushed
Salt and pepper
6 croutons frits*

Combine lentils, onion, clove, bay leaf, garlic, carrot, salt, and water in large saucepan. Bring to boil, reduce heat to simmer, cover and cook until lentils are just about tender (25-30 minutes); drain immediately; reserve liquid; discard bay leaf, garlic, and onion. Remove carrots (they may be added to soup or to lentils).

Sauté chopped onion in oil over medium heat until golden brown in heavy skillet; blend in tomato paste; sprinkle flour over; stir, add hot wine and liquid from lentils slowly and blend; add thyme, stir to blend. Cook over medium-low heat 3-4 minutes to thicken; add lentils and cook covered over low heat 5 minutes longer. Serve with hot *croutons frits*.

Croutons frits: Fried croutons — not croutons of the type found in American stores, but slices of French bread fried lightly in butter on both sides.

6 slices French bread
¼ cup or more butter or margarine

Place butter in heavy skillet; melt over medium heat. When butter is hot and foamy, add bread slices and sauté until golden brown; turn them over and fry other side. Add butter if needed. Drain on paper towels.

Artichauts à la barigoule   3
Stewed Artichokes

Artichokes are a dieter's good fortune. They are low in calories, (a medium-sized one contains 40 calories), rich in potassium, and contain vitamins A, B, and C.

This aristocrat of the vegetable kingdom came from Southern Europe. The ancient Greeks and Romans knew of it, and the wealthy Romans paid a high price to put artichokes on their tables. The artichoke was grown in Italy, France, and Spain as early as the fifteenth century and was introduced to the United States by the French in Louisiana and the Spanish on the West Coast, especially California.

The following recipe makes a satisfying and delicious luncheon dish.

(Serves 4)

8 small, tender artichokes, cleaned
Water to cover
Juice of ½ lemon
8 ounces mushrooms, cleaned and chopped
3 medium-sized onions, chopped fine
2 shallots, chopped fine (optional)
1 clove garlic, minced fine
½ teaspoon dried thyme leaves
1 tablespoon minced parsley
Salt and pepper
5 tablespoons oil or butter or margarine
⅓ cup dry white wine
¼ cup water

Remove coarse outer leaves; snip top of each artichoke ⅔ of the way down and remove the choke from the center. Soak artichokes for ½ hour in water to which lemon juice has been added. Remove from water and blanch them in boiling salted water for 5 minutes; drain; reserve artichokes.

Mix mushrooms, 2 onions, shallots, thyme, parsley, garlic, salt, and pepper in bowl; sauté this mixture in frying pan with 3 table-spoons of the fat over low heat for 5 minutes.

Stuff artichokes with this mixture; arrange them in Dutch oven with remaining onion, wine, and water and the 2 remaining tab-lespoons of fat. Sprinkle lightly with salt and pepper; bring to boil; reduce to simmer; cover and cook for 45 minutes to 1 hour.

Ratatouille   **3**
Ratatouille

The word ratatouille derives from the Provençal *ratatouia*—"poor man's stew." And what a colorful word! The sound of it evokes Provence, its melodious and sonorous language and its verbal people, Latin to the core, proud of their country and their origin.

This dish probably originated in the region of Nice. It is served either hot or cold and is very often taken on picnics after being thoroughly chilled, to be served between slices of French bread cut lengthwise.

(Serves 4-6)

2 medium-sized eggplants or 4 small Japanese eggplants, cut in 1-inch cubes
½ cup olive oil
2 medium-sized onions, skinned and chopped
2 medium-sized zucchini with skin, cut in 1-inch cubes
2 medium-sized green peppers, seeded and cut in narrow strips
3 large ripe tomatoes, skinned, seeded, and cubed small
2 garlic cloves, minced
2 large fresh basil leaves, minced, or 1 teaspoon dried basil leaves
1 teaspoon dried thyme leaves, crushed
1 bay leaf
1 tablespoon minced parsley
Salt and pepper
Oil-cured black olives, pitted and slivered (optional)

Sprinkle about ⅛ teaspoon salt over eggplant; set aside ½ hour. Drain liquid rendered, rinse under cold water, pat dry, set aside.

Sauté onion in large, heavy skillet in ¼ cup olive oil over medium heat until soft and transparent. Add another ¼ cup olive oil and eggplant; continue cooking for 5 minutes; add zucchini and green peppers; cook 5 minutes longer.

Add tomatoes, garlic, basil, thyme, bay leaf, parsley, salt, and pepper; increase heat to medium-high until mixture starts to boil*; reduce heat to low and cover tightly. Cook 35 minutes; if you wish to use olives, add now and continue cooking 5 minutes longer. The mixture should be thick; if too thin remove cover and cook 1 or 2 minutes more. Discard bay leaf; taste for seasoning; mash lightly with potato masher.

May be served hot as a vegetable or cold as an hors d'oeuvre. Also may be reheated the next day.

---

*Do not be alarmed by the consistency of the mixture at this point. The vegetables render their juices during cooking and the mixture will be thin for a while after the first ten minutes.

Fish, Crustaceans, and Mollusks

From Marseille to Monaco, strung along the coast and facing the waterfront, are miles of hotels and restaurants. They range from the three-star level to small bistros, all very Gallic and pungent with garlic and *pastis*, offering *bouillabaisses* and *soupes de poissons* redolent with olive oil and saffron, *loup de mer* (sea bass), grilled whole on a bed of fennel, and other specialties.

Not as glamorous and well-known as the Riviera, the western outposts of the South are now coming into their own. Languedoc and Roussillon, the two most southern provinces, are being rediscovered by tourists for their varied interest and beauty and for their distinctive cuisines.

From across the Pyrenean borders, the Catalan influence has found its way into the cuisine of the region. This is especially true of the Roussillon, where the rich harvest of fish, crustaceans, and mollusks is prepared with the help of garlic, tomatoes, saffron, and other spices.

As in all the Mediterranean countries, fish plays a leading role among the foods of the South. In all the coastal cities and villages, fish is brought to the markets or sold from the fishing boats the morning of the catch, thus ensuring freshness and flavor.

One of my fondest memories of Marseille, my home-town, is of sitting on the terrace of a restaurant at the Vieux Port, the old harbor, enjoying a *bouillabaisse*. The restaurant, owned by one of our friends, provided not only excellent seafood but a colorful and exciting view of the old city. Behind us, like a great river, the main artery La Canebière would flow with a cosmopolitan crowd, shopping, gesticulating, laughing in the brilliant sunshine, or watching the young men barking in praise of their respective bistro or café. To the left, on the hillside overlooking the sea, the Roman-Byzantine basilica of Notre Dame de la Garde stood reassuring and protective, pink in the voluptuous light found only in this part of the world. To the right, the ancient city with its warm rose tile roofs, its tortuous and narrow streets, teemed with people going back and forth to and from the harbor crowded with fishing boats, yachts, and noisy tourist boats.

The sultry breeze coming from the open sea would die down, breaking the water into tiny waves along the quays like myriad sparkling jewels, ever moving, ever changing. And over all this would float the pungent smell of a beautiful *bouillabaisse*, made of the freshest of fish brought that morning from the sea and presented triumphantly at our table, like a masterpiece.

The fish found in the Mediterranean waters are unique and impossible to export, but we in America also have all sorts of marvelous fish, and even if we live inland, with modern transportation fish can be flown to all parts of the country.

A FEW WORDS ABOUT FISH

A good way to recognize fresh fish is first of all through its odor; it should be fresh and mild. The eyes should be clear, not sunken. The flesh should be firm to the touch.

Cook fish the day of the purchase. If you use frozen fish, thaw it in the refrigerator and cook it as soon as it is thawed. If you cannot use it that day, wrap it in plastic, then surround it with ice cubes and place it in the refrigerator.

No kind of fish will stand overcooking. Fish is done when it flakes easily if pricked with a fork. A good rule to follow in baking fish is to measure it at the thickest part and bake at 350° for 10 minutes per inch.

To poach fish if you do not have a fish poacher, use a wide enameled or non-stick-surface frying pan half-filled with a simple *court-bouillon* or wine *court-bouillon* (see below). Heat it to boiling, then reduce to a simmer. Submerge a strip of foil, 5 inches wide and long enough to overlap the pan, in the liquid. Place the fish on the foil, cover pan and simmer 15 minutes per inch of thickness of fish. When the fish is done and flakes easily, lift up the foil with the fish on it and drain well. Prepare the fish with your favorite recipe.

A special note about stock-fish (or *estoco-fish*) that appears in some Provençal recipes: it is the dried and salted cod used in most cod-fish dishes in Southern France. In this country it can be found in the fish department of most supermarkets, packed in wooden boxes under the name "boneless salt fish." It has a very pungent flavor and gives more character to the dish. However, it should be soaked at least 2 days in cold water, and the water should be changed often (about 4 times).

When cooking this specially-treated fish, remember not to salt the dish until the end of cooking time and to taste it first. You will find that very often you do not need to add salt.

For the beginning cook, or the neophyte in the use of this kind of cod, it is recommended that fresh or frozen cod be used.

COURT-BOUILLONS

Simple court-bouillon (for poaching fish or fish *quenelles)*

(Makes 5 cups)

5 cups water
3 lemon slices
½ medium-sized onion, sliced
1 bay leaf
1 small carrot, scrubbed and sliced
Salt and pepper

Place ingredients in enameled saucepan; bring to boil; turn heat down to simmer and cook uncovered for 40-45 minutes. Strain before using, pressing hard to extract flavor. Can be kept in refrigerator 4-5 days.

Court-bouillon au vin (with wine; for poaching scallops, sole, delicate fish)

(Makes 5 cups)

5 cups water
¾ cup dry white wine
½ medium-sized onion, sliced
2 garlic cloves, skinned
1 bay leaf
1 teaspoon dried thyme leaves
3 sprigs parsley
1 medium-sized carrot, scrubbed and sliced
6 peppercorns
Salt to taste

Place ingredients in enameled saucepan; bring to boil; turn heat down to simmer and cook uncovered for 40-45 minutes. Strain before using, pressing hard to extract flavor. Can be kept in refrigerator 4-5 days.

Court-bouillon à base de poisson (or *fumet;* for soup base or to poach meaty fish—salmon, flounder, cod)

(Makes 5 cups)

1½ pounds fish trimmings (bones, heads, etc.)
5½ cups water
1 large onion, quartered
1 large carrot, scrubbed and sliced
1 bay leaf
1 teaspoon fennel seeds
2 cloves garlic, peeled
6 peppercorns
2 sprigs fresh thyme, or 1 teaspoon dried thyme leaves
¼ cup red or white wine vinegar
Salt and pepper to taste

Place ingredients in enameled saucepan; bring to boil; turn heat down to simmer and cook uncovered for 40-45 minutes. Strain before using, pressing hard to extract flavor. Can be kept in refrigerator 2 days.

Morue au four   1
Baked Cod

(Serves 4-5)

1½-2 pounds fresh cod fillets, or frozen thawed fillets
4 medium well-ripened tomatoes, skinned, seeded, and chopped
  fine
2 garlic cloves, minced fine
2 tablespoons minced parsley
2 large fresh basil leaves, minced, or ½ teaspoon dried basil
  leaves, crushed
Salt and pepper
3 tablespoons olive oil

Preheat oven to 350°.

Arrange fish fillets in oiled baking dish. Mix tomatoes, garlic, parsley, basil, salt, and pepper; spread over fish; drizzle with oil; bake in preheated oven for 30 minutes.

Morue aux olives　　**1**
Cod with Olives

(Serves 3-4)

1 pound fresh or frozen cod-fish fillets, thawed and cut into 3 or 4
　　pieces
1 medium onion or shallot, chopped fine
Salt and pepper
1 large ripe tomato, skinned, seeded, and chopped
½ teaspoon dried thyme leaves, crushed
1 garlic clove, minced fine
½ cup green olives, pitted and sliced
¼ cup olive oil

Preheat oven to 350°.

Place fish in bottom of oiled baking dish; sprinkle with onion; add salt and pepper to taste, then add tomatoes, thyme, garlic, and olives.

Sprinkle with olive oil and bake for 30 minutes.

Baudroie au champagne　　**1**
Monkfish or Angler Fish in Champagne

Known as *baudroie* in the South or *lotte* in other parts of France, this fish is called monkfish or angler fish in this country. Leave it to my mother's inventiveness to come up with this delicious recipe when she was faced one day with some leftover champagne which she could not bring herself to throw away. The dish has been my favorite ever since. Of course, *faute de champagne* (in the absence of), one may use any bubbly dry wine or a good dry white wine such as Chablis.

(Serves 4)

1½ pounds fresh or frozen monkfish or angler fish
3 tablespoons olive oil or vegetable oil
1 teaspoon dried fennel, crushed
½ teaspoon dried rosemary leaves, crushed
Salt and pepper
⅓ cup champagne or dry white wine (Chablis or Sauterne)

Preheat oven to 350°.

If fish is frozen, thaw and pat dry. If fresh, refreshen under cold water and pat dry.

Heat oil in heavy skillet over medium-high heat; sauté fish in hot oil for 2 minutes, turning to fry on both sides. Remove carefully with spatula to a well-buttered shallow baking dish.

Sprinkle with fennel, rosemary, salt, and pepper. Pour champagne or wine over fish. Bake in preheated oven for 20 minutes, uncovered. Serve on a bed of rice.

Bouillabaisse à la tunisienne   1
Bouillabaisse Tunis Style

This bouillabaisse was originally prepared by a friend of mine who gave me the recipe. She spent her youth in Tunis and adapted the traditional recipe for *bouillabaisse* to her own background.

The use of wine and hot pimiento and the final cooking done in the oven are radical departures from the *Bouillabaisse de Marseille*, which is boiled rapidly over the fire. (The word *bouilla-baisse* means "boiled down" in Provençal.) Usually the pimiento is not used in the *bouillabaisse* itself, but in the hot sauce, *la rouille*, which accompanies it; nor is wine an ingredient in the traditional recipe. Nevertheless, the unorthodox recipe below, which resembles a kind of Corsican *bouillabaisse*, is delicious, exhilarating, and worth the try. Serve this dish with a white Côtes du Rhòne such as Hermitage or Crozes Hermitage.

(Serves 6)

5-6 *pounds seafood (cod, sole, flounder, bass, small crabs, shrimp,*
    lobster—a combination of any)
3 garlic cloves, minced (or more, if you tolerate it)
2 medium-sized onions, quartered
2 well-ripened tomatoes, skinned, seeded, and coarsely chopped
¼ cup chopped parsley
⅛ teaspoon dried basil leaves, crushed, or 2 fresh basil leaves
⅛ teaspoon dried thyme leaves, crushed, or 1 fresh sprig thyme
1 piece orange rind 1½ inches in length
¼ teaspoon saffron
Hot water to barely cover
1½ cups dry white wine, heated to the steaming point
1 small dry hot pimiento (optional; not everybody can tolerate
    pimiento)
½ cup olive oil
Salt and pepper
6 slices day-old French or Italian bread
1 teaspoon chopped parsley

Preheat oven to 450°.

Place garlic, onions, tomatoes, parsley, basil, thyme, and orange rind in large, heavy baking casserole or Dutch oven. Arrange fish on top by layers, starting with soft fish and ending with firm fish and crustaceans. Dissolve saffron in hot water; add wine to it and pour over fish. Bring to rapid boil; place a piece of foil on top of casserole, then place the lid over to make everything airtight; place in preheated oven for 30-35 minutes. Remove firm fish to warm platter; keep warm.

Remove orange rind and pimiento, discard. Purée remaining soft fish and soup through sieve or food mill (do not use blender). Ladle over bread slices in individual bowls. Garnish with parsley.

Serve firm fish with an *aioli* or mayonnaise in which you have blended some grated garlic.

Crevettes aux herbes de Provence   1
Shrimp with the Herbs of Provence

Serve with a white Burgundy.

(Serves 4)

4 tablespoons olive oil
2 large shallots, minced fine
1½ pounds large fresh or frozen shrimp, shelled (leave tails on)
2 tablespoons finely chopped parsley
1 large garlic clove, minced fine
¼ teaspoon dried fennel or dill seed
½ teaspoon dried thyme leaves, crushed
Salt and pepper
¼ cup cognac
2 teaspoons tomato paste
½ cup dry white wine, heated
1 tablespoon butter

If shrimp are frozen, thaw out. Heat olive oil in large skillet over medium-high heat; add shallots and sauté until soft; add shrimp and continue cooking; shake the pan often until the shrimp turn to a pink shade. Add parsley, garlic, fennel, thyme, salt, and pepper; stir and cook 1 minute longer. Sprinkle cognac over and ignite, shaking the pan until the flames die out.

Add tomato paste and warm wine; blend well; reheat over low heat and cook 8-10 minutes or until very hot. Blend in butter and serve with rice and French bread.

Le revesset or bouillabaisse pauvre   1
Bouillabaisse of the Poor

In the past, when sardines were abundant in the Mediterranean Sea and therefore inexpensive; they were considered the food of the poor; hence the title.

(Serves 4)

2-2½ pounds smelts, fresh sardines, or herring—eviscerated,
*   scaled, head removed, and cleaned*
4 ounces spinach, cleaned, roughly chopped
4 ounces Swiss chard, cleaned, roughly chopped
3 sorrel leaves, chopped (optional)
1½ quarts water
2 tablespoons olive oil
8 thin slices French bread

Bring water to boil in soup kettle; add spinach, chard, sorrel, salt
and pepper. Cook until almost tender over medium heat.

Add olive oil and fish. Cook 15 minutes longer. Place 2 slices bread
in each soup bowl; pour bouillon and vegetables over. Serve fish
separately.

Escargots table du roy   1
King's Table Snails

This is an entrée of distinction. Serve it with white Beaujolais.

(Serves 3)

1 can snails (about 18) with shells
¾ cup soft sweet butter
2 tablespoons shallots, minced fine
2 garlic cloves, mashed or pressed through garlic press
1 tablespoon parsely, minced fine
⅛ teaspoon nutmeg
¼ teaspoon salt
⅛ teaspoon pepper
1 teaspoon cognac

Preheat oven to 375°.

Drain can, rinse snails in cool water. Pour boiling water over
shells, drain well until dry. Place one snail inside each shell.

Thoroughly mix butter, shallots, garlic, parsley, nutmeg, salt, pepper, and cognac, until you have a paste. Place a small amount of this paste (the size of a small walnut) inside each shell.

Arrange stuffed shells on a snail pan (found in department stores or kitchen stores) or in muffin tins, with the stuffing facing up. Bake in preheated oven until butter mixture starts bubbling, about 10 or 12 minutes.

Bouillabaisse de morue à la marseillaise   1
Codfish Bouillabaisse Marseille Style

This bouillabaisse made with cod is in my opinion as tasty as the traditional one. Serve it with a Côtes du Rhone.

(Serves 4)

3 pounds salted cod, freshened, or frozen fillet of cod, thawed (for
*   the handling of salted cod, see beginning of chapter)*
3 tablespoons olive oil
4 garlic cloves, minced
1 large onion, chopped
1 leek, white part, minced
1 large well-ripened tomato, skinned, seeded, chopped
2 pounds potatoes, peeled and cut in 1¼-inch cubes
Boiling water
1 bay leaf
1 sprig fresh thyme or ½ teaspoon dried thyme leaves
1 piece of orange rind about 1½ inches in length
¼ cup minced parsley
Pinch of saffron (about ⅛ teaspoon)
Salt and pepper
8 slices of day-old French or Italian bread

In large soup kettle sauté garlic, onion, and leek in oil over medium-low heat until golden brown. Add tomato and stir 1 minute; add potatoes, stir again 2 minutes; add boiling water to barely cover; add bay leaf, thyme, orange rind, parsley, and saffron. Bring to boil and cook on medium-high heat until potatoes are cooked but still firm. Add fish; salt and pepper to taste (watch salt!); continue cooking until fish flakes easily — just a few minutes.

Set fish and potatoes aside on warm serving platter; keep warm.

Strain bouillon; reheat and ladle onto bread slices (2 to each soup bowl). Fish and potatoes can be served with *aioli* (see index).

Friture du Golfe du Lion   2
Gulf Style Fried Fish (Smelts in Skillet)

This dish was originally prepared with fresh sardines. Because they have all but disappeared from the markets, I have substituted smelts (small if possible) which make a very satisfactory alternative.

(Serves 4)

24 smelts, fresh or frozen, with heads removed
½ cup milk
4 tablespoons all-purpose flour
⅛ teaspoon salt
2 garlic cloves, chopped fine
2 tablespoons parsley, finely chopped
1 tablespoon olive oil
Lemon wedges
Oil or fat for deep frying

Mix flour and salt in paper or plastic bag; shake to mix. If fish is frozen, thaw out and pat dry. If fresh, clean smelt, rinse, and pat dry.

Place milk in saucer. Dip smelt in milk, then in flour and salt mixture. Reserve.

In deep, heavy frying pan, bring fat to 350° or to the point where 2 or 3 drops of water make hot fat splatter. Slide smelts one at a time into hot fat, making sure not to crowd the pan. Fry 3 minutes, turning occasionally; fish should be golden brown. Remove to warm serving dish and keep hot.

Sauté garlic and parsley in olive oil briefly about 1 minute, over medium-high heat in small skillet. Sprinkle over smelts.

Serve with lemon wedges.

Morue à la catalane (Languedoc and Roussillon)   2
Spanish Style Codfish

(Serves 4)

1 pound freshened salt cod or thawed-out frozen cod
1 large leek, white part, or 3 shallots, chopped fine
1 small onion, chopped fine
2 tablespoons olive oil
3 garlic cloves, minced fine
2 large yellow potatoes, peeled and sliced
2 medium-sized tomatoes, skinned, peeled, and chopped
1 large green or red pepper, seeded and sliced thin
1 cup hot water
Salt and pepper

Preheat oven to 350°.

Pat fish dry and cut into several pieces about 2 inches in length. Reserve.

In heavy skillet sauté leek or shallots and onion in olive oil over medium heat until transparent; add garlic and stir until soft. Add fish to onion mixture and with wooden spoon or spatula stir fish for 2 more minutes. Remove skillet from heat and set aside.

Layer half the cod mixture, half the potatoes, half the tomatoes, half the green pepper, and a little salt and pepper in oiled oven-proof casserole; repeat the layers, ending with fish.

Pour hot water in skillet in which fish was cooked; be sure to get any bits and pieces of what is left of the onion-fish mixture, as they add to the flavor. Pour this water over fish mixture in casserole; add a little more salt and pepper; bake in preheated oven for 50 to 60 minutes.

Le loup à la provençale   **2**
Sea Bass or Grouper in the Style of Provence

Serve with a Muscadet from the Loire Valley, chilled.

(Serves 4)

1 2½- to 3-pound bass or grouper, eviscerated, cleaned, and dried
½ teaspoon fennel seeds, crushed, or (better) fresh fennel
2 tablespoons olive oil
Salt and pepper
2 tablespoons butter or margarine
½ lemon, peeled and sliced thin
¼ teaspoon dill weed, crushed
¼ teaspoon fennel seeds, crushed
½ cup dry white wine
Salt and pepper
Finely minced parsley
¼ cup Pernod (optional)

Preheat oven to 325°.

Heat olive oil over medium heat in skillet; sauté fish quickly, 1 minute, on each side. Place in well-buttered baking dish; add skillet juices; place in preheated oven. Bake 30 minutes or until fish flakes easily.

Melt the butter or margarine in small saucepan; add lemon slices, dill weed, fennel seeds, wine, salt and pepper to taste. Cook this sauce slowly over low heat 15 minutes; strain.

Sprinkle Pernod over fish to flambé. (This step is optional.) Ladle sauce over baked fish. Sprinkle with parsley.

Crevettes sauce aurore   **2**
Shrimp with Sunrise Sauce

Serve with a Riesling wine.

(Serves 4)

1 pound (3 cups) shelled raw shrimp
2 tablespoons butter or margarine
2 tablespoons brandy
¼ cup dry white wine
1 cup heavy cream
1 teaspoon tomato purée
Pinch of cayenne
8 fried or toasted bread triangles or 4 patty shells

Melt butter or margarine in large skillet over medium heat; add shrimp and sauté 2 minutes.

Heat brandy in small saucepan; add to shrimp in skillet and ignite; shake skillet until flames die out. Add wine, bring to a light boil and cook over medium heat until liquid is almost completely reduced. Remove from heat and set aside.

Combine cream and tomato paste in medium-size saucepan; heat slowly until very hot and steaming; turn down to simmer; add to shrimp and liquid in skillet; stir to blend and continue simmering, stirring constantly 4 or 5 minutes or until heated through.

Serve over fried or toasted bread or in patty shells.

Morue sauce tomate (Provence)   2
Codfish in Tomato Sauce

(Serves 3-4)

1 medium-sized onion, chopped
2 garlic cloves, minced
3 tablespoons olive oil
2 large tomatoes, well-ripened, skinned, seeded, cut up
2 large fresh basil leaves, or 1 teaspoon dried basil leaves
1 small sprig fresh thyme, or ½ teaspoon dried thyme leaves
1 tablespoon minced parsley
Salt and pepper
1 pound fresh cod fillets, or frozen and thawed, cut into large
    pieces
4 tablespoons flour
2 tablespoons olive oil

Sauté onion in skillet in olive oil over medium heat until soft and transparent; add garlic, stir. Add tomatoes, basil, thyme, parsley, salt and pepper to taste; cook over low heat, covered, for 10 minutes. Strain through food mill or whirl in blender (do not blend too long); return to skillet.

Place flour on paper toweling or wax paper; dip fish in flour to coat on both sides.

Sauté fish lightly on both sides in clean skillet in 2 tablespoons olive oil until lightly browned. Return fish to sauce. Simmer 15-20 minutes or until fish flakes with a fork.

Sole sauce béarnaise   2
Sole with Béarnaise Sauce

A Muscadet is recommended with this dish.

(Serves 3-4)

2 pounds (approximately) fresh fillets of sole*
1 cup dry white wine
½ cup water
1 small onion, peeled and sliced
1 large shallot, peeled and coarsely chopped
1 sprig fresh tarragon, or ½ teaspoon dry tarragon leaves
Salt and pepper
Béarnaise sauce (see index)
2 tablespoons finely minced tarragon or parsley

Roll fillets jelly-roll fashion and fasten with thread.

Combine wine, water, onion, shallots, tarragon, salt, and pepper in large skillet or wide saucepan. Bring to a boil; place fish rolls in liquid; cover and turn down to simmer; poach 5 minutes. Lift fish from liquid with slotted spoon to serving dish; keep warm.

---

*If you need to rinse sole, rinse briefly in lemon water or salted water (1 tablespoon lemon juice or ½ tablespoon salt to a quart).

Reduce liquid in skillet by boiling rapidly until ½ cup of the liquid is left—about 3-4 minutes. Strain liquid; reserve. Prepare Béarnaise sauce according to directions (see index), using strained liquid. Ladle over fish rolls on serving platter and sprinkle with finely minced tarragon or parsley.

Sole au vin blanc   2
Sole in White Wine

(Serves 4)

6 fillets of sole, or 3 pounds, fresh or frozen
2 tablespoons lemon juice
Salt and white pepper to taste
½ teaspoon dried tarragon leaves, crushed, or 1 tablespoon fresh
*   tarragon, chopped*
1½ cups dry white wine
2 tablespoons flour
2 tablespoons butter or margarine
½ cup heavy cream or light cream
2 tablespoons fine bread crumbs
1 tablespoon butter

Preheat oven to 350°.

If fish is frozen, thaw out. Rinse fillets under cold water; drain thoroughly and pat dry with paper toweling. Sprinkle with lemon juice, salt, and pepper.

Roll fillets jelly-roll fashion and fasten with thread and place them in a shallow, buttered baking dish. Sprinkle with tarragon and pour wine over. Cover with lid or heavy aluminum foil and place in preheated oven for 10 minutes. Drain wine into saucepan; keep sole covered in very low oven (warm).

Simmer wine until only half of it is left. Meanwhile, melt the 2 tablespoons butter or margarine in another saucepan; blend in flour; add cream slowly; stir to break and smooth out lumps. Cook over medium-low heat, stirring, until sauce starts to thicken, about 2 minutes.

Add reduced wine to cream sauce and cook over medium-low heat, stirring for 2 or 3 minutes or until thickened. It should have the consistency of thick cream.

Pour over fillets in baking dish; sprinkle with bread crumbs; dot with butter and place under broiler until light brown.

Coquilles St. Jacques gratinées   2
Broiled Scallops in Shells *

A very popular and decorative entrée.

(Serves 5-6)

1 slice white bread, crust removed
¼ cup milk
2 pounds sea scallops cut into small serving pieces
Juice of ½ lemon
1 tablespoon butter or margarine
3 shallots, chopped fine
2 garlic cloves, minced fine
8 ounces mushrooms, cleaned and chopped
2 tablespoons butter or margarine
¼ cup finely minced parsley
Salt and pepper
3 tablespoons dry white wine
Fine bread crumbs
1 tablespoon butter or margarine

Soak bread in milk until softened; squeeze bread thoroughly; chop and set aside.

Combine scallops and lemon juice in glass or porcelain bowl and set aside. Drain when ready to cook.

Melt 1 tablespoon butter in medium-sized skillet, add shallot and garlic; sauté until transparent over medium heat. Add mush-

---

* The shells can be found in the gourmet section of department stores or in gourmet shops.

rooms; stir to blend with shallot and garlic for 1 minute; remove from heat immediately and transfer to a bowl; set aside.

Place 2 tablespoons butter or margarine in same skillet; add scallops and sauté over medium-high heat for 3 minutes; add onion, garlic, mushroom, bread, parsley, salt and pepper to taste; stir 1 minute longer; add wine and blend. Remove from heat.

Spoon scallop mixture into shells or ovenproof ramequins. Sprinkle bread crumbs over; dot with butter; place under broiler, about 6 inches from heat; broil until golden brown. Serve with lemon wedges and parsley or any other green such as watercress or garden cress.

Sole arlésienne   3
Sole Arles Style

A very popular dish in Arles. Van Gogh must have eaten this at a small café where he took his meals.

(Serves 6)

Wine court-bouillon *(see index)*
6 fillets of sole or flounder, fresh or frozen
4 fresh young artichokes
2 tablespoons butter or margarine
¼ cup heavy cream
1 teaspoon tomato purée
1 garlic clove, mashed
Salt and pepper
1 tablespoon finely-minced parsley

Remove and discard the hard outside leaves of the artichokes; cut off the remaining tender leaves ¾ down. Cut each artichoke in half, each half in half again; remove fuzzy center chokes. Slice each quarter very thin; place chips in deep skillet with butter or margarine; sauté over medium-low heat until fairly tender; add cream and tomato paste; blend. Add garlic, salt, and pepper; simmer until artichoke chips are tender.

Meanwhile, place fillets of fish in frying pan; pour *court-bouillon* to cover fish by 1 inch; bring liquid to light boil; turn heat down to low and simmer 5-8 minutes or until fish flakes easily when tested with a fork.

Lift fish from liquid and arrange on warm serving platter. Reserve 2 tablespoons of *court-bouillon*; add to artichoke mixture; blend, reheat and ladle over the fish fillets. Sprinkle with parsley and serve.

Truites farcies   3
Stuffed Trout

Trout abounds in the fast streams crisscrossing the regions of Languedoc and Roussillon. This is one way they are prepared there. Serve with a rosé Côtes de Provence.

(Serves 4)

4 trout, fresh or frozen, cleaned
4 ounces fresh mushrooms, cleaned
2 tablespoons butter or margarine
1 slice white bread
¼ cup milk
¼ cup chopped parsley
1 tablespoon chopped shallot
1 teaspoon dried dill, crushed
1 teaspoon dried summer savory leaves, crushed
1 whole egg, slightly beaten
Salt and pepper
⅓ cup (approximately) dry white wine
1 bay leaf broken into 4 pieces
½ teaspoon dried thyme leaves
4 thin slices onion
Salt and pepper
1 tablespoon butter

Preheat oven to 325°.

Sauté mushrooms in butter over medium-low heat until tender; chop; set aside.

Soak bread in milk until soft; squeeze out milk and discard; chop bread.

Place mushrooms, bread, parsley, shallots, dill, summer savory, egg, salt, and pepper in bowl; mix well. Fill trout with this stuffing. Make 4 packets out of foil, place a trout in each; add 2 tablespoons wine, ¼ of the bay leaf, pinch of thyme, thin onion slice, and a little salt and pepper to each packet. Cover tightly. Arrange in baking dish and bake in preheated oven for 20 minutes.

Open packets before serving. Remove fish to hot serving platter; pour out juices and strain; return to baking dish. Add tablespoon butter; blend over low heat to warm again. When hot, ladle over trout and serve.

Moules à la marinière   2
Mussels Mariner Style

Serve with a white Côtes du Rhône.

(Serves 3-4)

1 can (8¾ ounces) mussels au naturel *(in salt and water)*
3 tablespoons olive oil
1 tablespoon finely chopped shallot
1 large garlic clove, minced fine
2 tablespoons finely chopped parsley
¼ cup dry white wine
Pepper
1 tablespoon lemon juice

Drain mussels; reserve ¼ cup of the juice. Set mussels aside.

Heat oil over medium heat in large skillet; add shallot and garlic. Sauté until limp and transparent, shaking the skillet often. Do not let it turn brown. Add parsley, wine, and the ¼ cup juice from mussels. Bring to a light boil and reduce to half by cooking rapidly, about 2 minutes. Add mussels, pepper, lemon juice, and salt if needed. Simmer 5 minutes; serve with *rizotto* or saffron rice.

La bourride   3
White Fish Bouillabaisse

This dish is called a white *bouillabaisse* because it does not come with tomatoes or saffron. For this reason the *court-bouillon* is loaded with pungent herbs. *Aioli* sauce is a must with it.

(Serves 4-5)

Aioli *sauce (see pages 21, 22)*
4 pounds mixed cleaned white fish such as cod, ocean perch, rockfish, whiting, haddock, or flounder
Wine court-bouillon *(see index)*
Piece of orange rind 1½ inches in length
3 egg yolks, lightly beaten
8-10 slices day-old French bread
¼ cup olive oil
2 cloves garlic, mashed

Make *aioli* sauce and set aside. Prepare wine *court-bouillon* according to directions and place in large enameled saucepan with orange rind. Heat gradually; when steaming hot (not boiling) add the fish. Bring to a boil and continue boiling rapidly for 8-10 minutes or until fish is tender but firm (do not overcook). If some of the fish cooks faster, remove immediately with slotted spoon to warm platter. Keep warm. When all the fish is done, remove to platter and keep warm.

Strain the bouillon; return to saucepan and keep on simmer.

Reserve 1 tablespoon per person of the previously made *aioli* sauce in a small serving bowl; set aside. Place remaining *aioli* in a large bowl; add the 3 egg yolks; mix gently with wooden spoon. Slowly, a small amount at a time, blend in the bouillon until the mixture is smooth and perfectly incorporated. Return to very low heat, stirring constantly with wooden spoon until creamy. (Do not let mixture come to a boil or it will curdle.)

Rub bread slices with olive oil and garlic on both sides; place 2 in each soup bowl. Ladle bouillon over. Serve the fish on the side with the reserved *aioli* sauce.

La brandade or gangasse   3
Codfish Purée

This fragrant, simple cod purée was first made in the monasteries of Provence. The monks baptized it *brandado* because of the strong wrist movement required to mix the ingredients. *Brandado* means "the thing you stir," while *gangasser* means "to pound." The monks mixed mashed potatoes with the purée to give it greater volume — lightening the dish and changing the flavor. Now it is served with or without the addition of mashed potatoes, as hors d'oeuvres with *croutons frits* (fried bread slices) or in patty shells (*vol-au-vent*).

In Languedoc the cod is cooked directly with the potatoes and garlic. Prepared this way it is called *morue à la languedocienne*. A Tavel or Côtes de Provence goes well with it.

(Serves 4)

1 pound salt cod freshened in cold water overnight
1 cup olive oil at about 75°-80° F
¾ cup milk or cream at about 75°-80° F
1 large garlic clove (more if you like the flavor)
Salt and white pepper
1 teaspoon lemon juice

Drain water from cod and cut in 6 equal pieces; place in saucepan and add cold water to cover. (Do not add salt to water, as cod retains some saltiness even after freshening.) Bring to boil rapidly and as soon as the scum rises to the surface, remove from heat and drain fish thoroughly.

Remove bones and flake fish. Purée the fish and garlic in blender in batches, or purée by hand in a mortar using pestle or wooden spoon. Transfer to a heavy saucepan and place over very low heat.

Beat the warm olive oil into the fish with wooden spoon or pestle with stirring motion, 1 tablespoon at a time, alternating with 1 tablespoon warm milk, stirring and pounding all the time until oil and milk are used up. At this point, mixture should be creamy and thick. Add white pepper, salt if necessary, and lemon juice. Blend again. Serve warm with *croutons frits* or in patty shells, or cold as hors d'oeuvres with crackers.

Langouste amoureuse   3
Amorous Lobster

A friend of my father, a businessman and a great cook, gave me this recipe but could not provide any history about the title. With tongue in cheek he offered his own explanation: the delicious quality of the dish together with its alcoholic content so predisposes one to a loving mood that even the lobster doesn't mind! The wine suggested is a white Burgundy: Meursault, Macon Villages.

(Serves 6-8)

12 ounces mushrooms and stems, cleaned and sliced
1 tablespoon butter or margarine
Court-bouillon *(see index)*
4 pounds frozen lobster tails
2 tablespoons olive oil
2 tablespoons butter
3 shallots, chopped fine
1 garlic clove, minced fine
1 bay leaf
½ teaspoon dried thyme leaves, crushed
2 tablespoons minced parsley
⅛ teaspoon cayenne pepper
⅓ cup vermouth or Pernod
2-3 tablespoons cognac or brandy
2 tablespoons tomato paste
1 cup heavy cream
Salt to taste

Thaw out lobster tails. Sauté mushrooms in butter in small skillet over medium heat for 1 minute. Set aside.

Bring *court-bouillon* to a rolling boil in kettle large enough for lobster tails, and boil 5-8 minutes. Drain. Carefully cut away underside membrane of lobster tails with scissors; pull out meat and cut into serving-size chunks.

Heat oil and butter over medium heat in large skillet; add shallots and garlic, sauté until transparent; add bay leaf, thyme, parsley, and lobster meat; sauté briefly over medium-high heat about 1 to 2 minutes; add cayenne and stir to blend.

Pour vermouth into stainless steel ladle; ignite and pour flaming alcohol over meat. Do the same with 2 tablespoons cognac; let it burn down. Blend in cream, tomato paste, mushrooms, and (optionally) 1 tablespoon cognac. Simmer 10 minutes; discard bay leaf. Serve over rice.

L'esquinade des pêcheurs   3
Fishermen's Crab

L'esquinade is the colorful Provençal word for a type of Mediterranean crab. This dish can be eaten as a main course with *risotto* or as an hors d'oeuvre with thin slices of French bread. With this dish a Côtes du Rhône or Côtes de Provence would be appropriate.

(Serves 4)

8 good-size crabs (frozen), thawed
Wine court-bouillon *(see index)*
2 egg yolks
1 teaspoon dry mustard or Dijon mustard
Juice of 1 lemon
Salt and pepper to taste
⅔ cup (or less) olive oil
1 tablespoon finely chopped parsley

Bring *court-bouillon* to a boil in large saucepan; add crabs and turn down to simmer for 30 minutes. Drain, cool crabs.

Cut crabs open, cutting around the shell to keep for later use. Discard the dark matter, keeping the meat and the eggs (called "coral"). Break the legs and remove the meat. Cut meat into bite-size serving pieces.

Place the eggs (coral), the egg yolks, mustard, lemon juice, salt, and pepper in a mortar or glass or porcelain bowl; pound to make a paste; gradually add olive oil until you obtain a thick, creamy mixture. Add parsley and blend.

Rub shells inside and out with what is left of olive oil. Place a helping of the meat in each shell; spoon sauce over or serve sauce in a separate dish to pass around.

Le loup farci Suzanne
Stuffed Sea Bass or Grouper

3

If you can get some fresh dill or fennel, or if you grow your own, this recipe will delight you.

(Serves 4-5)

2 slices white bread
¼ cup milk
2½- to 3-pound rock bass, sea bass, or striped bass (or any large
*   ocean fish such as mullet)*
1 large clove garlic, minced fine
2 tablespoons finely minced parsley
1 whole egg, slightly beaten
Pepper
1 tablespoon vermouth
1 large onion, skinned and sliced thin
Several fresh sprigs of dill or fennel
Salt and pepper
4 tablespoons olive oil
⅓ cup dry white wine, warmed
Minced parsley
Lemon slices

Preheat oven to 325°.

Soak bread in milk and set aside. Eviscerate fish by cutting the underside of the fish lengthwise from head to tail and removing entrails (or have the fish-market attendant do it). Clean inside and out, pat dry, and season cavity with salt and pepper.

Squeeze milk from bread thoroughly; discard milk; chop bread. Mix bread, garlic, parsley, egg, pepper to taste, and vermouth in a bowl. Fill fish cavity with this stuffing. Sew cavity shut with large needle and strong thread to prevent stuffing from oozing out during baking. Set fish aside.

Butter or oil a baking pan long enough to receive the fish, place onion slices in it, then arrange fennel or dill sprigs over to make a bed for the fish. Place fish, sprinkle with salt and pepper to taste, and drizzle with olive oil. Place uncovered in preheated oven for 35-40 minutes. Taste for doneness.

When done, remove fish carefully to a warm serving platter; keep warm. Pour wine in baking pan over herbs and onion; stir; strain juices into saucepan, squeezing with a spoon to get as much of the flavor from the herbs as possible. Reheat juices and ladle over fish. Sprinkle with parsley and arrange lemon slices around fish.

Serve with rice or buttered new boiled potatoes.

Moules à la provençale
(moules fraîches gratinées en coquilles)   3
Mussels Provençal Style

This dish is so popular in the South that it can be found practically anywhere in bistros along the coast from Roussillon to the Italian frontier. Serve it with a good dry white wine such as Côtes de Provence or Côtes du Roussillon rosé. It is even served in the South with reds from the Rhône Valley such as Côte-Rotie or Hermitage — those wines which go well with the garlic flavor. Use your own judgment and trust your own palate.

(Serves 4)

½ cup dry white wine
2 dozen fresh mussels in their shells
⅓ cup finely chopped parsley
3 cloves garlic, minced fine
½ cup fine bread crumbs
Salt and pepper
⅓ cup olive oil, or more

Check mussels and discard any that are not tightly closed. Scrub the mussels thoroughly with a stiff wire brush under cold running water. Cut off the "beard" with a sharp knife. Soak mussels in cold water for 2 hours; rinse them again in cold water and let them drain.

Place wine and clean mussels in large kettle; cover kettle and bring to a boil; continue cooking. As soon as mussels open, remove them with kitchen pincers; by the end of 6 minutes all the mussels should have opened.

Discard 1 shell from each mussel, keeping the shell with the mollusk in it. Place filled shells on large shallow baking dish or heavy cookie sheet; set aside.

Mix in a bowl the parsley, garlic, bread crumbs, salt, and pepper. Garnish each filled shell with some of this mixture. Drizzle with olive oil and place in large gratin or baking dish. Place under broiler until top is golden brown; watch carefully during last few minutes for scorching. Serve immediately with French bread.

Morue en raite   3
Cod in Raite Sauce

Raite (or *raito* in Provençal) is the name given to a sauce originally brought to the Mediterranean shores of France by the ancient Greeks who established bases there. Capers and pickles are added to give the sauce pungency.

(Serves 3-4)

1½-2 pounds frozen cod fillets, thawed out, or fresh fillets
4 tablespoons all-purpose flour
6 tablespoons olive oil
1 medium-sized onion, chopped fine
2 medium-sized tomatoes, well-ripened, skinned, seeded, and
    chopped fine
1 teaspoon tomato paste
1 rounded tablespoon all-purpose flour
¾ cup dry red wine, heated
½ cup hot water
1 bay leaf
¼ teaspoon dried thyme leaves, crushed
1 tablespoon minced parsley
2 garlic cloves, minced fine
Pepper to taste
1 tablespoon chopped capers
1 tablespoon chopped French cornichons or baby dill pickles

Dry cod well and cut into 3 or 4 equal pieces. Dip in flour on all sides.

Sauté cod in heavy skillet on both sides in 4 tablespoons olive oil over medium-high heat 3-4 minutes or until golden brown. Remove to warm platter; set aside, keeping warm.

Sauté onion in wide saucepan or skillet in 2 remaining tablespoons olive oil over medium heat until transparent. Add tomatoes and tomato paste, stir and continue cooking 5 minutes longer. Blend in flour, stirring to mix with tomatoes; add wine, water, bay leaf, thyme, parsley, garlic, and pepper. Cook over medium heat, bubbling lightly, about 15-20 minutes to reduce sauce, stirring quite often to prevent it from sticking. (It should be thick.)

Add capers and cornichons or pickles; put cod back in sauce; correct seasoning. Reheat over medium-low heat for 5 minutes or until heated throughout. Serve.

Quenelles de poisson   3
Fish Dumplings

May be served as an entrée for a light meal. Serve it with a white Burgundy.

(Serves 3-4; 12-14 dumplings)

2 pounds pike or flounder, fresh or frozen
6 cups water
½ teaspoon salt
¾ cup flour

Panade or base:
¼ cup butter or margarine
1 cup water
1 cup all-purpose flour
3 eggs
Salt to taste
⅛ teaspoon nutmeg
⅛ teaspoon pepper
2 tablespoons heavy cream

If fish is frozen, thaw out. Squeeze as much liquid from fish as you can. Dry thoroughly and chop fish in small pieces. Place in a mortar and with pestle or wooden spoon pound fish until you have a paste. Or—grind in food grinder or processor. Set aside.

To make base, place butter and water in saucepan; bring to a boil. Remove from heat. Add flour immediately and all at once. Stir vigorously with wooden spoon until mixture leaves the sides of the pan and forms a ball. Beat in eggs one at a time until well blended. Add fish, salt, pepper, nutmeg; mix well. Let rest ½ hour in refrigerator or other cool place; add the 2 tablespoons of cream; blend and refrigerate another hour.

Spread clean towel or paper toweling over work counter. Sift flour over it. Take dough mixture out of refrigerator, pick out small portions of dough and roll them in the wet palms of your hands to form small cork-like dumplings 2"x¾" (you should get 12-14 quenelles), and then roll them lightly in the flour; set aside on towel.

Bring water to boil in wide, large skillet, then reduce heat to low so that it barely simmers. Drop dumplings into the water one at a time; do not overcrowd the pan; cook, uncovered, 10 to 12 minutes or until firm to the touch and they float freely. Remove with slotted spoon to a colander, freshen a few seconds under cold water and drain well on paper towels. Continue cooking until all the dumplings are poached.

Place *quenelles* in a buttered baking dish and keep warm in a very low oven (250°) until ready to serve. To serve, cover with *sauce madère* (below) or *sauce tomate* (see index).

Sauce madère:
⅔ cup dry vermouth
4 teaspoons tomato paste
1 teaspoon lemon juice
Salt and pepper to taste
Cream

Simmer vermouth in enameled saucepan over medium-low heat until reduced to ½ cup. Blend in tomato paste, lemon juice, salt, and cream. Heat sauce again 5 more minutes over medium-low heat. Spoon over *quenelles* and serve.

La quinquebine   3
Codfish on Toast

This recipe comes from the region of the Camargue.

(Serves 3-4)

1 pound cod fillets, fresh or frozen (thaw out if frozen)
½ cup chopped leeks, white part only
2 garlic cloves, minced fine
1 tablespoon minced parsley
3 tablespoons olive oil
2 anchovy fillets, freshened and mashed
Pepper
1 level tablespoon all-purpose flour
1 cup milk
½ cup grated Swiss or Gruyère cheese
⅛ teaspoon grated nutmeg
Salt if needed
2-3 tablespoons butter or margarine
4 slices French or Italian bread

Fry bread in melted butter or margarine in a heavy skillet until light brown on both sides. Set aside; keep warm.

Dry fish well; cut into 3 or 4 pieces. Poach fish in a *court-bouillon* (see index) until fish flakes easily. Discard bouillon. Flake fish with a fork; reserve.

Sauté leek, garlic, and parsley in olive oil over medium heat in heavy saucepan until leek is transparent, about 3 minutes. Add anchovies and blend well, stirring while cooking 1 or 2 minutes. Sprinkle flour over, blend well, then add milk slowly; stir until flour is well blended; cook over medium-low heat until thickened, about 8-10 minutes.

Add flaked fish to sauce, then cheese, nutmeg, and pepper. Add salt only if needed. Cook on low heat 5 minutes longer. Serve very hot on fried bread slices.

La tarte Amphitrite   **3**
Seafood Pie

Amphitrite was the Greek goddess of the sea, wife of Poseidon. This quiche is an adaptation of a dish prepared in the Camargue.

(Serves 6)

1 9-inch pâte brisée, unbaked shell
1 tablespoon butter or margarine
½ pound small fresh or frozen shrimps, shelled
½ pound fresh or frozen sea scallops, halved
¼ pound fresh or frozen sole, cut into 1½-inch pieces
1 large garlic clove, minced
2 tablespoons finely minced parsley
4 ounces fresh mushrooms, cleaned and sliced
5 whole eggs, lightly beaten
¾ cup light cream
2 medium-ripe tomatoes, skinned, seeded, and chopped very fine
¾ cup grated Swiss or Gruyère cheese
Salt
Pepper (freshly ground if possible; be generous with it)

Preheat oven to 400°.

If fish is frozen, thaw out and pat dry; if fresh, pat dry. Prepare pie shell, prick bottom with fork; set aside.

Melt butter in large skillet; add shrimp, scallops, and sole; sauté over light heat 2-3 minutes or until shrimp turns pink, stirring often. Blend in garlic and parsley; stir 1 minute longer; add mushrooms and salt lightly. Stir 1 more minute; remove from heat, discard any liquids left, and spread over bottom of prepared pie shell; set aside.

Beat eggs and cream in large bowl until well blended; add tomatoes, cheese, salt, and plenty of pepper; beat again to blend. Pour over fish in pie shell. Just before baking, sprinkle top with 2 tablespoons grated Swiss or Gruyère cheese.

Place in preheated oven and bake 25-30 minutes. Do not overbake. Remove from oven while center is still on soft side. Cool 5 minutes and serve with lemon wedges.

Meats

The prerequisite of a good meal should be quality, not quantity. The same thing applies to meat. Moreover, it is not always the most expensive cut which offers quality and makes the meal memorable, but the way it is cooked—the know-how which brings out the flavor. Herbs, wine, and the mode of cooking are the elements that help transform simple and inexpensive cuts into a feast.

When people say they do not like meat cooked with wine, this is generally because of the misuse of the wine. It should be heated lightly before it is added to the meat, a process which volatilizes some of the alcohol, leaving the "bouquet," the flavor. The remainder is evaporated in the long process of cooking. In dishes which do not require long cooking, the amount of wine should be reduced by half, by gentle boiling, before use.

Wine, cognac, or brandy used in marinating serves a dual purpose: flavoring and tenderizing. When the alcohol penetrates the meat it breaks down the fibers, making the meat tender.

When preparing any meat for grilling or broiling, one should not salt it before or during the cooking process. Salt melts on contact with the meat, creating a humid "climate" which inhibits the searing action, thus letting the precious juices escape and making the meat tough. Salt it just before removing from the heat. For the same reason do not prick the meat with a fork in handling; use a metal spatula to turn it or move it around.

In the following chapter I have suggested some wines to accompany the meat dishes. These are of course French wines, but if any of them should prove hard to find, ask your wine merchant to suggest an equivalent in domestic wines.

BEEF

In the repertory of French cookery, beef plays an important role. France has beautiful, lush pastures and produces meat animals renowned throughout the world. It is no wonder its beef dishes are renowned as well! Who does not know, at least by name, such dishes as *boeuf bourguignon, boeuf à la mode, pot au feu*, to name a few!

In the South of France, lying west of the Rhône and bordered in part by the Mediterranean, is a rich alluvial plain known as the Camargue—a land that is neither earth nor water. Inhabited since prehistoric times by the wild horse and the wild bull, this land in modern times has been home for great *manades*, herds of horses and cattle, watched over by *gardians*—cowboys similar to the *gauchos* of South America.

In this corner of the South of France, the grass is not grown in rich pastures but is sparsely spread over vast areas and the cattle must wander far and wide to feed. It used to be that the meat of these animals was leaner and tougher than that of their northern cousins, and this is why the traditional dishes made from beef had names like *boeuf en daube, estouffade de boeuf* (French: *boeuf à l'etouffé*), *le fricot des guardians, daube a la niçarde*, etc. These dishes often required the maceration of the meat in wine or vinegar and were always braised slowly in a tightly covered earthen pot — a double process which resulted in tender and flavorful stews.

Methods of raising cattle have now improved, and some of the best beef is now being produced by crossing the Brahma bull and the French Charolais. This good meat is now sold in all parts of the South of France, leading the cooks of Dauphiné, Roussillon, and Languedoc to new adaptations of their old customary dishes made with lamb or mutton. From this beautiful, haunting, savage land with its rich past, a traditional cuisine has evolved, unique in the world.

On cooking a roast

"Pour faire un bon rôti il faut que le morceau soit épais" (the bigger the piece, the better the roast). This is one of the rules. Of course, not everyone can afford a baron of beef; however, the roast should weigh at least five or six pounds. Remember, roast beef leftovers can be utlized in many ways and can make at least one more meal.

If the roast is not to be cooked right after you bring it from the market, unwrap it and place it loosely covered in the refrigerator. Allow it to stand at room temperature at least thirty minutes before roasting.

The French methods of cooking a roast are as follows:

1. Sear the roast on all sides in very hot fat on top of the stove, then

transfer to the roasting pan, fat-side up, and place uncovered in an oven preheated to 325°.

2. Place the roast on a meat rack in the roasting pan, fat-side up, in oven preheated to 450°-500° until the surface is brown, then reduce the oven temperature to 325°.

The purpose of both methods is to sear the meat to form a crust which seals in the juices. Salt is added then — *not before* — and the meat is roasted until the meat thermometer inserted in the thickest part registers between 140° and 170°, depending on how well you like the meat done. The French prefer theirs rare, and that calls for 140°; I prefer mine between 160° and 170°.

I will never forget the delicious roast prepared by a French chef in a small restaurant years ago. When I asked him his secret he told me, " . . . *les herbes, Madame*" — and then proceeded to explain how he covers the roast with a thick mantle of herbs before roasting it. I have tried to recreate his recipe *à ma façon* (in my own way), and here it is:

1 6- to 8-pound boned and rolled rib roast
¼ pound butter or margarine at room temperature
½ cup all-purpose flour
1 tablespoon dry thyme leaves, crushed
3 tablespoons dry rosemary leaves, crushed
2 bay leaves, crushed
1 tablespoon dry marjoram leaves, crushed
1 tablespoon dry mustard
1 teaspoon ground black pepper

Pat roast dry with paper towel. Combine butter, flour, herbs and spices; work with fork or pastry blender to make a paste. Cover roast on its entire surface with this paste, working with your hands to make the paste adhere.

Place roast on meat rack in roasting pan, fat-side up; bake, uncovered, following previous directions. Salt 30 minutes before taking roast from oven.

Marinade pour viandes rouges et gibier
Marinade for Red Meat and Game Birds

A good marinade with its blend of pungent herbs can change an average piece of meat into a tender and wonderful cut.

When marinating use a glass or glazed bowl—never metal, as the acid from the marinade could react with the metal and create a toxic condition. Place the bowl and its contents in the refrigerator overnight in summer, in a very cool place in winter. Here is a marinade that I have used very successfully on many of our picnics and for home use in broiler cookery or for stewing meat.

½ cup sliced carrots
½ cup minced onion
2 minced shallots
¼ cup sliced celery
2 garlic cloves, peeled and cut in half
3 sprigs parsley
¼ teaspoon dried thyme leaves
1 bay leaf, crumbled
1 whole clove
⅛ teaspoon dried rosemary leaves
⅛ teaspoon dried sage leaves
Pepper, fresh ground
5 cups dry white wine
½ cup vinegar
2 tablespoons cognac, Armagnac, or other brandy
¼ cup olive oil or vegetable oil

In large, deep glass or ceramic container make a bed of half the carrots, onion, shallots, and celery. Place meat on top. Spread the rest of vegetables, herbs, and spices on top. Mix wine, vinegar, cognac or other brandy, and oil; pour over; cover and place in refrigerator or other cool place for several hours or overnight; turn occasionally.

For Stewing-Meat or Game

For a 2½-pound piece of meat or bird, remove meat from marinade; dry meat well; reserve and strain marinade. Salt and pepper meat;* brown in fat in large Dutch oven. Add two cups marinade and simmer, covered, for 2-2½ hours or until meat is tender. Add more marinade if necessary. (For a game bird, cooking time is reduced to about 1 hour.)

---

*In stewing, light salting is done first.

For Red-Meat Broiler Cookery

Sirloin steak: Drain meat, reserve and strain marinade. Place meat on a lightly-oiled grill 4 inches above white-hot charcoal. Grill 3-4 minutes per side for medium-rare individual steak, 7-8 minutes per side for medium-rare sirloin. Baste often with leftover marinade; salt just before serving.

Sirloin or flank-steak kabobs: Cut meat into 1½-inch cubes for sirloin. For flank steak slice diagonally. Marinate and proceed as above after placing meat on skewers. Slightly reduce cooking time for flank steak. Salt just before serving.

Boeuf bourguignon   1
Easy Beef Burgundy

I have included this famous recipe because it is so popular, even in the South, and well worth knowing about. This is a very easy version of the famous dish. Serve it with a good Burgundy or a Hermitage.

(Serves 4)

2-2½ pounds round steak or beef blade roast, cut into 1-inch
    cubes
3 tablespoons all-purpose flour
2 tablespoons vegetable or olive oil
⅓ cup diced salt pork or bacon, blanched and drained
2 large carrots, quartered then cut lengthwise in thick strips
2 medium-sized onions, sliced
2 garlic cloves, minced
2 tomatoes, cut into small cubes
1 tablespoon chopped parsley
1 bay leaf
1 teaspoon dried thyme leaves, crushed
2 cups dry red Burgundy wine, heated
Salt and pepper
1½ tablespoons demi-glace (optional) *

---

*If you have *demi-glace* on hand, dilute it in the gravy before serving; rewarm gently. Demi-glace is described on page 20.

Preheat oven to 325°.

Place meat and flour in paper bag; shake well to coat meat; shake off excess flour. Brown meat in oil over medium-high heat in heavy skillet.

Place meat in ovenproof casserole; add salt pork, carrots, onions, garlic, tomatoes, parsley, bay leaf, and thyme. Pour very hot wine over it; add salt and pepper to taste; cover tightly and place in preheated oven for 2½-3 hours, stirring once during cooking. Check for tenderness at end of 2 hours; continue cooking as necessary. Discard bay leaf before serving.

Entrecôtes à la marseillaise
Steaks Marseille Style

Entrecôte textually means "between the ribs" — hence, rib steak. A tasty way to prepare T-bone or sirloin steak is as follows:

(Serves 4)

4 T-bone or sirloin steaks
Salt and pepper
4 tablespoons olive or vegetable oil
1 large onion, sliced thin
3 tablespoons red wine vinegar
4 teaspoons Dijon mustard
4 tablespoons beef broth or bouillon
Salt and pepper

Trim excess fat from steaks; sauté steaks in large heavy skillet 2-3 minutes on each side in 2 tablespoons oil over medium-high heat for medium-rare, 2 minutes longer if the steaks should be well-done. Sprinkle lightly with salt and pepper. Transfer to warm platter.

Add 2 tablespoons oil to skillet; sauté onion slices over medium heat until transparent and soft; add vinegar, mustard, beef broth, salt, and pepper. Stir over low heat until sauce is very hot (about 1-2 minutes). Serve over steaks.

Feuilles de salades farcies

1

Stuffed Lettuce Rolls

Another use for the coarse outer leaves of lettuce.

(Serves 4)

8 large lettuce leaves from leaf or loose-leaf lettuce
1 pound ground beef
¾ cup bread crumbs
¾ cup milk, warmed
1 whole egg, slightly beaten
1 small garlic clove, minced fine
⅓ cup chopped parsley
Salt and pepper
6 large shallots, chopped fine
¼ cup butter or margarine
4 ounces dry white wine

Clean lettuce leaves; blanch rapidly by plunging them for a few seconds in boiling water; remove immediately and drain.

Spread leaves, two overlapping, on flat surface. Mix bread crumbs and milk in bowl until crumbs are softened. Add ground beef, egg, garlic, parsley, and salt and pepper to taste; mix well.

Fill lettuce leaves with meat mixture and wrap the leaves around; tie them securely. In deep, heavy casserole melt butter or margarine over medium heat; add shallots and sauté until transparent. Add lettuce rolls, wine, salt, and pepper. Cover tightly and simmer 40-45 minutes. Remove strings and serve on warm serving dish.

Le boeuf en daube provençal

2

Braised Beef Provençal

The term *daube* means braised meat. *Boeuf en daube* is a traditional dish; made all over the South. In Languedoc and Roussillon, the two provinces abutting the Béarn country, the pieces of beef are larded with small pieces of bacon, saturated with cognac or other brandy, then rolled in a mixture of minced garlic and parsley. The meat is cooked in the same manner as that indicated below.

This dish is even better if cooked one day ahead, cooled and refrigerated, then reheated slowly before serving. This way, you won't need to cook the day you are going to have company. Serve with Burgundy, Côtes du Rhône, or Hermitage.

(Serves 6)

½ pound lean salt pork or slab bacon, diced
2 pounds chuck meat, cut into 2½-inch pieces (a small amount of
    fat marbling the meat improves the dish)
¼ cup olive oil
2 large onions, chopped
1 medium onion studded with 1 whole clove
2 large carrots, pared and sliced thick
3 garlic cloves, minced
1 bay leaf
1 fresh sprig thyme or 1 teaspoon dried thyme leaves, crushed
3 sprigs parsley
1 strip orange rind 2 inches long
1 large ripe tomato, skinned, seeded, and chopped
1 teaspoon tomato paste
Freshly ground pepper
Salt
2-2½ cups dry red wine

Blanch pork or bacon in boiling water for 5 minutes; drain. Place olive oil and blanched salt pork in bottom of enameled Dutch oven; add meat pieces. Add onions, carrots, garlic, bay leaf, thyme, parsley, orange rind, tomato, and tomato paste. Sprinkle pepper and salt over; pour wine over meat and vegetables to barely cover. Bring to rapid boil; reduce heat to simmer; cover, first with piece of foil, then with lid on top of foil to seal pot; cook at least 5 hours or until meat is very tender.

Discard bay leaf, parsley, and whole onion with clove. Remove meat to warm platter; skim off fat; return meat to sauce; reheat and serve with macaroni.

L'estouffade de boeuf camarguaise   **2**
Braised Beef Camargue Style

Estouffade is a Provençal word equivalent to the French *à l'etouf-fé*, which can be translated as "cooked in a tightly covered pot." Marinating the meat overnight will tenderize it, and the slow cooking in a tightly covered pot will make it even more tender and moist. Serve with Côtes de Provence, Chateauneuf du Pape, or a Hermitage.

(Serves 6)

3 *pounds beef bottom round or chuck, cut into* 1¾-*inch cubes*
½ *cup olive oil*
1 *large carrot, scrubbed and sliced thick*
1 *large onion, coarsely chopped*
1 *teaspoon dried thyme leaves, crushed*
1 *bay leaf*
2 *tablespoons finely chopped parsley*
Freshly ground pepper
½ *cup red wine vinegar*
4 *ounces bacon, diced small*
2 *tablespoons olive oil*
3 *garlic cloves, minced fine*
2 *cups dry red wine, heated*
Salt
2 *teaspoons tomato paste*
½ *cup pitted green olives*
½ *cup pitted black olives*

Make a marinade of olive oil, carrot, onion, thyme, bay leaf, parsley, pepper, and vinegar in large glass or earthenware bowl; marinate meat in it in refrigerator or other cool place, 5-6 hours.

Sauté bacon in Dutch oven in the 2 tablespoons olive oil over medium heat until bacon is crisp. Remove bacon to paper towel to drain. Set aside.

Remove meat from marinade (save the marinade) and pat dry; add meat to hot fat in Dutch oven and sauté over high heat until meat is browned. Pour reserved marinade over meat; add garlic, heated wine, and salt (light). Bring to light boil; reduce to simmer; cover with piece of foil and place lid on top to make pot airtight. Cook for 2 hours or more, depending on the tenderness of the meat.

Skim fat; blend in tomato paste; add olives and reserved bacon crisps; heat again and simmer tightly covered 45 minutes. Serve with noodles or any kind of macaroni.

Le fricot des mariniers   2
Braised Beef Mariner Style

This dish was cooked by the boatmen (*mariniers*) of the Rhône travelling up and down the river on their barges. They carried their heavy skillets with them at all times and cooked their meals on board. Serve with a Rhône wine.

(Serves 4-5)

2 pounds beef round, cut into 12 3"x3"slices ½-inch thick
3-4 tablespoons olive oil
2 tablespoons wine vinegar
1 medium-sized onion, skinned and chopped fine
1 large garlic clove, minced
2 large sprigs parsley, finely chopped
2 tablespoons finely chopped capers
2 teaspoons tomato paste
½ teaspoon dry thyme leaves, crushed
1 bay leaf
Pepper
¾ cup dry red wine (a Rhône would be nice), heated
6 anchovy fillets, freshened, patted dry, and sliced lengthwise to make 12 fillets

Flatten meat slices with mallet until each slice has increased in size to about 4"x4". Heat olive oil in large skillet; brown meat quickly, 2 or 3 slices at a time. Transfer to large heavy skillet. Keep warm.

Add vinegar to first skillet and blend with meat juices, scraping the pan with wooden spoon to get all the brown bits. Add onion, garlic, parsley, capers, tomato paste, thyme, bay leaf, and pepper (do not salt). Blend in heated wine; bring to light boil. Pour over meat in heavy skillet; place one anchovy fillet over each meat slice; bring to a light boil again; cover with tight-fitting lid, or place a piece of foil over skillet and a lid over it, to prevent steam from escaping. Reduce heat and cook, bubbling gently, for 1 hour or until meat is tender. (In Provence, the cook places a shallow plate containing water over the skillet instead of a lid.)

When meat is tender, remove bay leaf; taste for seasoning; serve with macaroni or noodles, rice or mashed potatoes.

Bifteck au poivre   2
Pepper Steak

Serve with a Beaujolais or a Moulin à Vent.

(Serves 4)

4 individual boneless beef steaks (about 1½-2 pounds)
Salt
3 tablespoons whole peppercorns
2 tablespoons olive or vegetable oil
2 tablespoons butter or margarine
2 tablespoons brandy
½ cup heavy cream
½ teaspoon Dijon mustard

Place peppercorns in plastic or strong paper bags and crush with heavy object such as brick or bottom of a heavy skillet, or roll an empty bottle over, until a coarse texture is achieved. (Do not use pepper mill.)

Pat steaks dry with toweling; pat coarsely-ground pepper on both sides, pressing firmly to make it adhere.

Heat half the oil and half the butter in large heavy skillet over medium-high heat; when fat is hot, add 2 steaks; fry 2 minutes on both sides; transfer steaks to hot serving platter; keep warm. Add remaining oil and butter; heat as before and fry remaining steaks; sprinkle lightly with salt on both sides; transfer to serving platter.

Heat brandy until it steams; pour into juices in skillet; ignite; let flames die out. Pour in cream slowly, stirring until blended; add mustard; cook over medium heat until sauce is slightly thickened. Correct seasoning. Spoon over steaks and serve with *pommes de terre persillées* (page 132) and a salad.

Boeuf à la mode   3
Oven Baked Chuck

This beautifully flavored braised beef should be served with a St. Emilion or a Pomerol (Bordeaux) or a Burgundy such as Côte de Beaune.

(Serves 6)

4 pounds lean chuck roast, cut into 1½-inch cubes
3 cloves garlic, crushed
2 medium-sized onions, quartered
1½ teaspoons dried thyme leaves, crushed
½ teaspoon dried savory, crushed
½ teaspoon whole allspice
2 bay leaves
Freshly ground pepper
3 cups dry red wine (preferably Burgundy)
2 tablespoons oil
3 tablespoons brandy
1 cup beef broth (canned or homemade)
2 level tablespoons all-purpose flour
12 small fresh onions (about 10 ounces)
10 ounces fresh baby carrots

Preheat oven to 275°.

Place meat, garlic, onions, thyme, savory, allspice, bay leaves, and pepper in large glass bowl or earthenware casserole. Cover with wine and marinate overnight or at least 12 hours in warmer part of refrigerator or in other cool place. Drain meat well; reserve marinade.

Heat oil over medium-high heat in enameled Dutch oven; brown meat on all sides in hot oil; pour brandy over; ignite (watch carefully); when flames die, add marinade; bring to a very light boil; cover tightly and place in preheated oven. Cook 4½ hours. Remove meat from sauce; strain sauce, squeezing as much flavor out of it as possible; remove excess grease.

Return sauce to Dutch oven; blend flour with ¼ cup beef broth in small bowl, breaking all lumps; add to remaining beef broth; blend well and add to sauce in Dutch oven.

Return meat, small onions, and carrots to sauce; bring to light boil; reduce to simmer; cover tightly and continue cooking on top of stove another ½ hour or until meat is very tender. If sauce is too thick, add a little more beef broth. Serve with noodles.

This dish can be prepared a day ahead. Cool; chill overnight. Next day reheat slowly before serving time. It's even better the next day!

Boeuf en croûte   3
Beef in Pastry Crust

Because presentation is one of the prerequisites of an elegant meal, this way of fixing beef is well worth the effort. Any good dry red wine will do with this dish.

(Serves 8-10)

1 4-pound beef filet, rolled and tied (have butcher prepare it)

Marinade:
1 cup vegetable oil or ½ cup olive oil, ½ cup vegetable oil
Salt and pepper
½ teaspoon dried thyme leaves, crushed
1 bay leaf
1 medium-sized onion, sliced
1 tablespoon good wine vinegar

Mushroom filling:
2 tablespoons butter or margarine
8 ounces fresh mushrooms, cleaned and chopped fine
¼ cup dry white wine
4 ounces liver spread or pâté or liverwurst, mashed

Pastry:
2 cups all-purpose flour
½ teaspoon salt
¾ cup butter or margarine
4-5 tablespoons very cold water
1 egg, beaten
1 tablespoon water

Garnish (optional): watercress and mushroom caps

Step 1
Prepare marinade by combining oil, salt and pepper to taste, thyme, bay leaf, onion, and vinegar in a large, deep glass or ceramic bowl. Place prepared roast in marinade; turn meat in it to coat well; cover and place in refrigerator overnight or at least 10-12 hours; turn roast occasionally.

Step 2 (can be done the day ahead also)
Prepare mushroom filling: melt butter or margarine in medium-sized skillet; add mushrooms and sauté over medium heat until soft (about 1-2 minutes). Add shallots and wine; cook until liquid has evaporated; remove from heat and cool.

Add liver spread or pâté, or liverwurst, and blend well; set aside or chill in refrigerator until ready to use.

Step 3 (when ready to prepare roast)
Preheat oven to 425°. Remove roast from marinade; place meat on rack in shallow baking pan and roast 30-40 minutes. Meat should be on the rare side. Cool at least 30 minutes.

Step 4
Preheat oven to 400°.

Prepare pastry for crust: sift together flour and salt in large bowl; cut in butter or margarine until mixture resembles coarse meal. Sprinkle water over mixture and mix quickly until dough adheres. Shape into a ball; chill in refrigerator, covered, at least 30 minutes.

Roll chilled dough into a rectangle roughly 12"x14½" on lightly floured surface; spread with mushroom filling in a rectangle about 8½"x10½". Place meat in center of filling; bring long sides of pastry to overlap each other; press edges to seal; fold ends and press to seal. (Trim excess pastry — cutouts may be made from scraps to decorate top crust.)

Blend egg and water; brush pastry with this mixture. Place on heavy cookie sheet and bake 30-40 minutes or until pastry is a nice golden brown. Serve on large platter garnished with watercress and mushroom caps lightly sautéed in butter or margarine.

Bifteck grillé sauce tomate   2
Barbecued Steak with Tomato Sauce

(Serves 4)

2½-3 pounds sirloin or T-bone steak
Pepper
Vegetable oil

Sauce Provençale:
2 tablespoons olive oil
¼ cup finely chopped shallots
1 garlic clove, finely minced
1 teaspoon all-purpose flour
½ cup dry white wine, warmed
Salt and pepper
3 large well ripened tomatoes, peeled, seeded, and chopped
1 teaspoon fresh tarragon leaves, or ¼ teaspoon dried, finely
*   minced*
2 tablespoons finely minced parsley
1 tablespoon lemon juice
Pitted green olives (optional)

Brush steak lightly with oil, both sides. Sprinkle pepper over and broil under broiler or over charcoal until done.

Prepare sauce: heat olive oil in large skillet; add shallots; sauté until soft and transparent, over medium heat; add garlic and stir a few seconds; blend in flour and stir until very lightly browned; add warm wine, stirring until slightly thickened. Add salt and pepper to taste, tomatoes, tarragon, parsley, and olives (optional); cook over medium-low heat 8-10 minutes. Serve over meat.

Oiseaux sans tête   3
Beef Scallops (Birds without Heads)

May be served with a rosé sec such as Sancerre, or a light red such as Côte de Beaune or Côtes du Rhône.

(Serves 4)

1½ pounds bottom round steak, sliced by butcher in 8 thin slices
1 tablespoon butter or margarine
1 medium-sized onion, chopped fine
1 large garlic clove, minced fine
1 tablespoon finely minced parsley
¾ pound German or country sausage or sweet Italian sausage,
     casing removed
Salt and pepper
½ cup flour
2 tablespoons butter or margarine
1 medium-sized onion, chopped fine
½ cup dry white wine
2 tablespoons tomato sauce
½ cup chicken broth or bouillon

Place each slice of beef between 2 pieces of waxed paper and with wooden mallet pound lightly to get rectangles about 4"x5½"; set aside.

Melt 1 tablespoon butter or margarine in large skillet; add onion and sauté over medium heat until soft and transparent; add garlic and parsley; stir 1 minute; stir in sausage meat, breaking it with fork and blending it with onion and parsley mixture; season with salt and pepper to taste and cook 1 or 2 minutes, stirring. Remove from heat; drain grease.

Salt and pepper meat slices lightly; spread each slice with some stuffing; roll and tie securely at each end. (These little rolls will resemble small birds; hence the name.)

Place flour in large dish; roll each "bird" in flour; shake off excess. Melt the 2 remaining tablespoons butter or margarine in same skillet as above; brown birds on all sides over medium-high heat; remove to warm platter; keep warm.

Add onions to skillet; sauté over medium heat until golden brown; add wine, tomato sauce, and broth or bouillon; blend. Correct seasoning; return birds to sauce and bring to very light bubbling; turn down to simmer and cook 30-40 minutes or until tender.

To serve, remove strings from scallops and arrange on warm serving platter. Skim fat from sauce and strain it; reheat slowly and spoon over birds. Serve with mashed potatoes.

VEAL

Veal is the most delicate of meat, and requires a method of cooking different from that used with beef. Good veal is young veal; the animal should be under eight months of age, the meat a very pale pink. This type of meat lacks fat and connective fibers, a factor which prevents it from keeping moist during cooking. It is therefore up to the cook to provide either the fat or the moisture in the cooking process.

Veal is a blessing to dieters because it has a low calorie count. In France it has always been recommended for persons on special diets, those with delicate stomachs, and the very young and the aged.

Thin cuts of veal should be sautéed in hot butter or margarine; thicker pieces seared first in hot fat, then braised slowly in a basting liquid.

To roast a veal roast weighing about three pounds, place the meat on the meat rack of a roasting pan; sprinkle with salt and pepper; cover with 1 tablespoon butter or margarine and 1 tablespoon oil; place in preheated 325° oven for 1-1½ hours or until meat thermometer registers 175°. This requires 30-35 minutes a pound.

Fricandeau de veau
Braised Roast of Veal

1

Fricandeau is the name given to the rump of the animal and also to the way the meat is cooked—braised. A Vouvray would be a nice wine to serve with this dish.

(Serves 4-5)

2 pounds boneless loin or rump of veal tied to make a roast
3 tablespoons butter
2 tablespoons oil
⅓ cup finely chopped white parts of green onions
2 sprigs parsley
1 bay leaf
½ teaspoon dried thyme leaves, crushed
3-5 ounces beef or chicken stock, bouillon, or half dry white wine
*   and half water*
Salt and pepper
8 small carrots pared or 2 large ones thinly sliced
8 small white onions
1 tablespoon butter

Melt butter and oil over medium heat in enameled Dutch oven; add meat and sear on all sides to a golden brown color. Remove meat to a warm platter. Add green onions to fat in Dutch oven, stir one minute; add parsley, bay leaf, thyme. Return meat to Dutch oven; add bouillon, salt very lightly; add pepper. Cover tightly and cook on low heat 45 minutes.

Add carrots and small onions; cover again and continue cooking over low heat another hour, adding a little stock once or twice to avoid sticking. At the end of the hour, test for tenderness; cook a little longer if needed.

Remove roast and vegetables (carrots and onions) to warm serving platter; keep warm. Strain juices, return to pan; beat butter in; reheat and ladle over meat and vegetables.

If you enjoy the taste of turnips, add small, tender turnips when you add carrots and onions.

Côtelettes de veau sauce moutarde   1
Veal Chops in Mustard Sauce

Serve with a Rosé de Provence or a Vouvray.

(Serves 4)

2 tablespoons butter or margarine
1 tablespoon olive oil
4 veal loin chops
Salt and pepper
2 large shallots, minced fine
½ cup dry white wine, heated
½ teaspoon dry thyme leaves, crushed
¼ cup heavy cream
1½ teaspoons Dijon mustard or regular mustard

Melt butter in skillet; add olive oil; heat over medium-high heat; add chops; brown on both sides about 8 minutes. Add salt. Remove to warm platter; keep warm.

In same skillet sauté shallots in fat over medium-low heat until soft and transparent (about 2 minutes); add wine and thyme; cook, raising temperature to medium-high, until liquid is reduced to thick consistency (about 2 minutes). Return chops to skillet; cover and cook 8-10 minutes longer. Remove cover, transfer chops to warm serving plate; keep warm.

Blend cream slowly into juices in skillet; add mustard; taste for salt and add if necessary, with pepper. Reheat slowly until very hot. Ladle over chops and serve.

Foie de veau en brochette   1
Veal Liver on a Skewer

Veal liver is the best ever! If your butcher is willing to get you some, try this brochette recipe for a treat.

(Serves 4)

1 calf liver skinned and cut into 1½-inch cubes
1 teaspoon dried oregano leaves, crushed
⅓ cup lemon juice
Salt and pepper to taste
Thick bacon pieces cut into 1½-inch slices
¼ cup finely chopped parsley
Olive oil

Place liver cubes, oregano, lemon juice, salt and pepper in glass bowl. Marinate several hours or overnight.

Alternate liver and bacon on skewer, sprinkle with parsley, drizzle with olive oil. Grill over hot coals, turning often until done. Serve with mashed potatoes or rice.

Escalopes de veau niçoises
Veal Scallops Nice Style

2

Serve with a Hermitage (Côtes du Rhône) or a rosé Côtes de Provence.

(Serves 4)

8 veal scallops (about 1½ pounds), cut into 1½-ounce pieces
2 tablespoons butter
2 tablespoons olive oil
12 ounces fresh mushrooms, sliced
Salt
⅓ cup finely chopped onions or shallots
1 garlic clove, minced
½ cup dry white wine, heated
½ teaspoon dried thyme leaves, crushed
1 bay leaf
2 tablespoons finely chopped parsley
½ cup chicken bouillon
1 tablespoon tomato paste or purée
Salt and pepper to taste

Place each scallop between 2 pieces of waxed paper, pound gently with a wooden mallet.

Melt butter and olive oil over medium-high heat in a large skillet; add scallops and sauté on both sides to a golden brown color. Remove to warm platter.

Add mushrooms to same skillet; sauté over medium heat 2 minutes, stirring all the while. Add onion and garlic and sauté 3 minutes longer. Salt lightly; add hot wine, thyme, bay leaf, and parsley; stir and continue cooking 10 minutes over medium-low heat. Add broth and tomato paste, blend; add pepper and salt if needed. Return meat to sauce. Heat again slowly.

Discard bay leaf before serving. Serve very hot, with rice or mashed potatoes.

Côtelettes de veau au champagne   1
Veal Cutlets in Champagne

These delicious chops should be served with a Vouvray or white Burgundy such as Montrachet.

(Serves 4)

4 veal loin chops (about 1½ pounds)
2 garlic cloves, mashed
¼ cup olive oil
1 sprig fresh thyme or ½ teaspoon dried thyme leaves, crushed
1 sprig fresh rosemary or ½ teaspoon dried rosemary leaves, crushed
⅓ cup champagne (extra dry) or a good dry white wine
Salt and pepper
½ cup pitted green cracked olives

Pass the tines of a fork lightly over meat on both sides; rub garlic over both sides.

Heat olive oil over medium-high heat in heavy skillet, sauté meat on both sides until golden brown; add thyme and rosemary; pour champagne over it slowly and carefully; add salt and pepper; blend.

Bring to light boil; reduce heat to low and cook 15 minutes. Add olives, reheat 5 minutes; serve.

Paupiettes de veau provençales   **2**
Stuffed Veal Scallops Provençal Style

Serve this with a Bordeaux (St. Émilion, for example).

(Serves 6)

6 hard-boiled eggs, shelled
6 large veal scallops (about ½ pound)
6 thin slices Prosciutto ham or Westphalian ham
3 tablespoons butter or margarine
½ cup (scant) dry white wine
⅓ cup Madeira wine
3 teaspoons tomato paste
Salt and pepper
⅔ cup pitted green olives
1 pound small fresh mushrooms, cleaned

Place each scallop between two pieces of waxed paper and pound lightly until a rectangle of about 7 inches in length by 3½-4 inches in width is formed.

Wrap each shelled hard-boiled egg with slice of ham, then wrap each with a scallop rectangle; tie each roll securely with kitchen string, making neat little bundle.

Melt butter or margarine over medium-high heat in heavy skillet large enough to hold the meat rolls. Add meat rolls; sauté on all sides until brown. Remove meat to warm dish; keep warm.

Add white wine and Madeira to juices in skillet; bring to light boil; cook rapidly for 1 minute. Blend in tomato paste; salt and pepper to taste. Return meat bundles to sauce; turn them over to moisten throughly with sauce. Bring to light boil; cover tightly; simmer 30 minutes. Uncover and moisten again with sauce; add olives and mushrooms; cover and simmer another 30 minutes.

To serve, remove string, cut each roll in half widthwise; arrange halves around a serving dish (cut sides with yolk showing, on top); ladle sauce over; place mushrooms and olives in center. If sauce is too thin, reduce by boiling briskly one minute.

Poitrine de veau farcie
Stuffed Veal Roll

2

Serve with a rosé of Côtes de Provence or a Tavel.

(Serves 4-5)

3-4 pounds breast of veal, boned and butterflied
Salt and pepper
½ cup ground pork
½ pound cooked ham, minced fine
¼ cup parsley, minced fine
2 shallots, minced fine
1 whole egg, slightly beaten
2 tablespoons butter or margarine
1 medium-sized onion, sliced
1 carrot, pared and cut in four pieces lengthwise
1 sprig parsley
1 bay leaf
2 tablespoons cognac or other brandy

Preheat oven to 325°.

Pound the veal breast with wooden mallet; sprinkle with salt and pepper to taste.

Prepare stuffing by blending together pork, ham, parsley, shallots, egg, salt, and pepper. Spread mixture evenly over breast; roll up jelly-roll fashion and tie securely with strings.

Melt butter over high heat in roasting pan; brown the roll on all sides; sprinkle with salt and pepper; add onion slices, carrot, parsley, bay leaf, and cognac or brandy. Place in preheated oven and bake 2½-3 hours or until very tender, basting occasionally. Remove roll to a platter to cool thoroughly; then place in refrigerator to chill.

To serve, remove strings and slice.

---

*Split open and spread apart. (Butcher will probably do this at your request.)

Ragoût de veau Basses-Alpes　　2
Alpine Veal Stew

One of my grandmother's favorite recipes for veal. Serve it with a Côte de Beaune or Côtes du Rhône.

(Serves 4)

2 pounds lean stewing veal or breast cut into 1½-inch cubes
3 tablespoons vegetable or olive oil
1 medium-sized onion, thinly sliced
1 tablespoon all-purpose flour
1¾ cups water, warmed
1 teaspoon dried thyme leaves, crushed
1 bay leaf
Salt and pepper to taste
2 egg yolks, slightly beaten
1½ tablespoons wine vinegar or lemon juice

Sauté meat and onion slices in oil over medium heat in large heavy skillet until meat starts to color. Remove meat to warm platter.

Blend flour into skillet juices; add warm water slowly, stirring constantly to break flour lumps; add thyme, bay leaf, salt, and pepper and bring to a light boil. Return meat to skillet. Turn heat down to simmer, cover, and cook 1 hour or until meat is tender. Discard bay leaf.

Mix about ⅓ cup of sauce with beaten egg yolks; blend well; return this slowly to sauce, blending well again; cook on low heat 5 minutes longer; add vinegar or lemon juice; stir to blend. Serve at once.

Blanquette de veau　　3
Veal Stew

This delicious ragout has been named after its white (*blanc—blanquette*) sauce. Serve with a Loire wine such as Sancerre or a Muscadet.

(Serves 4-5)

2½ pounds veal stew or breast of veal, cut in 1½-inch cubes
1 medium-sized onion
1 large carrot cut in two, then cut in half lengthwise
1 bay leaf
1 large garlic clove
½ teaspoon dried summer savory, crushed
1 teaspoon dried thyme leaves, crushed
3 sprigs parsley
4 cups water
Salt (light) and pepper
2 tablespoons butter or margarine
¼ cup flour
½ cup dry white wine
2 egg yolks, slightly beaten
2 tablespoons lemon juice

Combine meat, onion, carrot, bay leaf, garlic, summer savory, thyme, and parsley in Dutch oven. Add enough water to barely cover (about 4 cups), salt, and pepper. Bring to boil over medium-high heat, skim if necessary; reduce heat to simmer; cover and cook 1 hour to 1¼ hours or until meat is very tender. Remove meat to warm platter; keep warm.

Remove carrots; reserve. Strain broth; reserve. Melt 1 tablespoon butter or margarine in same Dutch oven or large saucepan, blend in flour. Gradually add 1½ cups broth and ½ cup hot wine; bring to light boil, stirring constantly, and cook until sauce thickens slightly. Reduce heat.

In a bowl mix about ⅓ cup of sauce with beaten egg yolks, blend well; return this slowly to sauce, blend well again and cook on low heat 5 minutes longer or until sauce has thickened somewhat. Add 1 tablespoon butter and the lemon juice. Blend, return meat to sauce; reheat and serve immediately.

You may wish to add carrots to the stew. New boiled potatoes are good with this dish. If you have some broth left after reserving 2 cups for the sauce, add what is left to cooking water to boil potatoes.

Paupiettes de veau Suzanne   **3**
Veal Birds Suzanne

Serve these *paupiettes* on tomato halves or slices sautéed in butter.

(Serves 4)

8 veal scallops (about 1½ pounds)
10 large mushrooms with stems
1 tablespoon lemon juice
2 tablespoons butter or margarine
1 large onion, chopped fine
1 large garlic clove, minced fine
⅓ cup chopped parsley
1 egg white, slightly beaten
Salt and pepper to taste
½ cup all-purpose flour
3 tablespoons butter or margarine
1 large carrot, coarsely chopped
1 large onion, chopped fine
1 bay leaf
⅓ cup dry white wine, heated
½ cup chicken broth, canned or homemade, warmed
1 tablespoon tomato paste
1 tablespoon capers

Place each scallop between two pieces of waxed paper and pound lightly with wooden mallet to make 8 4"x5" rectangles.

Wipe mushrooms, remove stems. Cover 8 caps with lightly salted boiling water to which you add lemon juice. Set aside until ready to use. Chop 2 caps and stems fine; reserve.

Melt 2 tablespoons butter or margarine over medium-low heat in small skillet; add onion and sauté until transparent; add chopped mushrooms and parsley; stir 1 minute; add beaten egg white, stir rapidly to blend; add salt and pepper, stirring well.

Spread each slice of meat with a little of the filling. Roll and tie securely to make little sausages (*paupiettes*). Roll *paupiettes* in flour; shake off excess.

Melt 3 tablespoons butter or margarine over medium-low heat in large, deep, heavy skillet or Dutch oven; brown *paupiettes* on all sides. Remove to warm platter.

In same skillet sauté carrots and onions in fat over medium heat until lightly colored stirring often. Return *paupiettes* to skillet; add wine, broth, bay leaf, salt, and pepper. Bring to light boil, reduce to very low; cover and cook 30 minutes or until meat is tender. Remove *paupiettes* to warm platter; keep warm.

Discard bay leaf; test for seasoning, and correct if necessary. Blend in tomato paste and add capers. Return *paupiettes* to sauce; reheat. Remove string from *paupiettes*. Put 2 on each plate. Divide reserved mushroom caps in half; place one half on each side of *paupiettes*. Spoon sauce over *paupiettes* and caps.

Veau à la Marengo   3
Veal Marengo

This dish takes its name from the famous Chicken Marengo because of the similarity of its sauce. Serve the same wine as that used in the sauce.

(Serves 6)

4 pounds lean veal shoulder, cut into 1½-inch cubes
2 tablespoons butter or margarine
2 tablespoons olive oil
¼ cup cognac (optional)
1 large onion, chopped fine
2 tablespoons finely minced parsley
1 large garlic clove, minced fine
2 tablespoons all-purpose flour, browned lightly in dry skillet
2½ cups dry red wine, heated
½ cup chicken bouillon (homemade or commercial)
1 bay leaf
1 teaspoon dry thyme leaves, crushed
1 large ripe tomato, skinned, seeded, and chopped
1 teaspoon tomato paste
Salt and pepper

Melt butter or margarine in large Dutch oven or large deep skillet; add olive oil; heat over medium-high heat; add meat and sear on all sides.

Warm cognac, pour over meat, ignite, and let flames die out. Remove meat to warm platter; keep warm.

Add onion to leftover fat in same skillet; sauté over medium heat until light brown; add parsley and garlic; stir 1 minute; blend in flour; add wine and bouillon slowly to blend with flour; then add bay leaf, thyme, tomato, tomato paste, salt, and pepper. Return meat to skillet. Bring to light boil; cover skillet; turn to low and cook for 1-1½ hours or until meat is tender. Skim off fat; discard bay leaf. Remove meat to warm serving platter and keep warm.

Bring sauce to a light boil and reduce until thick. Spoon over meat. Serve with noodles or rice.

LAMB

Very popular with the French, lamb is served often, especially in Provence. The particular appeal of lamb in that part of the country is that the flocks graze all summer long in the mountains of Haute Provence on the scented herbs growing there, which impart flavor to the meat. What a beautiful sight it is to see the animals moving like great waves over the highways and meadows on their way to their summer range! So powerful a happening is this that only one of our most prolific Provençal writers, Jean Giono, could have adequately described it. In his book, *The Serpent of the Stars*, about the life of the shepherds of Provence, he describes in his unique epic style the departure of the great flocks for the high meadows:

The whole world was involved in this migration. The moving tide of animals seemed to be obeying the great world order, and I was filled with its overwhelming and monotonous sound as a sponge is filled with water. Lambs were tumbling like waterfalls along my arms, rustling like leaves through my hair, my chest weighted by their weight as by an enormous boot. Around me I could feel the dizzying rotation of the earth as in a dream. . .

Even if, after such a narrative, it sounds like sacrilege, we turn to the preparation of lamb for human consumption. The problem with lamb in the United States and its lack of popularity in the past stem from the fact that often the animals were butchered too late or the meat was improperly aged, giving it a strong, wool taste or making it tough. To be called *agneau*, the animal should not be over eight months old at the most.

When buying lamb, one should look for meat that is lean and pink. Dark red meat and yellow fat are the sign of the older meat, called mutton after the French *mouton*. Mutton is good meat too, but should be cooked a little differently — braised or in stews.

Because lamb is very low in cholesterol, in fact, the lowest of the red meats, it is recommended for low-cholesterol diets. (Remove the fat after cooking.)

Côtelettes d'agneau aux sarments   **1**
Broiled Lamb Chops (Grapevine Embers)

The *sarments* are the canes of grapevines, trimmed each year to give strength to new shoots. In Provence these canes are thoroughly dried and used to make an outdoor fire that will produce embers on which the lamb chops are grilled. They give the meat a unique delicious flavor and form the occasion for great picnics.

If you are fortunate enough to have grapevines, use the dry canes for this treat; or substitute a campfire built of dry wood. Small fruit tree branches are a good substitute for the *sarments*.

(Serves 4)

Olive oil
4 lamb chops
2 garlic cloves, crushed
*1 tablespoon dried rosemary leaves, or 1 tablespoon dried thyme
    leaves, crushed*
Fresh ground pepper
Salt

Rub meat on both sides with garlic. Sprinkle both sides with rosemary or thyme and pepper. Place in glass dish and drizzle with olive oil. Cover with foil and refrigerate, or place in cool spot, for 3-4 hours. When ready to broil, light canes or wood, and let fire burn to rich embers. Place meat on grill and grill on both sides; salt to taste.

My mother would serve this meat with fresh new peas and small potatoes, with a salad of corn-lettuce (*mache*) and young dandelion leaves.

La daube d'Avignon   1
Lamb Stew Avignon Style

Sometimes small pieces of bacon are inserted into the meat before marinating (this is called larding). Serve the *daube* with a Côtes de Provence or a rosé d'Anjou.

(Serves 4)

3 pounds boneless, lean lamb breast meat, cut into serving pieces
3 tablespoons olive oil
2 carrots, cut in half lengthwise, then in thick strips lengthwise
2 large onions, diced
3 garlic cloves, minced
2 bay leaves
1 teaspoon dried thyme leaves, crushed
2 sprigs parsley
1 piece orange peel 3 inches in length
Pepper
2½-3 cups dry white wine
¼ cup brandy
⅓ cup diced salt pork, blanched
Salt

Place meat in large glass bowl or earthenware casserole; add oil, carrots, onions, garlic, bay leaves, thyme, parsley, orange peel, pepper to taste, 2½ cups wine, and brandy. Mix well and marinate overnight.

Next day remove meat from marinade; reserve marinade, vegeta-

bles, and herbs. Arrange salt pork in bottom of large Dutch oven;
place meat on top and pour marinade, vegetables, and herbs over;
add salt to taste. Bring to light boil; cover and turn down to
simmer; cook 2-2½ hours or until meat is tender. Check once or
twice; if liquid evaporates too fast, add a little more wine, which
you must heat first. When meat is tender, discard bay leaf, orange
peel, and parsley; skim fat; reheat and serve with pasta—macaroni
or noodles.

Fricot de grand-mère   1
Grandmother's Stewed Lamb

A *fricot* is a simple stewed dish; but even in its simplicity this stew
is delicious and reminiscent of spring.

(Serves 4)

2½ pounds lean boneless lamb, cut into 1-inch cubes
3 tablespoons olive oil
1 large onion, chopped fine
1 garlic clove, minced
¼ cup finely chopped parsley
1 bay leaf
Salt and pepper
1½ cups hot water
1 package (10 ounces) frozen peas or the equivalent of fresh peas
Salt and pepper

Brown meat in oil over medium-high heat in large heavy skillet.
Remove to warm platter.

Sauté onion until golden brown in same skillet over medium heat;
add garlic and parsley; stir rapidly for 1 minute. Add hot water, bay
leaf, salt, and pepper. Bring to light boil; reduce heat to simmer;
cover tightly and cook 45 minutes.

Add peas (if frozen peas are used, break frozen lumps gently with
fork); simmer covered 10 minutes longer. Discard bay leaf. Serve
immediately.

Blanquette d'agneau   **2**
Lamb Stew

See *blanquette de veau*—same preparation.

Le gigot d'agneau rôti   **2**
Roast Leg of Lamb

Lamb roast, to be at its best, should be a bit on the rare side. Don't forget that the temperature in the center continues to rise for a short while after the roast is removed from the oven. Let the meat stand on the carving board 10-15 minutes in a warm place while you attend to the rest of your dinner preparations. Serve it with a white Burgundy (Macon Supérieur, Macon Village or Pinot Chardonnay) or a Loire (Sancerre).

(Serves 6-8)

1 leg of lamb, 5-6 pounds
3 garlic cloves, peeled and cut into slivers (about 8)
1 teaspoon dried thyme leaves, crushed
½ teaspoon dried marjoram or rosemary leaves, crushed
2 tablespoons vegetable oil or olive oil
3 tablespoons melted butter or margarine
Salt and freshly ground pepper

Preheat oven to 450°.

Wipe off roast with clean cloth. Cut small but deep (about 1-inch) slashes evenly over the surface with sharp knife. Insert slivers of garlic into slashes. Rub thyme and marjoram or rosemary over entire surface. Brush oil and melted butter over meat, covering entirely.

Place lamb on a rack in bottom of large, open roasting pan. Sprinkle with pepper; place pan in preheated oven and brown 15-20 minutes; reduce heat to 350° and continue to roast about 1½ hours or until thermometer inserted in the meaty part (away from the bone) registers 140° for medium-rare, 165-170° for well-done.

Remove leg from pan and let it sit on carving block as explained above.

Gravy:

Add 3 tablespoons very hot water to juices in roasting pan and scrape off the brown bits clinging to sides and bottom; skim off fat; heat again. Make flour gravy, or, as the French do, serve the natural juices in a gravy dish to be passed.

Serve with boiled small new potatoes sprinkled with a little chopped parsley.

Sauté d'agneau printanière   2
Sautéed Spring Lamb

Deliciously fragrant with the scents and taste of spring!

(Serves 4-6)

2½-3 pounds lean boneless lamb breast or shoulder, cut into
     1-inch cubes
1 large onion, chopped fine
2 tablespoons olive oil or vegetable oil
Salt and pepper
2 level tablespoons tomato paste
1 tablespoon all-purpose flour
1½ cups chicken broth
½ cup dry white wine, heated (optional)
1 fresh thyme sprig or 1 teaspoon dried thyme leaves, crushed
1 bay leaf
2 garlic cloves, minced
1 tablespoon minced parsley
12 small carrots, pared
12 small turnips, pared, or 4 turnips, cubed
¼ pound fresh green beans, sliced lengthwise
¼ pound fresh shelled peas (frozen beans and peas may be used)

Sauté meat and onion in oil over medium-high heat in Dutch oven or large kettle, stirring often. Add salt and pepper (salt lightly). Reduce heat to medium; add tomato paste and stir to coat meat. Sprinkle with flour, stir again; add chicken broth slowly to blend with flour; add warm wine, thyme, bay leaf, garlic, and parsley. Bring to light boil; reduce heat to medium and cook, covered, 40-45 minutes, depending on tenderness of meat.

Discard bay leaf; if you have used fresh thyme, discard. Add carrots and turnips; bring back to medium heat; cover and cook 15 minutes longer; add green beans and peas; cook another 15-20 minutes over medium heat. Serve with a salad.

Brochettes d'agneau   1
Lamb Brochettes

A good spring dish to serve with garlic toast and new peas and carrots.

(Serves 3-4)

2 pounds boneless lamb shoulder, cut into 2-inch cubes
¼ cup olive oil
1 tablespoon lemon juice
1 cup dry white wine
2 garlic cloves, mashed
1 bay leaf
1 teaspoon dried thyme leaves, crushed
¼ teaspoon dried rosemary leaves, crushed
⅛ teaspoon dried oregano leaves, crushed
Salt and pepper

Make a marinade of oil, lemon juice, wine, garlic cloves, bay leaf, thyme, rosemary, oregano, and pepper. Marinate meat in this mixture overnight or at least 8 hours, keeping in cool place or refrigerator in summer.

Arrange meat on skewer alternating with sprigs of fresh rosemary if you have this herb. Grill meat over hot charcoal embers or on electric grill.

Ragoût de mouton aux artichauts   2
Lamb Stew with Artichokes

(Serves 4-6)

3 *pounds lean boneless lamb shoulder or stew meat, cut into*
*   1-inch cubes*
3 *tablespoons olive oil*
2 *medium-sized onions, sliced thin*
2 *large tomatoes, ripe, skinned, seeded, and chopped*
1 *tablespoon flour*
1½ *cups warm water*
1 *tablespoon chopped parsley*
1 *bay leaf*
½ *teaspoon thyme*
1 *garlic clove, minced*
Salt and pepper
6-8 *artichoke bottoms, cooked if fresh,* or frozen*

Brown meat on both sides in oil over medium-high heat in deep,
heavy skillet. Remove to warm platter.

Add onion to same skillet and sauté until golden brown over
medium heat; add tomatoes and stir 2-3 minutes over medium
heat; sprinkle with flour; add warm water slowly and stir to blend
flour. Add parsley, bay leaf, thyme, garlic, salt, and pepper to taste.
Bring to light boil; reduce to simmer; cover tightly and cook 20-25
minutes or until meat is tender. Add artichokes and continue
cooking 25-30 minutes longer.

Côtelettes d'agneau farcies   3
Stuffed Lamb Chops

An especially elegant way of bringing this dish to the table is to
arrange the chops on a serving platter, leaving a space in the center.

---

*If fresh artichoke bottoms are used, drop them in salted boiling water; cover pot
and simmer between 35 and 40 minutes or until they are still very firm but almost
tender. Add to the ragout.

Just before serving fill this space with fresh, cleaned raspberries sprinkled with raspberry liqueur and briefly warmed. Arrange watercress around the dish.

(Serves 4)

4 thick rib lamb chops (about 1½ pounds)
4 tablespoons butter or margarine
½ cup dry white wine, warmed
1 pound fresh raspberries (optional)
3 tablespoons raspberry liqueur (optional)

Stuffing:
½ cup ground sausage meat
1 bread slice, torn into small pieces
¼ cup dry white wine
1 tablespoon finely minced parsley
2 shallots, chopped fine
½ cup cooked ham, chopped fine
½ teaspoon dry thyme leaves, crushed
1 teaspoon tomato paste
Salt and pepper
1 egg yolk, lightly beaten

Wipe chops with paper toweling; trim fat. Make a slash into the side of the meaty part of each chop with sharp knife, creating a pocket large enough to accommodate the stuffing. Set aside.

In medium-sized skillet sauté sausage meat over medium heat until it loses its pink coloring, about 3-5 minutes. Drain fat; reserve meat.

Place bread and wine in large bowl; let it soak until wine is absorbed and bread is soft. Mash bread; add parsley, shallots, ham, thyme, and reserved sausage meat; blend well.

Melt 2 tablespoons butter or margarine in same skillet used for sausage meat; add meat mixture; cook over medium heat 2 minutes, stirring often. Add tomato paste and salt and pepper to taste; stir; add beaten egg yolk and blend, stirring rapidly; cook 1-2 minutes longer or until mixture holds together. Remove from heat.

Divide mixture into 4 portions and stuff into lamb chop pockets.

Sew pockets with large needle and kitchen thread, or weave tooth-
picks through both sides of openings, to close.

Melt 1 tablespoon butter or margarine in large skillet over
medium-high heat; when sizzling, sear chops on both sides; salt
lightly. Add wine slowly (watch for spattering of grease); cook
rapidly over high heat for 1 minute, shaking pan to blend juices.
Turn heat to simmer; cover and cook 10-15 minutes or until
meat feels tender when pierced lightly with point of knife. Remove meat to hot serving platter; keep warm.

Add leftover tablespoon butter or margarine to juices in skillet;
blend and reheat. Spoon over meat and serve garnished with
raspberries and watercress. If berries are not available, serve with
julienne of carrots sautéed in butter.

To prepare raspberries: Clean berries, place in a sauté pan, sprinkle
with liqueur, and heat over medium heat until just warm, shaking
pan gently but consistently so as not to bruise the fruit. May also
be heated in a hot oven; place fruit and liqueur in shallow baking
dish; place in 375° oven until warm.

La gardiane à l'arlésienne   **1**
Lamb in the Style of Arles

Gardiane is the feminine form of *gardian*, or guardian in English
— the cowboys of the Camargue, where the bull is king over great
manades or herds, and the horses roam free. The traditional *gardiane* is made with beef. In Arles, this has been modified: lamb is
used instead of beef and potatoes are added.

(Serves 4)

4 lean shoulder lamb chops
3 tablespoons olive oil
2 large potatoes, peeled and sliced thin
1 large sweet onion, sliced thin
2 garlic cloves, minced fine
1 bay leaf
2-2½ cups very hot water
Salt and pepper

In deep, heavy skillet sauté meat in oil over medium-high heat until brown on all sides. Add potatoes, onion, garlic, bay leaf, hot water, and salt and pepper to taste. Bring to light boil; cover, leaving a little space between lid and skillet for steam to escape. Reduce heat to low and cook until meat is tender and potatoes are very soft (about 45 minutes to 1 hour). Serve.

PORK AND PORK DISHES

In the past, pork was mostly used in France to make sausages (*saucissons*) and cured hams. This was because of the short time span fresh pork could be kept without spoiling. Each farm family had one or two pigs which they would fatten for months, the butchering being done once a year. The meat from those animals was rich and fatty. For all these reasons fresh pork meat was not often cooked.

Today pigs are raised scientifically. The meat of the animals is leaner, healthier, and more digestible, and rich in the B vitamins and protein so that we may now use this wonderful meat without pangs of conscience. Also, pork is plentiful and the price often attractive.

The best buy is meat that looks lean; this is also the most healthful. If you are not going to cook the pork right away, remove the wrapping and place the meat in the refrigerator, lightly covered to prevent bacterial spoilage. If any pork is left over after cooking and serving, wrap or cover it and refrigerate *immediately*.

Pork should always be cooked *well*. Pork roasts should be cooked at 325°, with the meat thermometer inserted in the fleshiest part of the roast reading 170° F or 77°C and usually 30-35 minutes per pound for a loin roast, 40-45 minutes for a sirloin or crown roast.

The roast should be placed uncovered in the roasting pan, fat-side up; do not add water to the pan. When the roast is done and before carving, let it stand as for lamb roast 10-15 minutes in a warm place.

Marinating is recommended for persons who have a problem digesting pork. Place the meat in a marinade of dry white wine and herbs such as thyme, bay leaf, and sage for 2 hours before cooking.

Haricots aux saucisses   1
Fresh Beans and Sausage

A dish that is fragrant and also very inexpensive and rich in protein.

(Serves 3-4)

8 garlic, German, or country sausages
2 cups shelled fresh shelling beans (in season, found in vegetable
department, in plastic bags) or fresh blackeyed peas
Boiling salted water
1 medium-sized onion, chopped fine
1 tablespoon oil
½ teaspoon dried thyme leaves, crushed
1 bay leaf
1 tablespoon minced parsley
1 teaspoon tomato paste
Pepper
Salt if needed

Prick sausages and place in skillet with a little water; bring to boil and cook over medium-high heat until water has evaporated; then cook, covered, over low heat for 20 minutes; set aside.

Add beans to boiling water in saucepan; continue cooking, boiling gently until beans are almost done but still very firm. Drain, reserve liquid; keep beans warm.

Cook onion in fat in heavy skillet over medium heat until golden; add beans, thyme, bay leaf, parsley, tomato paste, and pepper; add enough of the reserved cooking liquid to barely cover; cook uncovered over low heat until liquid is almost absorbed and beans are tender. Add sausages to beans 5 minutes before serving; add salt if needed.

La potée montagnarde   1
Mountain Stew

When one speaks of Provence, visions of easy living, beautiful beaches, emerald waters, and a riot of flowers come to mind; but Provence also has its high, arid plateaus and mountains covered with evergreens where winters are so severe and snow so deep that the *cols* (passes) are closed most of the time.

This harsh land was once cultivated by the Ligurians, plundered by the hordes sweeping in from the North on their way to the coastal villages, tamed by the Romans, and evangelized by the monks. This rich and tumultuous past has forged a strong people who till their small plots of land, raise their flocks, and brave nature's wrath in a stoic manner. Their food reflects their character — simple and hearty.

This stew was originally cooked in an earthen pot; hence the name *potée*.

(Serves 6-8)

2 pounds boneless lamb shoulder, cut in 1½-inch cubes
1 pound boneless pork shoulder, cut in 1½-inch cubes
1 pound lean smoked salt pork, diced
1 medium-sized cabbage
2 turnips, pared and quartered
2 large carrots, pared, quartered, and cut in long strips
2 leeks (white only), chopped
2 garlic cloves, minced
1 bay leaf
¼ cup chopped parsley
½ teaspoon dried thyme leaves, crushed
Salt and pepper
Boiling water
2 pounds potatoes, peeled and cut into 1¼-inch cubes
6-8 pieces country sausage 5 inches in length (optional)

Preheat oven to 325°.

Layer meats in bottom of large Dutch oven; add cabbage, turnips, carrots, leeks, garlic, bay leaf, parsley, thyme, and pepper; salt lightly. Add enough boiling water to almost cover; place piece of foil over Dutch oven, then lid, to make it airtight; place in preheated oven and bake 2 hours. Add potatoes (and country sausage if you like). Bake 30-45 minutes longer. Taste for seasoning and serve. (If too much fat is rendered, skim.)

Filet de porc aux navets
Pork Roast with Turnips

2

Serve this with a Côte de Beaune or other light red wine.

(Serves 6)

3½-4 pounds boneless pork loins, rolled and tied
1 teaspoon dried thyme leaves, crushed
1 small bay leaf, crushed
1 large garlic clove, mashed
Salt and pepper
2 dozen small turnips, pared
1 tablespoon sugar

Preheat oven to 325°

Mix thyme, bay leaf, garlic, salt, and pepper in small bowl. Pound and mix together well. Wipe roast with a damp paper towel; rub on all sides with this mixture. Let roast stand in cool place 1-2 hours before cooking.

When ready to bake roast, place it fat-side up in roasting pan or baking dish without rack; bake in preheated oven 1 hour and 40 minutes.

Parboil turnips in large saucepan in lightly-salted water for 6-8 minutes or until almost tender but firm. Drain well. Arrange turnips around meat in roasting pan; sprinkle turnips with sugar (it neutralizes their slightly bitter taste); spoon juices from roast over turnips; put roast back into oven; bake 35 minutes longer, turning roast and basting turnips once during baking.

To serve, remove string from roast; slice meat and arrange on warm serving platter with turnips around it.

Choux aux saucisses
Cabbage with Sausages

2

This is a very hearty dish that you will make often if you enjoy cabbage.

(Serves 4-6)

1 pound Savoy cabbage
4 ounces bacon, diced
1 medium-sized onion, chopped fine
Enough country or German sausage for 4-6 people
3-4 tablespoons hot bouillon or water
Salt and pepper

Prick sausages and place in skillet with a little water; bring to boil and cook over medium-high heat until water has evaporated; then cook, covered, over low heat for 20 minutes; set aside.

Core cabbage and discard coarse outer leaves; separate leaves and blanch 20 minutes in salted boiling water; drain and squeeze cabbage dry; chop; set aside and keep warm.

Render fat from bacon in saucepan or heavy frying pan over medium heat until bacon is almost crisp. Remove bacon; set aside. Add onion to fat in same saucepan and cook over medium heat until onion is soft and transparent. Combine cabbage, bacon, sausages, salt, pepper, and water; cook covered over low heat for 15 minutes.

Le cassoulet   3
Lamb-Bean-Pork Casserole

This dish has its origin in the Languedoc region. The best known is the *cassoulet de Castlenaudary*. It is prepared with different sorts of meats and white beans slowly cooked in an earthen pot which is called a *cassole*. (We still use the word *cassolette* for a small porcelain dish in which hors d'oeuvres or entrées are individually served.) The authentic *cassoulet* is made with the addition of *confit d'oie* (potted goose) — a long, complicated process which has been omitted here to simplify preparation.

(Serves 8-10)

1 1-pound package dried white Great Northern Beans
1 large onion, studded with 2 whole cloves
1 carrot, pared

4 garlic cloves, minced
4 sprigs parsley
1 bay leaf
Pinch of salt
¼ teaspoon pepper
1 pound Polish or garlic sausage
8 ounces salt pork, cut in 1-inch cubes
4 tablespoons butter or margarine
2 pounds boneless lean breast or shoulder of lamb, cut in large
     cubes
1½ pounds boneless lean pork shoulder cut in large cubes
Pinch of salt
⅛ teaspoon pepper
Hot water
4 tablespoons tomato paste
1 teaspoon dried thyme leaves, crushed
1 garlic clove, minced fine
1 whole garlic clove, mashed
3 tablespoons bread crumbs
Butter or margarine

Soak beans overnight in cold water to cover. Next day, drain, place beans in 4-quart kettle; cover with fresh water; add studded onion, carrot, garlic, parsley, bay leaf, salt, pepper, and Polish or garlic sausage. Bring to boil; turn down to simmer; cook 30 minutes, covered. Remove sausage and set aside. Return beans to simmer and cook 1 hour longer.

Blanch salt pork in saucepan of boiling water to cover for 5 minutes; drain, pat dry, and set aside.

Melt butter or margarine in large heavy saucepan or deep skillet; add lamb and pork meat and sauté over medium-high until lightly browned. Pour off excess fat; salt lightly and add ⅛ teaspoon pepper; set aside. Drain beans; discard parsley and bay leaf.

Place lamb, pork, and salt pork over beans in kettle; add hot water to cover, tomato paste, thyme, and minced garlic clove. Bring to boil; turn down to simmer; cover and cook 1 hour; add sausage; return to simmer; cook 45-60 minutes longer or until meat and beans are tender. Add a little more hot water if mixture dries out too fast while cooking.

Rub bottom and sides of large casserole with the mashed garlic clove; remove meat and sausage from kettle; cut sausage into ½-inch slices. Place half the meat and sausage slices in bottom of casserole; pour bean mixture over; add leftover meat and sausage on top. Sprinkle with bread crumbs; dot with butter; place under preheated broiler about 3 inches from heat until golden brown.

Le tian   3
Vegetable and Pork Pie

A *tian* is a deep dish in Provençal. For this purpose use a quiche pan 1½ to 1¾ inches deep.

(Serves 6)

1 9-inch unbaked pâte brisée *(basic pastry for quiches; see index)*
5 tablespoons olive oil
1 pound yellow zucchini, cleaned and sliced thin
1 pound green zucchini, cleaned and sliced thin
1 pound ground sausage meat
1 cup cooked long-grain rice
2 tablespoons finely minced parsley
1 large clove garlic, minced fine
1 teaspoon dry thyme leaves, crushed
2 whole eggs, beaten lightly
½ cup grated Gruyère cheese
Salt and pepper
2 tablespoons fine bread crumbs

Preheat oven to 400°.

Prepare pie crust according to directions; roll out dough in an 11-inch circle on floured surface and fit into quiche pan. Trim pastry, leaving an overhang of about ½ inch; turn under and flute edge. Prick bottom with a fork and prebake for 10 minutes in a preheated 400° oven; remove immediately and cool on a rack.

Preheat oven to 375°.

Heat 3 tablespoons olive oil over medium heat in large skillet; add yellow and green zucchini; sauté 1 minute; stir well; cover and cook 5 minutes over medium-low, stirring once or twice during cooking. Remove to large bowl; reserve.

In same skillet sauté sausage meat over medium heat, mashing
with fork; cook until meat has lost its pink color, 5 to 7 minutes.
Remove from heat; drain grease; add meat to zucchini in bowl; add
rice, parsley, garlic, thyme, eggs, cheese, salt and pepper to taste.
Mix lightly and pile into pie shell; sprinkle with bread crumbs;
drizzle with oil; place in preheated oven for 30-40 minutes. Serve
hot.

Le sou-fassum (chou farci) de Grasse   3
Stuffed Cabbage of Grasse

(Serves 4-6)

1 large cabbage, Savoy or regular (Savoy preferred, as leaves are
    looser and easier to work with)
⅓ *cup pork sausage*
⅓ *cup veal, chopped fine*
⅓ *cup lean bacon, chopped fine*
1 onion, chopped fine
1 clove garlic, minced
2 sprigs parsley, chopped
¼ *cup grated Gruyère or Swiss cheese*
1 cup cooked rice
2 eggs
Heart of the cabbage
Salt and pepper

Bouillon:
1 carrot, cut up in large chunks
1 onion, quartered
1 garlic clove
1 bay leaf
1 sprig thyme or ¼ *teaspoon dry thyme leaves*
¼ *cup olive or vegetable oil*
Pepper

Remove coarse outer leaves and discard; blanch cabbage in boiling
water for 5 minutes; drain and cool; spread leaves apart; cut out
heart and chop fine; mix with it the pork, veal, bacon, onion, garlic,
parsley, cheese, rice, eggs, salt, and pepper.

Spread leaves and put stuffing between them and in center of cabbage. Place cabbage in one layer of cheesecloth and tie secure-ly.* Put cabbage in deep pan with lightly salted water to barely cover; add carrot, onion, garlic, bay leaf, thyme, oil, and pepper; simmer slowly, covered, for 3 hours. Once in a while moisten top of cabbage. When done, remove cabbage to serving platter and serve with a tomato sauce. The bouillon may be made into a vegetable soup.

Pâté campagnard   3
Country Style Pâté

This is the perfect food for a summer picnic. Serve with French bread and *crudités* or a salad. Serve a Châteauneuf du Pape or a Côte-Rôtie.

(Serves 6-8)

3¾ cups all-purpose flour
1⅛ teaspoons salt
1 cup unsalted butter or margarine
1 egg lightly beaten
½ cup cold water
½ pound fresh lean pork cut into ¾-inch cubes
1½ pounds lean veal, cut into ¾-inch cubes
1 pound cooked ham, cut into ¾-inch cubes
½ cup chopped onion
¼ teaspoon dried summer savory leaves, crushed
½ teaspoon dried thyme leaves, crushed
⅛ teaspoon ground allspice
1 large garlic clove, minced fine
⅛ teaspoon freshly ground pepper
½ cup cognac or other brandy
Salt to taste
4 small dill pickles or French cornichons

Glaze:
1 egg, beaten, with 1 teaspoon water

---

*In Provence, the net used for this operation is called a *fassumier*.

Aspic:
¾ *cup chicken or beef broth*
1 envelope unflavored gelatin
1 tablespoon cognac or other brandy

Day before:
Mix pork, ham, veal, onion, summer savory, thyme, allspice, garlic, pepper, cognac, and salt in large glass or ceramic bowl. Let stand in refrigerator, covered, overnight.

Next day:
Preheat oven to 375°.

Sift flour with salt in large bowl; cut butter into flour until mixture resembles corn meal. Beat egg and water lightly and add to flour mixture, mixing rapidly to form a ball. Place on floured board and knead for 1-2 minutes (do not over-work); put back into bowl; cover and chill 25-30 minutes. Drain marinade from meat and set aside.

Remove dough from refrigerator. Cut about ¼ of the dough and set aside for the top crust. Roll remaining dough on floured board to about 3/16-inch thickness; lift gently and press into a lightly buttered or greased 9"x5"x3" loaf pan. Some of the dough will hang over edges; trim off excess and set aside.

Place ½ of the meat mixture in bottom of pastry-lined pan; arrange pickles in straight line over meat; place another layer of meat over, pressing lightly to remove air bubbles. Brush dough edges of pâté with egg glaze.

Roll out the remaining dough into a 9"x5" rectangle. Lift gently and place over meat; fold edges to seal, pressing together. Cut out leaves or other decoration of your choice with the leftover pastry; arrange in a pleasant pattern on top of crust.

Make opening in top crust by cutting a ¼-inch circle in the center with scissors. Insert a funnel made with foil in this opening, for steam to escape. Brush top of pastry and decorative design with remaining egg glaze.

Place in preheated oven and bake 1 to 1¼ hours (20 minutes to a pound); the crust should be golden brown (if edges brown too fast, cover them with foil and remove a few minutes before pâté is done). Cool pâté (with funnel still in) 20-25 minutes.

Add chicken or beef broth to leftover marinade and gelatin and place in enameled pan. Heat over medium-low heat until gelatin dissolves, stirring all the while. Remove from heat; add cognac and stir. Remove foil funnel and replace with small plastic or metal funnel; pour gelatin mixture through it slowly and carefully.

Refrigerate pâté at least 12 hours before cutting. It is always better to cook pâté 2 days in advance if possible, as it improves with age. Unmold pâté to serve and slice. Keeps well 4-5 days in refrigerator.

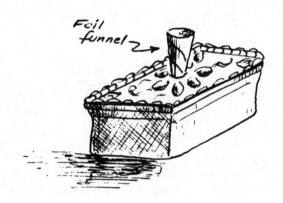

Foil funnel

Poultry and Rabbit

The history of poultry cookery goes all the way back in the history of man. The Romans, Greeks, Egyptians, and all the Mediterranean peoples were known to use poultry. Wherever olive trees grew, poultry was roasted in olive oil.

Of course, our barnyard fowl is a far cry from its ancestors, which were in all probability scrawny and tough from running and scratching all day for food. Poultry was moreover an expensive item to put on the table and was used only on special occasions and mostly by the wealthy and powerful.

Around the year 1300, Taillevant, *chef de cuisine* for the court of French King Charles VI, was using some 14,000 chickens a week. We can imagine the work that went into rounding up that many birds, and we can be sure that the poor farmers who raised them were eating mostly vegetables in order to please the king. If a chicken was consumed, it was in all probability a hen which was too old to lay eggs or a rooster dying of old age anyway!

It was not until 1600 that King Henry IV of France, sensitive to the plight of his subjects and their poverty and a gourmet himself, declared there should be "a chicken in every pot" on Sundays. Napoleon, very food-conscious—a gourmet and a gourmand—made poultry forever famous when his personal chef, who followed him in battle, concocted *Poulet Marengo* during his Italian campaign. But it was the great French chef, Escoffier, who around 1900, perhaps more than any other great cook, brought poultry to a place of prominence in the world of *haute cuisine*.

Since poultry is so universal as a staple, it was indeed logical that the Southern Provinces of France would come up with their own special ways of preparing it, and they have: *poulet aux olives à la niçoise, poulet à la languedocienne, poulet à la catalane, pintade* (guinea-hen) *à la provençale*, to name a few.

Today, thanks to modern conveniences, refrigeration, and large-scale breeding methods, the chicken in every pot has become a reality. Chicken is an excellent choice when it comes to finding a good source of meat protein. It also has an important place in a diet low in cholesterol and calories.

Moreover, you can make chicken as fancy or as simple as you wish. It can be served with an aura of luxury to an honored guest or very simply as a nourishing and pleasing dish for the family. It can be stretched and transformed. Magic can be performed with left-over soups, pâtés, etc.

Breeds never before available are now abundant on the market—for example, the Cornish hens that lend themselves to all kinds of preparation and which are fairly inexpensive.

Rabbit is becoming more popular in this country. In Europe generally and in France in particular it has long been a popular favorite, raised for its delicate meat. The taste for it is acquired, and I can understand the reluctance to eat these charming animals; but if and when you manage to overcome any reluctance, you are in for a treat!

Poulet à la crème   **1**
Chicken in Cream Sauce

The combination of evaporated milk, eggs, and juices from the chicken creates a delightfully smooth sauce.

(Serves 4)

2½-pound whole broiler-fryer
4 tablespoons butter or margarine
Salt and pepper
1 tablespoon lemon juice
1¼ cups evaporated milk
2 egg yolks, slightly beaten
1 tablespoon cornstarch
½ cup crème fraîche or sour cream

Preheat oven to 400°.

Wash and pat chicken dry inside and out. Sprinkle cavity with salt and pepper. Melt 2 tablespoons butter and sprinkle inside. Melt remaining 2 tablespoons butter in roasting pan and turn chicken in pan to coat it all around. Sprinkle lemon juice, salt, and pepper over chicken.

Place in 400° preheated oven and roast ½ hour; reduce heat to 375° and roast another ½ hour, basting twice or until fork-tender. Reduce temperature to 300°; cover with aluminum foil for 15 minutes. Remove chicken from roasting pan to carving board; cut into serving pieces and keep warm. Turn oven off. (Use neck and bones to make stock for soup.)

Blend evaporated milk with egg yolks in mixing bowl. Gradually add to cornstarch until well blended. Discard extra grease from pan, keeping the brown juices. Add milk-egg mixture to roasting-pan juice, scraping sides and bottom of pan to get all of the brown gravy.

Heat slowly on top of stove, stirring constantly, over medium heat. Cook until thickened. Add sour cream, salt, and pepper; blend well; reheat over low heat. Coat chicken pieces with sauce and serve at once. Good with buttered carrots and rice.

Poulet à la moutarde   1
Chicken in Mustard Sauce

Really easy, delicious, and perfect for company. A light red wine such as Moulin à Vent from the Beaujolais region or a Loire wine would be good with this dish.

(Serves 4)

3-pound broiler-fryer cut into 8 pieces
1 teaspoon salt
¼ teaspoon pepper
4 tablespoons butter or margarine
⅔ cup dry white wine
2 tablespoons brandy or applejack
½ cup crème fraîche *or heavy cream*
4 tablespoons Dijon mustard

Pat chicken pieces dry. Season chicken parts with salt and pepper. Melt 2 tablespoons butter in large heavy skillet. Add chicken pieces and sauté over medium-high heat until brown on all sides, adding 2 more tablespoons butter if needed, and turning the pieces to brown evenly. Reduce heat to low and cook, covered, 15-20 minutes longer, or until fork can be inserted easily in meat pieces. Transfer pieces to warm dish; keep warm.

Add wine and brandy to pan juices in skillet; blend, scraping bottom and sides; boil on high heat for 5 minutes. Add cream slowly and carefully; bring to boil again, stirring constantly for 3-4 minutes to reduce sauce. Remove from heat; add mustard; blend well. Return to low heat; add chicken pieces and simmer for 5 minutes. Serve with green beans or peas.

Poulet aux olives à la niçoise   1
Chicken with Olives in the Fashion of Nice

As olives are an important ingredient in the dish, it would be better to use the cracked olives sold in specialty markets. The recommended wine is white Côtes du Rhône.

(Serves 4)

3½- to 4-pound broiler-fryer, cut into serving pieces (or the same
   amount in chicken parts)
½ cup flour
⅓ cup olive oil
1 medium-sized onion, chopped fine
2 garlic cloves, minced fine
4 tablespoons minced parsley
4 medium-ripe tomatoes, skinned, seeded, and chopped fine
3 anchovy fillets, freshened and mashed
⅔ cup dry white wine, heated
1 teaspoon dry thyme leaves, crushed
2 large fresh basil leaves, minced, or 1 teaspoon dry basil leaves
   crushed
¾ cup green cracked olives, pitted, or ¾ cup regular green pitted
   olives
Salt and pepper

Shake chicken well in flour to coat in paper or plastic bag. Shake off excess flour.

Heat olive oil over medium-high heat in large heavy skillet or Dutch oven and sauté chicken pieces on all sides until deep golden brown. Remove chicken to warm platter.

Sauté onion until transparent over medium heat in same skillet; add garlic and 2 tablespoons parsley; stir for 1 minute (do not let garlic burn); add tomatoes; stir another minute; add anchovy and blend; add hot wine, thyme, basil, olives, and pepper. Taste for salt as anchovy and olives are somewhat salty, add if needed. Return chicken to sauce.

Bring to light boil; reduce to simmer; cover and cook 35-40 minutes or until tender. Transfer chicken to serving platter; ladle sauce over and sprinkle with remaining parsley.

Poulet au vinaigre   1
Chicken with Vinegar Sauce

Poulet au vinaigre is not a traditional recipe, but in recent years it has become a favorite in the South. It is simple to prepare, and delicious, especially if you can get some raspberry vinegar. A Bordeaux (Graves-Margaux) or a red wine from Champagne (Bouzy, for example) would be excellent with this dish.

(Serves 4-5)

2½- to 3-pound broiler-fryer chicken, cut into serving pieces, cleaned and dried
3 tablespoons vegetable oil
1 tablespoon butter
4 large shallots, minced fine (⅓ cup)
2 unpeeled garlic cloves
9 tablespoons red wine vinegar or raspberry vinegar
Salt and pepper
2 tablespoons tomato sauce
1 tablespoon butter, divided into small pieces

Heat oil over medium heat in large skillet; add chicken pieces and sauté until nicely browned on all sides. Remove to warm platter.

Reduce heat to low. Add butter, shallots, and unpeeled garlic cloves to same skillet; sauté over medium-low heat until shallots are golden brown, about 7-10 minutes, stirring often. Away from heat, add 3 tablespoons vinegar, salt, and pepper. Return to heat; cover and simmer for 10 minutes.

Return chicken pieces to skillet; add remaining 6 tablespoons vinegar; cover and cook over low heat 25-30 minutes more or until fork-tender. Remove chicken to serving dish; keep warm. Discard garlic; add tomato sauce to juices in skillet and blend over very low heat; beat in butter pieces one at a time; reheat slowly; serve over chicken. Decorate with parsley or watercress.

Fricassée de lapin aux olives   3
Rabbit Fricassee with Olive Sauce

This makes a distinctive dish with a deliciously fragrant sauce. The wine to accompany it could be a light red Burgundy.

(Serves 6)

3- to 4-pound rabbit, cut into serving pieces
4 cups dry red wine
5 tablespoons olive oil
2 fresh thyme sprigs or 1 teaspoon dried thyme leaves
1 bay leaf
2 whole cloves
5 small carrots, sliced thick
2 medium-sized onions, sliced
⅛ teaspoon pepper
1 medium-sized onion or 3 large shallots, chopped fine
¼ cup cognac or Armagnac
Salt and pepper
1 cup pitted green olives or green cracked olives (found at specialty food stores)

Make a marinade by blending wine, 2 tablespoons oil, thyme, bay leaf, cloves, carrots, onions, and pepper. Pour over rabbit in large glass dish and marinate covered and in refrigerator 1 or 2 days.

Remove rabbit pieces from marinade; drain well. Remove carrots from marinade; strain and save.

Sauté chopped onion or shallots in 3 tablespoons oil over medium heat until transparent in Dutch oven or deep, heavy skillet; add rabbit pieces and sauté until golden brown on all sides. Pour cognac or Armagnac over rabbit and stir rapidly for 2 minutes. Add marinade and carrot slices to rabbit; bring to light boil; cover; reduce to simmer and cook 1 hour. Add olives and simmer, covered, 25-30 minutes longer or until rabbit is tender.

Poulet à la Marengo   2
Chicken Marengo

Napoleon always took his own chef with him on his campaigns. During his Italian venture and while in Marengo, so the story goes, the chef having run out of staples went about the countryside to gather what was available and created this now-famous French dish. Serve a red Bordeaux, Graves, for example, with this dish.

(Serves 4-6)

2 2-pound broiler-fryer chickens, cut into serving pieces, or the
    equivalent in legs, breasts, etc.
5-6 tablespoons olive oil
1 large onion, chopped
2 tablespoons flour
4 tablespoons tomato paste
⅔ cup dry white wine, heated
¾-1 cup chicken broth, warmed
1 clove garlic, minced
2 tablespoons minced parsley
1 bay leaf
½ teaspoon dried thyme leaves, crumbled
½ pound small button mushrooms, cleaned, or canned mush-
    rooms, drained

Pat chicken pieces dry and season with salt and pepper to taste. Heat oil in large heavy skillet; brown pieces on all sides over medium-high heat. Remove chicken to warm platter; keep warm.

Sauté onions in pan juices in same skillet until golden brown. Add flour to onions in skillet. Stir in tomato paste, wine, hot broth, garlic, parsley, bay leaf, and thyme; blend until smooth.

Return chicken to sauce; bring to light boil; reduce heat to low; cover and cook for 1 hour or until chicken is tender. Add mushrooms and cook 15-20 minutes longer. (If canned mushrooms are used, cook only 5 minutes longer.) Taste for seasoning. If sauce becomes too thick during cooking, add a little more hot water or broth. Serve with rice, pasta, or potatoes.

Le poulet au fromage de chèvre (ou de Roquefort) 2
Chicken in Goat (or Roquefort) Cream Cheese Sauce

The beautiful, sensual sauce makes this dish a perfect main course for a company meal. Sautéed buttered zucchini and carrot *batonnets* (sticks) and asparagus or leek vinaigrette would be a nice accompaniment. A Beaujolais Villages wine is appropriate with this meal.

(Serves 2-3)

1½-pound broiler-fryer, cut up in serving-size pieces or the equivalent in parts
1-1½ tablespoons butter or margarine
Salt and pepper
2 tablespoons chicken broth
1½ tablespoons finely minced shallots
⅓ cup dry white wine
½ cup light cream, lukewarm
1-2 tablespoons Roquefort cheese, mashed (better flavor than any other blue cheese; I have however prepared this dish with soft goat cheese with great results)
1 tablespoon butter
1 tablespoon Dijon mustard or moutarde blanche

Melt butter or margarine in large skillet; sauté chicken pieces in hot fat over medium-high heat until nicely browned on all sides. Sprinkle with salt and pepper (salt lightly); add chicken broth; cover tightly and cook 20 minutes over low heat. Uncover, remove chicken to warm dish. Set aside; keep warm.

Reduce juices in skillet until fairly thick over high heat, 2-3 minutes; add shallots and cook 2 minutes longer. Blend in wine and reduce by half, about 3 minutes. Lower heat to simmer; add cream slowly and blend, stirring constantly; heat thoroughly (sauce should not be boiling). Return reserved chicken to pan and cook 12 minutes longer or until fork-tender.

Remove meat to serving platter and keep warm. Blend Roquefort, butter, and mustard together; add to sauce in skillet; scrape every bit of brown juice from sides and bottom of skillet to retain the nice flavor. Blend thoroughly; reheat until hot but not boiling. Ladle over chicken and serve with rice or small pasta.

Gardiane de lapin   2
Rabbit Gardian *Style*

For an introduction to the *gardians* of the Camargue (feminine *gardiane*), see the section on beef. For this dish a full-bodied red wine is in order; for example, a St. Émilion or Pomerol from Bordeaux, or a Hermitage from the Côtes du Rhône.

(Serves 4)

4 cups dry red wine
1¼ cup dried pitted prunes
2 whole cloves
¼ cup butter or margarine
2 tablespoons olive oil
3 pounds rabbit meat, cut in 1½-inch pieces
Salt and pepper
4 ounces salt pork, cut into small pieces
1 pound small onions, skinned
1 teaspoon dried thyme leaves, crushed
1 large bay leaf

Bring wine to lukewarm over medium-low heat in enameled saucepan; remove from heat, pour over prunes in glass or ceramic bowl; add cloves and let the prunes steep or marinate overnight.

Next day, drain wine; reserve for sauce; set prunes aside. Melt butter or margarine in large Dutch oven; add olive oil; heat over medium-high heat; add rabbit pieces and sauté until meat is golden; salt and pepper meat. Add salt pork, onions, thyme, and bay leaf; stir 2-3 minutes or until onions start to color lightly. Slowly pour in wine; bring to light boil; turn down heat to simmer and cook, covered, 1 hour. Add prunes; return to simmer and continue cooking, covered, ½ hour longer. Serve with long-grain rice or wild rice.

Le poulet sauce tomate   2
Chicken in Tomato Sauce

(Serves 3-4)

2½- to 3-pound whole broiler-fryer
2 tablespoons vegetable oil, butter, or margarine
Salt and pepper

Sauce tomate:
3 tablespoons olive oil
1 medium-sized onion, chopped fine
2 large well-ripened tomatoes, skinned, seeded, and chopped fine
1 tablespoon finely minced parsley
2 garlic cloves, finely chopped
⅓ cup warm water
1 teaspoon dried thyme leaves, crushed
1 bay leaf
1 teaspoon dried basil leaves, crushed, or 3 large fresh basil leaves,
*   chopped*
½ teaspoon dried summer savory, crushed, or 1 sprig fresh sum-
*   mer savory, chopped (optional)*
Salt and pepper

Preheat oven to 400°

Wash chicken, pat dry; sprinkle cavity with salt and pepper to taste. Heat oil or fat in roasting pan on top of stove over medium heat. Place chicken in hot fat and turn it on all sides to coat with fat. Sprinkle with salt and pepper. Place in preheated oven and roast, uncovered, 1-1¼ hours or until a fork inserted into the thigh comes out easily and juices escaping run clear. Remove chicken to carving board; cut into serving pieces; keep warm. (Bones may be added to water and vegetable to make broth.)

Sauce:
Heat oil in large skillet; add onion, sauté over medium heat until soft and transparent. Add tomatoes, parsley, and garlic; stir 1 minute over medium heat; add water, thyme, bay leaf, basil, summer savory, salt, and pepper. Bring to light boil; reduce heat to low and cook, uncovered, 15-20 minutes. Discard bay leaf. Sauce may be whirled briefly in blender or used as is (if too thick, add a little more water).

Poulet aux quarante gousses d'ail   2
Forty Clove Garlic Chicken

"More bark than bite," the garlic is kept unpeeled, lending only a delightful aroma and subtle flavor to the gravy. Fresh herbs are better than dried for this dish, but dried herbs may be used and the results will still be delicious. Serve a good Bordeaux or a Côtes du Rhône.

(Serves 4)

3- to 3½-pound broiler-fryer chicken, whole
2 fresh rosemary sprigs or 1 teaspoon dried rosemary, crushed
Salt and pepper
2 tablespoons butter or margarine
3 tablespoons oil or olive oil
2 fresh thyme sprigs or 1 teaspoon dried thyme leaves, crushed
1 bay leaf
4-5 large fresh basil leaves, or 1 teaspoon dried basil leaves, crushed
40 cloves garlic, unpeeled (2 or 3 heads)
¼ cup dry white wine
2 teaspoons hot water

Preheat oven to 400°.

Wash and pat chicken dry; sprinkle cavity with salt and pepper. Place some of the fresh rosemary leaves in cavity or sprinkle dried rosemary.

Melt butter and oil in covered roasting pan. Place chicken in melted fat and turn in fat to coat well all over, ending with breast down. Add leftover rosemary leaves, herbs, and unpeeled garlic cloves. Place piece of foil over pan to cover completely, with lid over foil to seal pan. Place in preheated oven for 1-1½ hours, basting with pan juices twice during baking. Uncover pan during last 15 minutes; chicken is done when a fork inserted into thigh comes out easily and juices oozing out run clear. Remove chicken to warm platter; discard herbs (if you use fresh herbs) and bay leaf; save garlic cloves.

Heat wine in small saucepan until it starts to steam; add hot water; pour into roasting pan; boil 3 minutes, scraping sides and bottoms of pan to melt all the brown bits of gravy.

Carve chicken; serve garlic cloves with chicken and gravy. Let your guests suck the garlic pulp (squeeze cloves with a fork to get pulp out, or pick up cloves and squeeze them into the mouth). Serve with plain rice to enjoy the full flavor of the gravy. If some is left over, it can be used with *sauce tomate* (see *Poulet sauce tomate*).

Le risotto à la toulonnaise 2
Chicken and Rice Toulon Style

Risotto comes from our neighboring Italy, where the ways to prepare it vary with the provinces.

(Serves 6)

5- to 6-pound stewing chicken, cut up into serving pieces
3 tablespoons butter or margarine
Hot water to cover
1 large onion, skinned
1 bay leaf
3 peppercorns
2 tablespoons olive oil
1 small yellow onion, chopped fine
1½ cups long-grain rice
⅛ teaspoon saffron, powdered
½ teaspoon dried thyme leaves, crushed
Salt and pepper

Heat butter or margarine in deep kettle over medium-high heat; add chicken pieces, including neck, and sauté until golden brown. Carefully pour in hot water to cover; add onion, bay leaf, and peppercorns. Bring to boil; skim; reduce heat; cover and simmer for 1½-2 hours or until tender. Remove chicken from broth and keep warm; strain broth; reserve; keep hot.

Heat oil in large skillet and add onion; sauté over medium heat until soft and transparent; add rice; stir, coating the rice thoroughly, for about 3 minutes. Add 3 cups hot broth, saffron, thyme, salt, and pepper. Bring back to light boil; reduce heat; cover and simmer 15 minutes or until broth is almost absorbed. Add chicken pieces, minus the neck, and gently mix. Increase heat slightly; cover and cook 5 more minutes or until rice has completely absorbed the broth.

Poussins au vinaigre   3
Cornish Hens in Vinegar Sauce

A *poussin* is a very young chicken. A good red Bordeaux such as Graves, or a Côte-Rôtie or Hermitage (Côtes du Rhône) will go well with this.

(Serves 4)

4 small Cornish hens or quails halved lengthwise
3 cups water
½ cup red wine vinegar
3 cups coarsely chopped celery stalks
2 tablespoons minced parsley
2 medium onions, coarsely chopped
2 garlic cloves, minced
10 juniper berries, crushed, or 2 whole cloves
1 bay leaf
Salt and pepper
3 tablespoons butter or margarine
½ cup cracked olives
2 teaspoons tomato paste

Blend water, vinegar, celery, parsley, onions, garlic, juniper or whole cloves, bay leaf, salt, and pepper in large glass bowl or ceramic casserole. Add Cornish hens or quails and marinate at least 9 hours, turning occasionally.

Remove hens from marinade, dry well, reserve hens. Place marinade in enamel saucepan; heat slowly to the steaming point and boil lightly for 2 minutes. Strain, squeezing as much of the essence out of it as possible; reserve.

Melt butter over medium-high heat in large heavy skillet; add hens; sauté on all sides until well browned. Being very careful, slowly add 1¼ cups of the marinade; cover immediately and simmer 45 minutes. Reserve remaining marinade.

Add olives and simmer 15 minutes longer; blend in tomato paste; correct seasoning. If sauce is too thick, add a little more marinade; spoon sauce over hens; cover and heat again. Serve with wild rice or long-grain rice.

Poussins en fricassée   3
Cornish Hen Fricassee

This dish was originally prepared with a very young chicken. Since it is impossible to find a sufficiently young bird now, I have substituted Cornish hens. This makes it also a very economical dish.

(Serves 4-5)

2 Rock Cornish hens (about 2 pounds)
½ cup flour
Salt and pepper
1 cup sliced mushrooms
1 tablespoon butter or margarine
4 tablespoons olive oil
2 shallots, chopped fine
1 medium-sized onion, chopped fine
2 garlic cloves, minced fine
¾ cup dry wine
¼ cup good brandy or vermouth
2 tablespoons chopped parsley

Cut hens into small serving pieces; mix flour, salt, and pepper in paper bag; add hen pieces; shake well to coat; shake off excess flour; set aside.

Melt butter or margarine in saucepan; add mushrooms; sauté over medium heat; remove from saucepan; set aside and keep warm.

Heat olive oil over medium-low heat in large, heavy skillet or Dutch oven; add shallots and onion; sauté until transparent; add Cornish hens to onion in skillet and sauté until golden brown on all sides. Add garlic, stir 1 minute; add ¾ cup hot wine and brandy, cognac, or vermouth. Bring to light boil; reduce heat to simmer; cover tightly and cook 25-30 minutes or until tender. Add mushrooms and correct seasoning; reheat 2-3 minutes; add parsley. Serve with wild, brown, or long-grain rice.

Le caneton aux olives
Duckling with Olives

3

A Riesling is an excellent wine with this dish.

(Serves 4)

3½-pound tender duckling
Salt and pepper
⅛ teaspoon dried thyme leaves, crushed
6 ounces salt pork, cut in ½-inch cubes
2 tablespoons olive oil
1½ cups small white onions
1 cup dry white wine, heated
¼ cup hot broth or chicken bouillon in hot water
¾ cup pitted green olives

Preheat oven to 325°

Trim wing tips and cut off neck of duckling; wipe inside and out and cut in half along the back; season cavities with salt, pepper, and thyme.

Melt butter in baking pan on top of stove; place both halves of duckling on rack in baking pan; roast in preheated oven, uncovered, 45-50 minutes at the most (meat should be slightly pink).

Blanch salt pork in boiling water 2-3 minutes. Drain and pat dry; place in large saucepan with olive oil and sauté 5 minutes on medium-low heat; add onions; cook, covered, 15-20 minutes or until onions are tender but not too soft, shaking pan once in a while; when done, set aside.

Remove duckling pieces from oven when done; transfer to chopping board and cut each half in half again to total 4 pieces; set aside and keep warm.

Pour broth or bouillon in baking pan; scrape to get all juices out; add wine; bring to light boil; remove from heat and degrease by dragging a piece of toweling over the surface. Return sauce to the saucepan with the onions and salt pork; add olives; heat over medium heat for 8-10 minutes. Taste for seasoning. Place duck pieces on serving platter and pour hot olive-sauce over. Serve with young tender peas.

Chaud-froid de volaille en gelée   3
Jellied Chicken Breasts

An anomaly, the name *chaud-froid* (hot-cold) implies that the chicken has been cooked first, then prepared and served chilled.

(Serves 6)

3 *chicken breasts, halved*
1½ *cups chicken broth (canned or homemade)*
2 *medium-sized carrots, pared and halved*
1 *small turnip, pared and halved*
1 *medium-sized onion, skinned*
2 *teaspoons dry tarragon leaves or 1 sprig fresh tarragon*
2 *sprigs parsley*
3 *peppercorns*
1 *envelope unflavored gelatin*
Canned sliced pimientos, cut into narrow strips

3 hard-boiled eggs, peeled and halved
6 black olives, pitted

Place chicken breasts in large saucepan, along with broth, carrots, turnip, and onion. Place tarragon, parsley and peppercorns in a square piece of cheesecloth; tie securely. Add to broth and bring slowly to a light boil. Cover and reduce heat to low; cook 30-35 minutes or until chicken is tender. Remove chicken to wire rack placed over a pan to drain and cool. Skin the breasts when cool.

Strain broth and chill in refrigerator; when fat has hardened on the surface, skim off.

Soften gelatin in ½ cup of broth in medium-sized saucepan. Heat slowly, stirring constantly until gelatin is completely dissolved; stir in remaining broth. Chill ½ cup of mixture in refrigerator until it is of the consistency of unbeaten egg whites; reserve the rest.

Pour small amount of chilled mixture over each breast with ladle and spread evenly with a brush to coat. Arrange pimiento strips on each breast to resemble petals of a flower. Chill until set; when set, pour out another ½ cup of gelatin mixture and chill until thickened. Spread new batch of gelatin mixture over breasts, being careful not to disturb the flower decoration. Chill until set and firm.

If some broth-gelatin mixture is left over, chill until firm; chop. Just before serving, arrange Bibb lettuce leaves on large platter; place jellied chicken breasts on top, garnish with chopped *gelée* and halved hard-boiled eggs topped with black olives.

Caneton aux cerises   3
Duckling with Cherries

Because a *caneton* is small it is more tender than regular duck; cooking time will vary with its size and age. After an hour of cooking, start tasting for doneness. A fruity rosé would be perfect for this. Try a Tavel or Rosé de Cabernet.

(Serves 4)

*1 pound fresh sour cherries, preferably pitted, or pitted frozen
    cherries*
4-pound duckling
Salt and pepper
Peel of 1 lemon cut in julienne strips
3 tablespoons butter or margarine
1 medium carrot, pared and quartered
1 medium onion, peeled and quartered
½ cup sherry wine
½ cup chicken broth or bouillon, heated
1 teaspoon cornstarch
1 tablespoon water
Juice of ½ lemon
¼ cup sugar
¼ cup vinegar
¼ cup Grand Marnier or cognac (optional)

If frozen cherries are used, thaw out. Peel skin thinly from lemon, using paring knife; cut into very fine strips, like thin filaments (julienne).

Place julienne of lemon in cold water to cover in small saucepan; bring to boil and cook 3 minutes; strain water and reserve peel.

Rub duckling inside and out with salt and pepper; truss it. It will roast evenly if first sections of wings are tucked under; legs are placed against the breast; and string is slid under the tail, then under leg joints, then above wings and tied securely.

Melt butter or margarine over medium-high heat in large Dutch oven; add duckling, carrot and onion; brown duckling on all sides. Add wine and continue cooking over medium-high heat to reduce the wine, about 2 minutes. Add chicken broth; bring to light boil; cover and reduce heat to simmer; cook 1-1½ hours or until duckling is tender. Remove bird to carving block and cut into serving pieces. Keep warm.

Discard onion and carrot; skim off fat. Scrape up any brown particles from sides and bottom of Dutch oven; blend in the juices — they will add to the flavor.

Dilute cornstarch in the ¼ cup of water and add slowly to the juices in Dutch oven, stirring all the while; add hot broth or bouillon and blend well. Cook over medium heat for 3-4 minutes or until thickened; add lemon juice and heat again. Keep warm.

Bring sugar and vinegar to a light boil in small skillet; reduce heat to low and cook, watching carefully, until the mixture is of the color and consistency of light caramel. Pour small amount of thickened gravy in this caramel and blend; return the whole to the gravy in the kettle; stir to blend; add lemon julienne and cherries; cook over low heat until hot throughout.

Flambé Grand Marnier or cognac and add to gravy. Spoon hot cherry sauce over duck pieces in serving platter. Serve with brown or wild rice.

Lapereau en gibelotte   3
Stewed Young Rabbit

Gibelotte derives from *gibier*, game. (Also interesting: the Old French was *gibelet*, a stew of game, from which the English takes the word giblet.) Serve a Châteauneuf-du-Pape or Hermitage.

(Serves 4)

20 (approximately) small fresh white onions, in season, or canned
*   small onions*
¾ cup flour
Salt and pepper
2½- to 3-pound tender rabbit, cut into serving pieces
¾ cup salt pork, cut into small pieces
3 tablespoons olive oil or vegetable oil
2 tablespoons butter or margarine
1 medium-sized shallot, chopped fine (2 tablespoons)
1 medium-sized onion, chopped fine
2 cloves garlic, minced fine
2 tablespoons minced parsley
1½ cups dry white wine, heated
½ cup chicken broth, heated
1 teaspoon dried thyme leaves, crushed
1 bay leaf
2 cups mushrooms, cleaned and sliced
2 tablespoons cognac (optional)

If you use fresh small onions, peel and place in boiling water to cover, boil gently 5 minutes; drain water, reserve onions. If you use canned small onions, drain liquid, rinse onions under cold water and reserve.

Put flour, salt, pepper, and rabbit pieces in paper or plastic sack; shake well to coat rabbit; reserve.

Blanch salt pork in boiling water to cover in small saucepan for 2 minutes; drain water, dry salt pork in paper toweling.

Melt butter and olive oil over medium heat in large enameled-iron Dutch oven; add salt pork and sauté until crisp. Remove salt pork and set aside.

Add shallots and onion to fat in Dutch oven; sauté over medium heat until light brown; add floured rabbit pieces and sauté, increasing heat to medium until rabbit pieces are golden brown on all sides. Add garlic and parsley; stir well; add hot wine, hot broth, thyme, bay leaf, and salt and pepper to taste; bring to light boil; cover, reduce heat to very low and cook 30 minutes.

Add mushrooms, reserved onions, and salt pork; cook, covered, over low heat 15-20 minutes longer or until rabbit is very tender.

If you add cognac, warm it in small saucepan and drizzle rabbit with it; ignite to flambé; let the flames die down and serve.

For an elegant dinner, serve this dish surrounded by bread triangles fried in a small amount of oil and accompanied by steamed, parsleyed potatoes. For a regular meal, serve with parsleyed noodles.

La poule au pot farcie   3
Stuffed Chicken in the Pot

We have Henry IV to thank for the declaration of the 1600s, "A chicken for every pot every Sunday." In the Béarnais, the province of the good King Henry, the *poule au pot* is traditionally served with thick tomato sauce and small green pimientos. I have included this recipe because it has become a French classic and is prepared all through the South.

(Serves 6)

5- to 6-pound stewing chicken
2 tablespoons butter or margarine
1 large onion, chopped fine
1 clove garlic, minced fine
3 tablespoons minced parsley
1 cup chopped cooked ham
2 cups soft bread crumbs
2 eggs, beaten lightly
⅓ cup cognac or other brandy
1 teaspoon thyme
Salt and pepper
1 onion stuck with 2 cloves
1 bay leaf
2 sprigs parsley
1 clove garlic
6 carrots
6 turnips
1 small cabbage
Hot water to cover

Remove liver and heart; chop them fine if you want to add to stuffing. Wash and pat chicken dry; rub cavity with salt and pepper.

Sauté chopped onion in butter in saucepan over medium heat until transparent; add garlic, parsley, ham and bread crumbs; blend in eggs, brandy or cognac, thyme, and salt and pepper to taste. Mix well; add chopped liver and heart (optional). Stuff chicken cavity with mixture; truss chicken by sewing tightly and securely (see page 250, *Canetons aux cerises*); stuffing should not escape while cooking. Place trussed chicken in large kettle with studded onion, pepper, bay leaf, parsley, and garlic tied in cheesecloth. Bring to rolling boil; skim foam; reduce heat; cover; simmer gently over low heat for 1½-2 hours.

Add carrots, turnips, cabbage, and salt to taste; bring back to light boil; cover and simmer gently for 1 hour longer or until vegetables are tender.

Serve broth as *potage* with toasted croutons, and chicken, stuffing, and vegetables as main course.

Salmis de faisan   **3**
Pheasant in Wine Sauce

Originally a *salmis* was a dish consisting of barnyard or game birds cooked in wine, with the sauce prepared at the table in front of the guests. Appropriate wines include Côte de Beaune, Nuits-St. Georges, Pommard, or a good Beaujolais.

(Serves 4)

2 young pheasants weighing 2-2½ pounds each
4 slices lean bacon
4 tablespoons butter
Salt and pepper
3 shallots, chopped fine
1 carrot, coarsely chopped
1 bay leaf
½ teaspoon dried thyme leaves, crushed
Pepper
2 cups dry red wine (Burgundy)
2 cups chicken broth
1 tablespoon all-purpose flour
2 tablespoons water
2-3 truffles, sliced thin (optional)
Fried croutons

Pluck, clean, and singe birds. Sprinkle pheasant cavity with salt and pepper; truss them; wrap 2 slices bacon around each bird; tie securely. Melt butter in large Dutch oven, place birds in butter and coat well by turning them in the melted butter, ending breasts down.

Cook covered, over medium-low heat (turning birds twice) about 20-30 minutes, depending on tenderness of birds. Remove strings and bacon strips; cut birds into service pieces: 4 legs, 4 wings, and the meat from the breasts; keep the bones to add to the sauce.

Place shallots, carrot, bay leaf, thyme, pepper, and bones in saucepan. Add wine and bring to very light boil; reduce heat to low and let it simmer until it has reduced by about ¾, 30-35 minutes. Strain sauce and return to saucepan.

Blend flour in water, dissolving any lumps; add to chicken broth; blend well. Add this to reduced wine sauce; salt sauce and heat slowly, stirring constantly. Cook on low heat 30 minutes longer until satiny. Return pheasant pieces to sauce; add truffles; heat again without bringing to boil. Serve with slices of bread, crust removed and cut diagonally into triangles, fried in butter.

Salads

For the *méridional* (person from the South), as well as for the average French person, a salad is a glorious addition to a meal; in fact a meal is not complete without it. Moreover, it serves the purpose of clearing the palate before the cheese and dessert are served; thus, the salad comes after the meat and vegetable course.

In the summer months, combination salads were and still are an important element in the cookery of the South. The hot weather made it uncomfortable for the housewife to cook. The salad was a beautiful alternative to the main dish and nourishing as well. A perfect example is *salad niçoise*, where all the elements that enter into its composition can either be cooked in the cool of the evening or prepared in the early morning hours and put together to be kept in the cellar (or refrigerator) until time for the noon meal. This salad provides the needed protein, carbohydrates, vitamins, minerals, and fiber.

To return to the green salad—only greens enter into it: Bibb (Boston) lettuce, escarole, endive, lamb lettuce (also called *mâche*) or a combination of these.

A good salad starts with a good dressing! The traditional French dressing consists of vegetable oil (olive or peanut); red wine vinegar, white wine tarragon vinegar, or lemon juice; salt; freshly ground pepper; garlic; and sometimes in the South, herbs—fresh in summer, dry in winter. Mustard is also sometimes used.

In the South garlic is rubbed over the tines of a fork in the bottom of the *saladier* (wooden bowl); then the oil and vinegar are added, followed by salt and pepper. The greens, having been shaken completely dry (*essoré*) are added at the last minute. (Drying the greens is most important for if any water is left it will dilute the dressing and make it watery.)

Addition of a *chapon* to the greens helps the garlic flavor permeate the salad. The *chapon* is a piece of fresh crusty French bread, rubbed thoroughly with a bud of garlic cut in half.

The salad should be tossed at the last minute to prevent the vinegar from "cooking" the greens. Only *crudités* are marinated ahead of time.

To dry the lettuce if you do not have a device called an *essoreuse*, which spins the greens dry, do as Provençal housewives do (and as I do): spread a square clean dishtowel that you keep for the purpose, place the rinsed lettuce on it, bring the corners of the towel together to make a neat bundle, hold the top together tightly so that none of the lettuce escapes. Swing the bundle vigorously forward and backward a few times. The moisture will go through the towel and the lettuce will be perfectly dry. (This operation should take place outdoors or in the garage. If you have no place to swing it, pat it dry with the clean towel.)

History of the olive tree

Cultivation of the olive tree is as old as the history of humankind. Its roots run deep in the soils of Mesopotamia, Greece, Rome, and the countries bordering the Mediterranean Sea. Their people cultivated it, ate its fruits, and extracted its oil as far back as three to six thousand years ago.

Around 600 B.C. the southern coast of Gaul, now known as Provence, was populated by the Segobrigii, a Ligurian tribe that had come from the North. They were a primitive people, living on their flocks of sheep and goats and on fish from the sea. The coastal waters were often visited by the Phoenicians, Egyptians, Rhodians, and Phoceans who came peacefully as traders. It was Protis Euximos, chief of a Phocean expedition, who first introduced the olive tree to the South of Gaul. On his ship painted red, the sailor's auspicious color of the time, he carried the wheat stalk, the grapevine, and the olive tree as gestures of friendship. After his marriage to Gyptis, daughter of the Ligurian king, the alliance of the two countries was sealed. This was the step that led to the foundation in the enclave of Lacydon of Massilia, now the great port of Marseille.

The second and most important step after the introduction of the olive tree was the cultivation of the tree to produce oil. This innovation changed the course of history for Provence, its industry, its commerce, and its traditional cooking. Provençal olive oil is now the best in the world. It is still produced as it was centuries ago, with some few changes such as more modern presses.

The fruity taste of this oil makes it an invaluable asset in the cooking of the South. In Provence, first-pressed oil—green in color—can be bought directly from the farmer. To taste this oil is an experience in itself. Unfortunately we cannot obtain it here, but some very good Provençal oil is to be found in specialty stores. I recommend your indulging yourself by buying some, even at some expense, to find out how good olive oil really is! Olive oil is a must for good Provençal dressing and for the preparation of some traditional dishes. For other dishes, olive oil can be cut with a good grade of vegetable oil, neutral in taste; the fruity taste of the olive will come through and you will have saved some money in the process.

Vinaigrette provençale 1
Provençal Salad Dressing

(Serves 3-4)

1 medium-sized garlic clove, mashed against tines of a fork resting against bottom of the bowl
4 tablespoons olive oil
Salt and pepper
1 tablespoon red wine vinegar
1 fresh basil leaf, chopped, or ⅛ teaspoon dried basil leaves
1 sprig fresh summer savory or ⅛ teaspoon dried summer savory
A chapon *(optional)*

Add oil and vinegar to bowl with mashed garlic in it. Add salt, pepper, red wine vinegar, basil and summer savory; mix. Place *chapon* in bottom of bowl and add lettuce. Toss gently but thoroughly and serve.

Vinaigrette simple 1
Simple Vinaigrette

1 medium-sized garlic clove, mashed against tines of a fork resting against bottom of the bowl
4 tablespoons olive or other oil
1 tablespoon wine vinegar
Salt and pepper

Add oil and wine vinegar to bowl with mashed garlic in it. Add salt and pepper. Add greens just before serving and toss lightly.

I sometimes blend ½ teaspoon commercial mayonnaise (not salad dressing) to the vinaigrette. The combination is delicious, and the slight departure will only add smoothness and a slightly tangy flavor.

Vinaigrette à l'estragon   1
Tarragon Vinaigrette

---

1 medium-sized garlic clove, mashed or put through garlic press
4 tablespoons olive or vegetable oil
1 tablespoon tarragon vinegar
1 teaspoon Dijon mustard
Salt and pepper
1 teaspoon tarragon leaves, minced fine (in season)

Add oil and vinegar to bowl with mashed garlic in it. Add salt, pepper, and mustard; mix. Add greens just before serving and toss lightly. Sprinkle with tarragon leaves. This vinaigrette is excellent on plain Bibb or romaine lettuce salad.

Salade de haricots verts   1
Green Bean Salad

A very popular and refreshing summer salad.

(Serves 4-5)

2 10-ounce packages frozen French-cut green beans or equivalent
*   in fresh green beans, French-cut, cooked and drained*
¼ pound fresh mushrooms, cleaned and sliced thin
Lemon juice
1 medium-sized sweet white onion, sliced thin
1 clove garlic, mashed or minced fine
1 tablespoon red wine vinegar
4 tablespoons olive oil
¼ teaspoon dry mustard
Salt and pepper

Mix mushrooms and a few drops of lemon juice; toss lightly; set aside. Cook beans according to package directions if you use frozen beans; drain.

Mix beans, mushrooms, onion, garlic, vinegar, oil, salt, and pepper. Toss and keep refrigerated for at least one hour before serving.

Coeurs de laitue   1
Hearts of Lettuce

A very decorative as well as refreshing salad.

(Serves 4)

4 large hearts of Bibb lettuce
4 tablespoons olive oil
1 tablespoon red wine vinegar
1 tablespoon Dijon or regular mustard
Juice of ½ lemon
2 anchovy fillets, mashed to a paste
¼ cup finely chopped parsley
1 egg yolk, lightly beaten
Pepper (no salt needed—anchovies will provide)
½ cup garlic croutons
2 hard-boiled egg yolks, chopped or sieved

Arrange one lettuce heart in each individual salad bowl; spread the petals lightly like an open flower.

Mix oil, vinegar, mustard, lemon juice, anchovy, parsley, beaten egg yolk, and pepper to taste. Blend well. Sprinkle dressing over lettuce hearts; garnish with croutons and sieved hard-boiled egg yolks.

Concombres à la crème   1
Cucumbers in Cream Dressing

An interesting departure from the regular dressing is the use of *crème fraîche* instead of oil. It marries perfectly with the sweetness of the cucumber and coats it to give it a velvety surface.

(Serves 3-4)

2 *medium-sized cucumbers, peeled and sliced very thin*
1 *medium-sized white onion, sliced very thin*
1 *teaspoon salt*
1 *cup* crème fraîche *or 1 cup sour cream diluted with 2 table-spoons heavy cream*
1 *clove garlic, minced fine*
2 *teaspoons white vinegar*
½ *teaspoon dill weed, crushed, or 1 tablespoon finely chopped fresh dill weed*
White pepper
Salt

Mix cucumbers and onion in a glass or porcelain bowl; add salt and let stand 10 minutes; drain the liquid, squeezing as much of the excess as you can without crushing the cucumbers.

Add *crème fraîche* or sour cream, garlic, vinegar, dill, and pepper. Mix lightly and taste for salt; add if needed. Chill thoroughly in refrigerator before serving.

Salade de févettes   1
Baby Lima Bean Salad

Févette is the diminutive for *fève,* or *fava,* which was discussed in the chapter on vegetables. Because it is almost impossible to find fresh young *fava* unless you grow your own, I have substituted lima beans, a member of the broad bean family to which the *fava* belongs.

(Serves 4)

1 package (10 ounces) frozen baby lima beans
2 hard-boiled eggs, chopped
1 clove garlic, minced fine
Vinaigrette provençale
2 anchovy fillets, freshened and chopped (optional; in Marseille
    anchovies are always used in this recipe)

Cook lima beans according to package directions, but cut cooking time to 5 minutes. They should be firm. Drain liquid and rinse beans immediately in cold water to stop cooking process. Drain well.

Mix lima beans, hard-boiled eggs, garlic, anchovies, and vinaigrette in salad bowl. Toss lightly and serve.

Salade de Noël   1
Christmas Salad

This salad is served at Christmastime with the traditional turkey. Truffles are used with it, but considering the price and rarity of truffles, I have substituted mushrooms, which give the salad a delicate flavor.

(Serves 4)

2 cups celery hearts and tender stalks, sliced
1 cup mushrooms, cleaned and sliced
3 tablespoons lemon juice
1 head Bibb lettuce, fairly large
4 anchovy fillets, freshened and patted dry
½ cup olive oil
Salt and pepper

Mix celery and mushrooms; add 1 tablespoon lemon juice; toss and set aside. Place lettuce leaves in salad bowl; add celery and mushrooms.

Mash anchovies in small bowl; add olive oil, a small amount at a time, mixing with pestle or wooden spoon. Add salt and pepper and drizzle over the salad. Toss gently and serve.

Fromage de tête en salade
1
Head Cheese Salad (a summer salad)

If you like head cheese, this salad is deliciously refreshing and a great addition to the picnic basket.

(Serves 3-4)

2 cups head cheese, cubed in 1-inch pieces·
⅔ cup sliced cornichons or tiny dill pickles
1 medium-sized sweet onion, sliced very thin
⅔ cup black pitted olives, sliced
Vinaigrette dressing (simple or Provençal)
2 hard-boiled eggs, sliced

Combine head cheese, cornichons or pickles, onion, and olives in salad bowl. Add vinaigrette and toss; add hard-boiled eggs and toss again lightly. Chill and serve on Bibb or head lettuce nest, with French bread.

Salade à l'huile de noix
1
Walnut Oil Salad

In Haute Provence, where walnut trees grow in abundance, each family makes its own walnut oil and uses it as the base for its salad dressing. No herbs are used, as the oil lends the flavor. If you are willing to try this deliciously different dressing, walnut oil may be found in health food or specialty food shops.

(Serves 4)

Bibb or Boston lettuce for 4 persons
3 tablespoons walnut oil
1 tablespoon cider or white wine vinegar or regular vinegar
Salt and pepper
Garlic (optional)

Blend oil, vinegar, salt and pepper in salad bowl. Wash and dry lettuce thoroughly. Enhance dressing by adding ½ cup walnut halves; toss.

Walnut oil can be kept in the warmest part of the refrigerator. This oil can also be used successfully to sauté vegetables such as zucchini, beans, carrots, and celery.

Sardines en salade   1
Sardine Salad

The term sardine is applied to small herring, pilchard, and sprats, depending on the country in which the product is caught and canned. In any event these small fish are rich in protein and nucleic acids, and because of their small size are low in pollutants.

Usually, canned sardines come in two sizes: small, about 12 to a can, and large, with 6 to the can. For the salad below I much prefer the larger, firmer size that do not crumble when tossed with the greens. Also, they should be packed in olive or soya oil for this recipe. This inexpensive, good summer salad is one of my favorites.

(Serves 4)

2 4-ounce cans sardines, drained of their oil
½ cup olive oil
1 cup garlic croutons
1 medium-sized sweet white onion, sliced thin
2 tomatoes cut in wedges
1 head Boston, romaine, or iceberg lettuce
1 egg yolk, slightly beaten
2 tablespoons lemon juice
2 tablespoons grated Parmesan cheese
Salt and pepper

Add half of olive oil to croutons and mix gently until saturated. Combine onion slices, tomatoes, lettuce, egg yolk, lemon juice, salt, and pepper. Toss gently but thoroughly. Add sardines, croutons, and cheese. Toss gently again and serve.

Poivrons en salade

1

Green Pepper Salad

When red peppers are in season, substitute 2 red peppers for the green peppers and you'll get a slightly different flavor and a colorful salad.

(Serves 3-4)

4 medium-sized bell peppers or 4 large Italian sweet peppers
½ cup olive oil
4 hard-boiled eggs, quartered lengthwise (optional)
¼ cup parsley, minced fine
Vinaigrette provençale

Cut green peppers in half lengthwise. Remove seeds. Soak peppers in olive oil for 1 hour. Drain and place on a cookie sheet. Put under broiler 1 inch away from heat source until they sizzle and blister, and start to change color. Remove from broiler and cool 2-3 minutes; place in a plastic bag and let them stay for 15 minutes so that they will peel more easily. Peel and slice in thin strips.

Mix green pepper strips, hard-boiled eggs, parsley, and vinaigrette in a bowl.

Morue en salade

2

Codfish Salad

Surprisingly refreshing and delicious in summer.

(Serves 4-6)

4 hard-boiled eggs, peeled and sliced
1 pound red thin-skinned or white potatoes (long or round), boiled
1 pound freshened salt cod or frozen cod, thawed
Vinaigrette provençale
Lettuce leaves
4-6 lemon slices
Capers (optional)

Boil potatoes (for directions see page 116). Cool thoroughly, peel and slice; set aside.

Place cod cut into 4-5 pieces in saucepan; cover with cold water by 1 inch. Bring slowly to a boil, removing scum as it floats to surface. When water reaches a boil, remove immediately; drain in colander and cool cod thoroughly.

In large bowl mix potatoes, cod, hard-boiled eggs, and vinaigrette; toss well. Line a serving bowl with lettuce leaves; arrange cod mixture in center; decorate with lemon slices and capers (optional). Refrigerate until serving time.

La salade niçoise   1
Salad of Nice

Often sliced cold boiled potatoes are added to this salad to make it more substantial.

(Serves 6)

1 head Bibb lettuce, washed and dried
2 large tomatoes, skinned, seeded, and cut in wedges
1 large cucumber, peeled, seeded, and sliced thin
2 large green peppers, seeded and sliced thin
1 heart of celery, sliced
1 medium-sized sweet white onion, sliced thin
1 cup baby lima beans, fresh (preferably), or frozen baby lima
    beans, cooked for 5 minutes only and freshened im-
    mediately under cold water
1 8-ounce can chunk tuna, drained
6 anchovy fillets, freshened and sliced in half lengthwise
16 black olives, pitted
3 hard-boiled eggs, cut in large wedges
2 basil leaves, chopped, or 1 teaspoon dried basil leaves, crumbled
¼ cup chopped parsley
5 tablespoons olive oil
1 tablespoon red wine vinegar
Salt and pepper

Arrange lettuce leaves around and in bottom of large, shallow serving dish. Decorate lettuce with tomatoes; then add cucumber, green peppers, celery, and onion, leaving the center to be filled with lima beans. Place large chunks of tuna on top of lima beans; finish with anchovies, eggs, and olives. Sprinkle basil and parsley over the whole. Mix oil, vinegar, salt, and pepper; drizzle over the salad. Toss gently and serve immediately.

La salade de pommes de terre chaude au cervelat 2
Hot Potato Salad with Garlic Sausage

This is a winter salad.

(Serves 4)

4 *medium-sized potatoes, scrubbed, peeled, quartered, and thickly sliced*
Boiling water
Salt
8 *thick slices* cervelas *(about ¼ thick)* *
2 *tablespoons finely chopped parsley*
Vinaigrette provençale

Cover potatoes with boiling water in saucepan; add very little salt; bring back to boil. Cook uncovered over medium-high heat until tender but not soft. Watch and test with fork, this cooking takes very little time. Drain, reserve bouillon; keep potatoes warm.

Return bouillon to pan; add *cervelas* slices. Warm for 5 minutes over medium-low heat. Remove *cervelas* with slotted spoon, add to potatoes. (The bouillon may be used as the base for a *potage* or soup.)

Place potatoes in salad bowl. Arrange *cervelas* over it. Sprinkle with parsley and pour vinaigrette over it. Toss gently and serve immediately.

---

*One finds *cervelas* (or *cervelat*), a French garlic sausage, in specialty stores or the delicatessen section of some supermarkets.

Salade d'asperges mimosa   **2**
Mimosa Asparagus Salad

Asparagus is a member of the lily family and has been on earth for thousands of years. It still can be found in its wild state in all the countries of Europe and Asia. The Romans cultivated it and used it for food and medicinal purposes. In France, Louis XIV was so fond of this vegetable that his royal gardener kept a special bed of asparagus growing for the sole user, the king.

Here in the United States wild asparagus grows in abundance along streams and in meadows. Every spring it is a ritual for me to go in search of the slender stalk. It becomes a celebration and a game to track it hidden among the grasses, and when I have enough I make a delicious salad.

Asparagus is low in calories and full of vitamins and minerals such as calcium and potassium. It is a natural diuretic and a mild laxative.

(Serves 4-6)

2 pounds asparagus—the thin, green kind, wild or domestic
Simple vinaigrette
3 hard-boiled eggs
3 quarts boiling water
1 teaspoon salt

Trim tough stems, wash gently. Tie them in small bundles, about 10-12 to a bundle.

Bring 6 quarts salted water to rapid boil in large, deep enameled or stainless steel pan or kettle. Drop asparagus gently into boiling water. Bring back to boil, cook, uncovered, 10-15 minutes or until stems are almost tender when pierced with a fork. Lift bundles from water, rinse under gently running cold water until cold. (This stops the cooking process and retains the color.) Refrigerate.

When ready to serve, arrange on a pretty serving platter into a wheel pattern, the asparagus being the spokes (the stems toward the center, the tips touching the "rim of the wheel").

Separate the yolks from the whites of the hard-boiled eggs. Sieve or chop the yolks; chop the whites coarsely. Place yolk in center of asparagus wheel, over the stems; sprinkle the white around the yolk. Just before serving sprinkle vinaigrette over asparagus and eggs.

Salade campagnarde de légumes   2
Country Vegetable Salad

(Serves 3-4)

1 ½ cups cooked green beans, fresh or frozen
1 cup boiled potatoes, sliced
2 medium-sized tomatoes, seeded and sliced
⅔ cup green peppers, sliced and seeded
½ cup pitted black olives
1 tablespoon capers
4 anchovy fillets, freshened and cut into thin strips
1 tablespoon chopped parsley
1 large basil leaf, chopped, or ⅛ teaspoon dried basil leaves
4 tablespoons olive oil or vegetable oil
1 tablespoon wine or tarragon vinegar
Salt and pepper

Mix all ingredients in salad bowl and toss. Refrigerate for 1-2 hours before serving.

Salade de pissenlit   1
Dandelion Salad

Yes, the lowly dandelion is regarded in France as not only good but healthful, since it is a rich source of vitamins A and C and iron. It is eaten in salad and sometimes added to spinach or chard in omelets. Of course it is gathered in the spring, when it is at its most tender stage, and in meadows away from pollution.

I recommend mixing dandelion greens with other types of greens — lettuce, etc. — to start with, as dandelion is an acquired taste.

If you live in the country or away from any source of pollutants or insecticides, herbicides, etc., pick enough young plants (before they have bloomed) to mix with your salad greens. Remove roots and any soiled leaves, wash well and dry thoroughly. Use regular or Provençal vinaigrette on it. Delicious with buttered French bread.

Salade provençale   1
Salad of Provence

Summer in Provence would not be the same without this delicious salad.

(Serves 4)

2 tomatoes, ripe but firm, sliced thin and seeded
1 medium-sized cucumber, peeled and sliced thin
1 medium-sized green pepper, sliced thin
1 medium-sized sweet white onion, skinned and sliced thin
1 tablespoon finely minced parsley
1 tablespoon capers
½ cup pitted black olives, whole or sliced
1 serving Vinaigrette provençale

Mix first seven ingredients in salad bowl; spoon dressing over and toss lightly. Refrigerate at least 1 hour before serving.

Salade de pois chiches   1
Chickpea Salad

(Serves 4)

1 large can garbanzo beans, drained and refreshed under cold
      water; or home-cooked chickpeas*
1 large clove garlic, chopped fine
1 medium-sized sweet white onion, chopped coarsely, or coarsely
      chopped shallot

*See Soupe de pois chiches et d'épinards if you want to start with dry chickpeas.

1 tablespoon chopped parsley
1 small fresh sweet red pepper cut in narrow strips, or a 2-ounce
    can red pimientos, drained and cut into narrow strips
1 large tomato, skinned, seeded, and cubed small
4 tablespoons olive oil
2 tablespoons red wine vinegar
Salt and pepper

Mix all ingredients in salad bowl. Chill at least 6 hours. Serve on lettuce leaves or as is.

Salade aux aubergines   **3**
Eggplant and Lettuce Salad

A delectable, interesting salad that can become habit-forming.

(Serves 4)

3 medium-sized eggplants, peeled, sliced thin lengthwise
Salt
Olive oil, or a mixture of ½ olive oil, ½ bland vegetable oil*
1 head Bibb or Boston lettuce
2 garlic cloves, peeled and minced fine
¼ cup finely chopped parsley
Salt

Salt eggplant on both sides and let drain for 30 minutes. Freshen under cold water to remove salt and pat dry. Fry the slices in hot olive oil in heavy frying pan (do not crowd the pan). You will need to watch carefully, as they burn easily; they should be a deep golden brown. Remove and drain on paper towels. Add more oil if necessary. Reserve what is left of the oil.

Arrange lettuce leaves all around and in bottom of flat serving platter; place eggplant slices artistically on top of lettuce in pinwheel fashion. Salt very lightly. Mix garlic and parsley, sprinkle over eggplants; drizzle warm oil over them.

---

*Because the eggplant has the ability to absorb oil like a sponge, and olive oil is expensive, one can cut the olive oil by half.

Salad de lentilles
Lentil Salad

Sometimes when I cook lentils for soups or for a vegetable dish I cook enough to put some aside and keep refrigerated to make this salad later in the week.

(Serves 4-6)

1½ cups lentils, washed and picked
3½ cups cold water
1 medium-sized onion
1 bay leaf
1 sprig parsley
1 sprig fresh thyme or ⅛ teaspoon dried thyme leaves
2 cloves garlic, peeled
Salt and pepper
1 tablespoon chopped parsley
2 shallots, chopped fine
Vinaigrette provençale

Put water in large saucepan; add lentils and onion. Tie bay leaf, parsley, thyme, and garlic in muslin or cheesecloth; add to mixture with salt and pepper. Bring slowly to a boil. Reduce heat and simmer covered for 30-35 minutes or until lentils are tender but firm, not soft. (Test at the end of 30 minutes.) Remove onion, garlic and herb bag; drain over bowl (bouillon can be used as a base for a soup); cool lentils.

Mix lentils, shallots, chopped parsley, and vinaigrette in salad bowl. Toss and serve immediately, or serve chilled.

Salade de pommes de terre à la crème
Potato Salad in Cream Dressing

An unusual and delicious salad my grandmother made in the summer when apples were at their best.

(Serves 5-6)

2 *tart red apples (red Delicious, Rome Beauty, or McIntosh),*
    peeled, halved, and sliced thin
1 *teaspoon lemon juice*
2 *pounds round red or long white potatoes in their jackets*
¼ *cup minced sweet red onion or sweet white onion*
¾ *cup* crème fraîche *or sour cream mixed with some thick cream*
1 *tablespoon cider or white vinegar*
Salt·and white pepper

Mix apples with lemon juice in glass bowl and set aside.

Scrub potatoes in cold water with a brush; remove any green spots
(they are toxic) and any spoiled spots. Do not peel potatoes. Drop
into boiling water to cover by about ¾ inch; cook covered and
boiling gently until tender when pierced with the point of a sharp
knife. Drain and let cool completely. (You may chill them until
ready to prepare them.) Peel and slice.

Combine sliced potatoes, sliced apples, and onion in a large glass or
earthenware bowl. Add *crème fraîche* or sour cream, vinegar, salt,
and pepper. Mix lightly and chill at least 1 hour before serving.

Salade de choux-fleurs   **2**
Cauliflower Salad

(Serves 3-4)

2 *cups tightly packed cauliflower flowerets (the white buds of the*
    cauliflower head)
Salted water
Tarragon dressing
Bibb lettuce leaves, washed and dried
1 *small fresh red sweet pepper, cut into narrow, thin strips, or 1*
    2-ounce can pimientos, drained
2 *tablespoons finely minced parsley*

Place cauliflower flowerets in saucepan and cover with salted
water. Bring to a boil and cook in rapidly boiling water for 5
minutes or until tender but still crunchy. Drain, freshen under
cold water; pat dry with clean towel or paper towel. Place

flowerets in a bowl and mix in dressing. Set aside. Arrange lettuce leaves in and around the bottom of a salad bowl. Place cauliflower and dressing mixture on top of lettuce, garnish with pimiento or red sweet pepper strips, sprinkle with parsley, and serve.

Salade de riz   3
Rice Salad

A traditional salad of the South.

(Serves 4)

2 cups cold cooked rice
1 medium-sized green pepper, seeded and cut into narrow strips
3 tablespoons olive or vegetable oil
¼ cup canned pimientos, drained and cut into narrow strips
1 large tomato, skinned, seeded, and cubed
⅓ cup pitted black olives, cut up
1 tablespoon capers, drained
2 hard-boiled eggs, sliced (optional)

Dressing:
8 tablespoons olive oil
2 tablespoons vinegar
1 small garlic clove, mashed
½ teaspoon Dijon mustard or other mustard
Salt and pepper

Sauté green pepper in olive oil or vegetable oil in heavy skillet over medium-low heat until tender but firm, about 8 minutes. Remove with spatula to paper towel to drain. Cool thoroughly.

Put cold rice in serving bowl; add green pepper, pimientos, tomatoes, olives, and capers. Add dressing and toss well. Keep refrigerated until serving time. Serve on lettuce bed garnished with hard-boiled egg slices.

Cheeses

Say "cheese" to people who have visited France, and visions of large platters filled with arrays of fragrant, creamy, hard or soft cheese will come to their minds.

France is the home *par excellence* of good cheeses. Its citizens from time immemorial, from the highest to the most humble, have praised cheeses and delighted in their aroma, flavor, and taste.

When touring the French countryside it is delightful to discover a new cheese made in a small *hameau* (hamlet), lost in the middle of nowhere. It is believed that more than five hundred cheeses are made in France, in all sizes and shapes. Their versatility makes them suitable to use with a variety of foods. They are the perfect answer for a relaxed party among good friends: all you need for its success is a variety of cheese, some crusty bread, and good wine.

From the earliest times cheese has played a major role in the history of civilization. We know for a fact that over two thousand years ago France, then called Gaul, was producing and exporting cheeses which figured prominently on the tables of Roman and Greek patricians. In countries throughout the world where the raising of herds of cows, goats, lambs, llamas, reindeer, and other animals is practiced, the surplus milk has been used for centuries in the making of cheeses.

Even with modernization the manufacture of cheese still follows the same basic procedure as that used by our ancestors, except that in some steps mechanization replaces the human hand. The principle remains the same: the curdling of milk by the addition of lactic acid and/or a natural enzyme called rennet (*la pressure*); in France it is the extract of the lining of the calf's stomach.

The origin of the milk—ewe, goat, cow, etc.; the different cooking processes; the various natural transformations or the addition of molds of penicillin (*moisissures selectionnées*); the aging process, sometimes resulting in a natural enzyme transformation; or the formation of natural molds (*moisissures non-selectionées*) are all factors which give the distinctive flavor and quality to the various cheeses.

To name all the French cheeses made at the present time would be an impossible task; furthermore, many cheeses do not travel well. Therefore I will limit my list to the cheeses you will most likely find in your local cheese shop or supermarket. Following is a description of the several types of cheeses.

The Creamed Cheeses—*fromages frais*

Rich, soft, uncured cream cheeses or double or triple *crèmes* such as *Neufchâtel, Petit Suisse, Boursin, Boursault,* or *Bellétoile,* plain or herb-seasoned.

The Soft Ripened Cheeses With a Rind Called *Fleurie*

Very delicate in flavor when they are fresh, more robust when ripened; for example, *le Brie* and *Coulommiers.*

Camembert, highly praised and loved by Napoleon, who gave it its name from the location where it originated in Normandy. When fresh it is creamy, but not too soft, mild in flavor; when ripened, it is more pungent and has a yellowish tint.

The Semi-soft Cheeses

These cheeses have a smooth texture and mild flavor, on the tangy side, deepening with age. Excellent for their melting quality, they are used not only for eating with bread or crackers but for sauces, to top casserole dishes, and for grilled sandwiches. The following belong in this category:

Bonbel, round with a yellow wax protective covering; light, buttery shade; tangy.

Roquefort is the best known. It is made from ewe's milk in the Rouergue region of the southern part of France. It is slightly crumbly, spicy, and unique in flavor. It should be called the "grandfather of cheeses." The Romans and Greeks knew and used it and went to great expense and trouble to have it brought from the central part of France, where it was made and cured in limestone caves. One legend has it that an amorous shepherd, meeting his beloved in one of these caves, forgot in his ardor to eat his lunch of bread and cheese and left it there. Much later upon returning, he

found what has become the precursor of our present Roquefort —
the cheese had combined with the bread in a molding process.

Bleu d'Auvergne. Made in the Auvergne region of central France
from cow's milk, it is rather sharp.

The Goat or Ewe's Cheeses

Firm or soft, as the *Banon de Provence*. Named after a small town,
this cheese is wrapped in grape or chestnut leaves, or sometimes is
covered with winter savory. Or the *St. Marcellin*, larger than
Banon. Both have a mild fragrance and flavor and a firm texture.
Before these cheeses are left to dry in cool cellars, they are soft and
moist; at this stage they are sold on the spot under the name of
tomme fraîche, fresh cheese.

The region of les Deux Sèvres in the Poitou Province produces the
Pyramide, a soft goat cheese with a whitish crust and a creamy,
smooth, buttery interior.

Niolo, a cheese made in Corsica from ewe's and goat's milk.

The Process Cheeses

These are cheeses made from a Gruyère base with a blend of
various cheeses melted together with butter, milk, or cream added.
They are soft and creamy and are sometimes flavored with a
liqueur such as cherry. Best known are:

La Vache Qui Rit (laughing cow), which comes in wedges, large or
small, wrapped in foil; soft and easy to spread, it is great for
canapés, snacks, picnics, and lunch boxes.

Gourmandise has a cherry-liqueur flavoring.

Tomme au Marc. A large round cheese, delicate in flavor, creamy
in texture, with a crust covered with roasted grape seeds; a dessert
or snack cheese.

Pont l'Evêque, a square cheese with light yellow-orange rind;
wonderful aromatic flavor which brings to mind the country of its
origin, Normandy.

Port Salut was created originally by the Trappist monks in the

Champagne region. It has a bright red rind; a pressed, uncooked cheese with a mild flavor.

Reblochon, a round cheese from the mountains of the Savoie region, takes its name from the word describing the second milking of the day the cheese is made. Fragrant, with a delicate, smooth texture and a slightly nutty taste which makes it a superb accompaniment for fruits, or delightful as an appetizer.

The Semi-hard Cheeses

Yellow in color, firm but supple when sliced or grated, with rinds hard and greyish-brown. They have large or small gas holes and a nutlike flavor. Great for melting, sauces, fondues, soufflés, casseroles, salads, desserts—grated or diced. From the Franche-Comté and Jura regions, the best known are:

Gruyère de Comté, with small gas holes called the "eyes"; comes in a large round wheel.

Emmental, more tangy in flavor, with large gas holes; also comes in large wheels.

The Hard Cheeses

These are very firm, not resilient. They slice and grate well; can be used in sauces, fondues, casseroles, and as desserts. *Cantal* is one of these. Very old (in fact probably one of the oldest of French cheeses), it is sharp in flavor.

The Blue Cheeses

These types are marbled with blue-green veins produced by the addition of penicillin; they are made from cow's or ewe's milk. They keep well and are served in appetizer dips, spreads, salads, or vegetables, or as dessert cheese.

THE CHEESES OF THE SOUTH

Roquefort (as described under Semi-Soft Cheeses).

Banon de Provence: Soft when fresh, firm when aged. Named after the town of Banon in the Alps of Haute Provence, it is made of goat's or ewe's milk and flavored with savory or black pepper, wrapped in chestnut leaves, and tied with raffia.

Pèbre d'Ail: Obtained from the milk of ewes pasturing in the high mountains of the lure in Haute Provence on fragrant grasses. It is sometimes covered with wild savory.

Tomme d'Annot: In the Var region (Haute Provence), this cheese takes its name from the delightful little town of Annot. It is a kind of Gruyère made of goat's or ewe's milk.

Brousse: A fresh goat or ewe cheese made all over the South.

Brousse du Rôve: Renowned in Marseille and its environs; made in the Rôve, a suburb of Marseille.

Tomme d'Arles: A soft cheese made with sheep's milk in the Camargue area.

Fromage des Pyrenées. A semi-hard cheese with a gray-brown rind, made of cow's milk in the eastern part of the Pyrenees region.

Because cheeses are changeable and are affected by temperature, wrap them separately in plastic wrap or foil and store them in the warmest part of the refrigerator. *Never* freeze them. To serve, bring them back to room temperature at least one hour beforehand.

La brousse du Rôve   3
A Cream Cheese

This soft cheese used to be sold in the streets of Marseille early in the morning. Pushing a small cart, the vendor would advertise his or her wares by singing the name of the cheese through the city. It was and still is made in an area near Marseille called le Rôve — hence the name. An excellent substitute can be made at home very simply.

If you do not have the small heart-shaped perforated molds for *coeur à la crème*, make your own by using small (6½-ounce) tuna cans or others. Remove the tops completely, wash the cans well with soap and water, rinse and dry. With a clean nail, perforate the bottom in several places (20-25 holes), to obtain a perforated mold. Line the cans with a double thickness of cheesecloth.

2 cups rich cow or goat milk (goat gives authentic taste)
½ cup buttermilk

Place the milk and buttermilk in a heavy saucepan; heat over low heat until it reaches 90° — no more. Remove immediately, or it will start to curdle. Pour into a clean jar which has been kept at about 90° temperature in warm water or oven. Cover and keep in warm place until curds form, about 1-1½ days.

Place curds in double layer of cheesecloth; holding the corners bring them together and tie securely to form a bag. Hang over a pan or place in a colander over a pan to let the whey run out. When the curds are dry, remove from bag and spoon curds into the molds. Let the cheese drain several hours or overnight. This delicious cheese can be eaten with sugar or fruits such as strawberries or raspberries.

Le boursin   1
Herb Cream Cheese

The real *boursin* is a double-crème cheese flavored with herbs and distributed all over France. Because of the difficulty of finding it in this country sometimes, and prompted by my longing for this fragrant cheese, I came up with a blend of ingredients that most favorably approaches the flavor of the real thing.

(Makes one 9-ounce cheese ball)

1 8-ounce package cream cheese, softened at room temperature
¼ cup sweet butter or sweet margarine, softened at room temperature
1 large clove garlic, mashed or minced very fine
1 scant teaspoon each dried basil, rosemary, summer savory leaves
½ teaspoon each dried thyme and oregano leaves

¼ *teaspoon dried marjoram leaf*
1 *teaspoon fresh chives, chopped very fine*
Light pinch of salt
½ *teaspoon cognac or good whiskey (optional)*

Blend cheese, butter, and garlic in a bowl until smooth. Place all
the herbs in a fairly fine-mesh strainer; stir the herbs with a spoon
until only the coarse parts are left. The fine powdered herbs will
have gone through. Blend the powdered herbs and chives with the
cheese and salt until smooth. Add cognac or whiskey, blend again.
Refrigerate a few hours to let the flavor of the herbs permeate the
mixture.

When ready to serve, form into a ball and place on a pretty dish
with crackers or slices of French bread around it, or use to stuff
small tomatoes.

Breads

It is a tradition of long standing — even a ritual — for French families to purchase their daily bread at the neighborhood bakery. It is a custom observed in every town and city throughout France.

Everyone is familiar with a picture of the little boy or girl carrying the long *baguette* home. Once I was one of those little girls, and many a time I was severely reprimanded for bringing home a *baguette* with a substantial piece missing. The fresh-baked bread smelled so good, it was like having some of the summer wheat in your arms. It was very difficult to resist tasting the delicious crunchy golden crust!

In the past, however, in remote villages bread was prepared and baked at home. Also, during the war, farmers who were lucky enough to have some wheat would bake their own bread. One of my wartime experiences involves such home preparation. Cut off from my family by the destruction of the railroads and finding myself stranded in the country, I stayed with a family on their farm and was taught by the farm wife how to bake bread. It was a revelation for a young city girl and an experience never to be forgotten.

I am still making bread at home every week, and it is delicious. Following is the recipe for one type of home bread.

Pain de provence
Provençal Bread

3

(Makes 2 loaves)

Starter sourdough:
1 package dry yeast
½ cup warm water, 95-100°

1 teaspoon salt
1½ tablespoons sugar
2 cups lukewarm water
2¼ cups unbleached white flour

Dissolve yeast in the ½ cup warm water; add salt and sugar. Stir in the 2 cups warm water, then the flour; beat until free of lumps. Let stand uncovered at room temperature (about 72°) 4-5 days. By that time the starter should have a yeasty smell. Transfer to glass or crockery jar; cover and refrigerate; place in lower part of refrigerator until ready to use. Let it mature for 2 days before use. Now you are ready to make the leaven.

Leaven:
1 cup sourdough starter
½ teaspoon salt
1 teaspoon sugar
2 cups warm water, 95-100°
2½ cups unbleached white flour

Take 1 cup from your sourdough starter jar; return the rest to the lower part of the refrigerator. Let the cup of starter warm at room temperature before you mix the batter.

Place starter in bowl that has been rinsed in warm water and wiped dry. Add salt, sugar, and warm water; stir until thoroughly mixed. Add flour and blend until free of lumps. Cover bowl with plastic wrap; wrap bowl again with piece of woolen cloth; place in warm, dry place, away from draft (a cupboard, for example); let it rest for 12 hours or more, undisturbed. Batter is then ready to use.

Before using primary batter to make bread, be sure to return 1 cup of this leaven to the sourdough starter in your refrigerator; it will keep your starter going. If you are unable to use the starter at least twice a month, add a little sugar (about ½ teaspoon). At this point you are ready to make the bread.

Bread:
1 package active dry yeast
1½ cups warm water, 95-100°
5-5½ cups unbleached white flour
3 cups primary batter at room temperature
2 tablespoons olive oil
1 tablespoon salt
1 tablespoon sugar

Using wooden spoon, dissolve yeast in warm water; set aside. Place primary batter in large, warm bowl (about 4 quarts capacity). Blend in 1 cup of the flour, stir until free of lumps; add the yeast-and-warm-water mixture, olive oil, salt, and sugar, then 4 more cups of flour; stir until dough is too stiff to stir any longer.

Turn dough onto well-floured board and knead until smooth and elastic, additional flour being added as needed. Dough should not stick to your hands.

Turn into greased 4-quart bowl; cover with plastic wrap; place in warm, dry place, away from drafts, until the dough has doubled, about 2 hours. With a floured fist, punch dough down; cover again and let rise until doubled again, about 35-40 minutes.

Preheat oven to 375° 10-15 minutes before baking time.

Thoroughly grease 2 loaf pans. Turn dough onto floured board and divide in 2 equal parts. Shape dough into 2 loaves and place in greased pans. Brush top with small amount of melted butter or margarine. Place in warm spot away from draft and let rise until double in bulk, about 1½ hours.

Bake in preheated oven, center-rack, for 40 minutes; turn oven off and leave bread in another 5 minutes. Remove pans immediately.

Les cressins   3
Breadsticks

These crisp breadsticks are sometimes eaten in place of bread. They are often served with meals in small cafés along the coast. A tradition in Provence, I suspect their origin is Italian.

(Makes about 30)

1 package dry yeast
2 cups warm water, 95-110°
2 teaspoons salt
5 cups sifted all-purpose flour (approximately)
1 tablespoon olive oil

1 egg yolk, slightly beaten
1 tablespoon water

Preheat oven to 425°.

Soften yeast in ¼ cup warm water (see temperature above); let
stand 5 minutes. Place 1¾ cups warm water in large bowl; add
salt; stir in about 3 cups flour and blend. Stir the yeast into flour
mixture and blend well.

Add 1¼ cups flour to yeast-flour mixture; beat until fairly smooth;
add olive oil; work again to incorporate the oil; turn out dough
onto floured working surface (use the ½ cup flour remaining).
Knead until shiny and smooth, bringing in small amount of flour
from working surface as you knead. Shape into a ball and place in a
deep bowl, lightly buttered; turn once to grease entire surface of
dough. Cover bowl with towel and let dough rise in warm place
(80°) until double in size, 1-1½ hours.

Punch down with fist and knead lightly again on floured surface for
1-2 minutes. Grease 4 baking sheets or cookie sheets. Divide
dough into 3 equal parts, and work each part into small balls.
Using the palms of your hands, roll balls into long cigar-shaped
sticks 8 inches long by ¼ inch thick. Place sticks 1½ inches apart
on greased baking sheets.

Mix egg yolk and ¼ cup warm water; brush sticks lightly with this
mixture; let sticks rise, covered, in warm place (80°). Bake in
preheated 425° oven for 5 minutes; reduce heat to 350° and bake
10-15 minutes longer until golden brown; turn oven off and leave
sticks in for 5 minutes longer until they are very crisp.

Desserts

As a young girl, when I was visiting my grandmother in her village in the Alps of Provence, a great joy for me was to go with her to the baker's. *Grandmaman* would take all sorts of mouth-watering desserts to have them baked for her in his oven. This was the custom among the village housewives. The baker was not a *patissier* (pastry-man), but he did have the best oven in town and always had some room after the bread was done to bake some tarts and cakes and pies.

In the cities all through France, however, the pastry shops were and still are full of wonderful baked goods made daily. Pastries, cakes, *petit-fours*, *croissants*, and *pains-au-chocolat* are purchased each day as gifts for visits to friends or relatives, for anniversaries or birthdays, or to be consumed on the spur of the moment when temptation overcomes you as you pass by one of those wonderful windows. Or you may want to take them home for the *quatre-heures* (four-o'clock break) with the traditional *café au lait*.

Following the daily meal, however, what will be served will more likely be fruits, particularly in the South, where they grow in abundance owing to the mild and sunny climate. But come Sunday or on occasions when friends or relatives are visiting, the cook will proudly end the meal with a sweet dessert in the form of a fruit tart, some *oeufs à la neige* (floating island), or a *flan, crème caramel*, or *clafouti*.

In the summer months it will very likely be a fruit sherbet (*sorbet aux fruits*) bought at the *glacier* (ice-cream store). On occasions such as Christmas, Easter, etc., special cakes, fritters, cookies, and candies are made at home too, served to the family or taken to friends' houses to wish them happy holidays. These endearing customs and traditions are still followed throughout the South; what better way to celebrate the renewal of life!

Clafoutis aux poires à ma façon   **1**
Pear Clafouti *"My Way"*

The *clafouti* is a classic dessert which claims its origin as the Limousin region on the Central Plateau of France. Originally made with cherries, it now contains seasonal fruits of the other regions to which it has migrated, including the South.

(Serves 8-10)

3 large pears (about 1½ pounds), partially ripe
2 tablespoons lemon juice
4 tablespoons unsalted butter, melted and cooled
1 cup milk
3 eggs
⅔ cup sugar
½ cup sifted all-purpose flour
2 teaspoons vanilla
1 teaspoon pear liqueur, cognac, or Triple Sec

Glaze:
⅓ cup peach preserves
½ teaspoon grated lemon rind
¼ teaspoon cinnamon
1 tablespoon Triple Sec or other fruit liqueur
Confectioner's sugar

Preheat oven to 375°.

Butter a 10-inch quiche pan, 1½ inches deep; set aside. Peel, core, and slice pears (drop them in lemon juice to prevent discoloration). Arrange slices neatly, wagon-wheel fashion, in quiche pan.

Place butter, milk, eggs, sugar, flour, vanilla, and liqueur in blender; blend until smooth. Pour batter gently over pears. Place in preheated oven and bake 30-35 minutes or until firm on the surface but still custard-like; remove from oven. The *clafouti* will puff up during baking and come down during cooling.

While *clafouti* is baking, place all glazing ingredients but Triple Sec in small pan and heat slowly until hot but not boiling. Remove from heat; blend in Triple Sec; spread over top of *clafouti*; sprinkle confectioner's sugar all around edge. May be served warm or cold.

Crème anglaise   1
English Cream (a dessert cream)

(Makes about 2 cups)

4 egg yolks, slightly beaten
½ cup sugar
Pinch of salt
2 cups milk
1 teaspoon vanilla extract

Combine egg yolks with sugar in a bowl and work with wooden spoon until light.

Scald milk in large saucepan, add to egg mixture slowly, and stir to blend. Place over medium heat and cook, stirring until it thickens. Do not let it boil. Remove from heat; add vanilla. Cool, stirring once; then refrigerate, covered.

When ready to serve, pour into individual dessert glasses or serve over fruit such as pears, peaches, or apricots poached in syrup, or canned fruits.

Fraises au vin   1
Strawberries in Wine

Excellent on warm days when you need a light, easy dessert.

(Serves 6)

2 pints strawberries, cleaned and hulled
2 teaspoons lemon juice
⅓ cup sugar
1 cup red Bordeaux or Beaujolais wine

Before hulling strawberries, wash them (they won't get soggy). Slice in two, or four if very large. Place in glass or ceramic bowl; sprinkle with lemon juice. Sprinkle sugar over them and shake lightly to coat each strawberry; pour wine over and macerate at least 3 hours in refrigerator.

With slotted spoon remove strawberries to dessert glasses, filling to about ½-inch from brim; pour wine syrup over and serve.

Macédoine d'oranges   1
Macédoine of Oranges

What could be quicker and easier than this refreshing dessert?

(Serves 4-5)

4 California oranges, peeled and white membranes removed
Powdered sugar to taste
⅓ cup kirsch or cognac

Slice oranges thin; place in bowl with sugar and cognac or kirsch; mix together. Let stand 1 hour in refrigerator before serving. Pile into dessert serving glasses.

Mousse de marrons   1
Chestnut Mousse

This elegant, delicious dessert is simplicity itself. It can also be served without raspberries, but the fruit adds a distinctive flavor and charm.

(Serves 6)

1-pound tin chestnut spread (crème de marron)
¼ cup (2 ounces) semi-sweet baking chocolate, broken into pieces
3 tablespoons milk or light cream
2½ ounces or ⅓ cup sweet butter or margarine at room temperature
1¼ cups fresh or frozen raspberries
Whipping cream, whipped
Grated semi-sweet baking chocolate

Melt chocolate with milk or cream in small saucepan over low heat. Place chestnut spread in a bowl; pour chocolate mixture over, blend well. Add butter or margarine and blend until smooth and creamy.

Spoon into individual dessert glasses; top with raspberries and whipped cream in that order. Sprinkle grated chocolate over whipped cream. May be served immediately or may be refrigerated in lower part of refrigerator.

Coupe aux framboises   1
Raspberries in Cream Sauce

I have always thought of the raspberry as fruit for the gods — and I am sure the gods would enjoy this dessert as much as I do.

(Serves 4)

⅓ cup superfine granulated sugar
Pinch of salt
2 tablespoons cornstarch
2 cups whole milk
1 large egg, well beaten
1 tablespoon sweet butter (if you use regular salted butter, omit
    the pinch of salt)
2 tablespoons cognac or other brandy
8 ounces fresh or frozen raspberries
Whipping cream
1-ounce square semi-sweet chocolate

If frozen raspberries are used, thaw out, strain juice (use juice later to flavor drinks or to make jelly).

Blend dry ingredients in large saucepan. Slowly add milk, then beaten egg; stir with wooden spoon until smooth. Place over medium heat and cook, stirring constantly until mixture thickens and starts to bubble. Remove from heat; blend in butter; stir until melted; add cognac or brandy; cool thoroughly; chill in refrigerator until ready to serve.

Divide fresh or frozen raspberries among 4 dessert glasses; place in bottom, reserving a few for garnish. Spoon chilled cream over raspberries. Whip cream and float spoonful over cream in each glass. Shave chocolate curls with vegetable peeler; sprinkle over whipped cream; add a few raspberries for color and eye appeal.

Pâte brisée   2
Pastry

Basic dough for pies or quiches.

(Makes one 9- or 10-inch pie crust)

1⅓ *cups all-purpose flour*
⅛ *teaspoon salt*
1 stick (8 tablespoons) unsalted butter or margarine
5 tablespoons ice water (approximately)

Preheat oven to 350°.

Sift flour and salt together in large bowl; with pastry blender or tines of a fork cut in butter or margarine until mixture resembles coarse meal.

Sprinkle the water over mixture; blend quickly until dough adheres. (Do not overwork it; the more you handle it, the tougher it will become.) Press firmly all particles of dough together; form a ball. Refrigerate ½ hour.

Roll out dough between 2 sheets of waxed paper to fit a 9-inch pie pan or a 1½-inch *flan* ring, sprinkled with flour. Insert over pan; shrink crust into pan, working the dough with your fingers (this will avoid shrinkage). Trim off edges and pinch to flute; remaining pie dough can be made into decorative designs to place on top of pie.

For prebaked shell:

Line dough with foil, shiny side up; fill with rice or beans to prevent base from swelling. Bake in 350° preheated oven for 8-10 minutes. Remove rice or beans; bake 2 minutes longer to color bottom.

Pâte brisée sucrée pour tartelettes ou barquettes* 2
Sweet Pastry for Individual Tartlets or Barquettes

(Makes 12)

2 cups all-purpose flour
¼ teaspoon salt
3 tablespoons sugar
¾ cup or 10 tablespoons unsalted butter or unsalted margarine,
    cold
2 egg yolks, slightly beaten
3-5 tablespoons ice water

Preheat oven to 375°.

Sift flour, salt, and sugar into large bowl. Cut butter into small
pieces and work in flour mixture with pastry blender or tines of a
fork until mixture resembles coarse meal. Add egg yolks and work
in the mixture until blended. Sprinkle ice water over, 1 tablespoon
at a time; knead lightly until dough holds together; press and form
a ball. Sprinkle lightly with flour; chill, wrapped in wax paper, at
least 1 hour.

When ready to make tartlets, divide dough into 12 pieces; roll out
each piece on floured surface to make circles 5 inches in diameter.
Fit each circle into lightly floured tartlet pans.** Prick bottom
with fork, place them on large cookie sheet or piece of heavy foil;
bake in preheated oven 10-12 minutes or until golden brown.
Remove from oven; cool 5 minutes; turn them carefully in the
palms of your hands and place them open-side up on a cake rack or
piece of foil to cool completely.

---

*See *Barquettes aux fruits.*
**Tartlet pans are small individual versions of tart pans. A muffin pan can substi-
tute: cut the dough into circles with a pastry wheel; fit the circles over the
bottoms of the individual cups of a muffin pan turned upside down; prick the
bottom of the dough in several places and bake as above. Both barquette and
tartlet pans may be obtained from special gourmet stores, some hardware stores,
or the gourmet section of department stores.

Granité aux framboises   2
Raspberry Ice

This *granité*, or sherbet, would be excellent as a refresher between the hors d'oeuvre and the main course of an elegant dinner.

(Serves 4)

1 package (10 ounces) frozen raspberries, thawed
1 cup sugar
1 ¾ cups water
Juice of 1 large orange
Juice of 1 lemon

Purée thawed raspberries and sieve through a fine-mesh sieve to remove seeds; set purée aside.

Blend sugar, water, and orange juice in enameled saucepan; bring slowly to a very light boil over medium heat; cook, stirring frequently with wooden spoon, for 5 minutes. Remove from heat and let mixture cool. Add lemon juice and raspberry purée; refrigerate until thoroughly chilled.

Pour into ice-cream maker and freeze according to manufacturer's instructions. Or pour into ice-tray and freeze in freezer unit of refrigerator until slushy; remove and beat mixture with electric beater or hand beater until smooth. Freeze again until slushy; beat again. Repeat the process one more time, then let it freeze to sherbet consistency.

Barquettes aux fruits (airelles ou framboises)   2
Blueberry or Raspberry Barquettes

These individual tartlets (called *barquettes* because they are in the shape of small boats) are pretty to serve at a buffet-style supper. The *barquette* shells are to be found, all prepared and packed in boxes, in specialty stores.

(Makes 12 *barquettes*)

12 pâte brisée sucrée barquettes or *tartlets, baked*
8 ounces cream cheese
4 tablespoons heavy cream or coffee cream
3 tablespoons sugar
2 tablespoons Triple Sec or almond liqueur
¾ to 1 pound fresh blueberries or raspberries
½ cup raspberry or strawberry jelly
Whipping cream, whipped

Beat cheese, cream, sugar, and liqueur until smooth in medium-size bowl. Divide among tartlets or barquettes and spread in bottom. Arrange fruits on top of cheese mixture in each *barquette*.

Heat jelly slowly in small saucepan until it melts. Pour over fruits; decorate with whipping cream.

Mayonnaise au chocolat   2
Chocolate Mousse

Incorrectly called mayonnaise, the name has probably been given to this mousse because of its creamy consistency.

(Serves 6-8)

½ cup unsalted butter at room temperature
⅓ cup sugar
6 ounces semi-sweet chocolate cut in pieces
4 egg yolks
4 egg whites
1 teaspoon dark rum

Beat the sugar and softened butter until light and fluffy in a bowl. Place in blender container; set aside.

Melt chocolate in top of double-boiler; cool slightly; add to butter-sugar mixture and beat at high speed until blended. Add egg yolks, one at a time, until well blended; add rum, blend again.

Beat egg whites in large bowl until stiff and firm peaks form when beater is lifted. Blend carefully into chocolate mixture with rubber spatula, using an up-and-down motion. Blend until no white streaks are left.

Spoon into *pots de crème* (demitasse-size French dessert cups) or individual dessert glasses; refrigerate at least one hour. It freezes well.

Tarte aux bananes   **2**
Banana Pie

(Serves 6-8)

1 9-inch pâte brisée *crust, unbaked*
6 bananas, ripe but firm
4 tablespoons sugar
3 tablespoons rum
1 tablespoon Curaçao or brandy
⅓ cup apricot preserves

Preheat oven to 350°.

Peel 3 bananas, slice in ⅛-inch slices; place in glass or ceramic bowl with 1 tablespoon sugar and 2 tablespoons rum. Stir gently to coat; set aside.

Peel 3 leftover bananas and purée in blender or sieve through food mill; add 2 tablespoons sugar and 1 tablespoon rum; blend.

Prick bottom of unbaked pie crust with fork; sprinkle bottom with leftover 1 tablespoon sugar. Spread mixture of mashed bananas over sugar.

Arrange sliced bananas over in a pleasing overlapping pattern. Place in preheated oven and bake for 15 minutes; raise temperature to 400° and continue baking for 5 more minutes or until crust is golden brown. Remove from oven and set aside to cool slightly while you prepare the glaze.

Warm preserves in saucepan over medium-high heat until melted; remove from heat; add Curaçao or brandy; blend and spread over top of pie to glaze; cool. Serve with or without whipped cream.

Crème patissière

Cream Filling (for tarts or cream puffs)

2

(Makes about 2 cups)

½ cup all-purpose flour
½ cup sugar
2 whole eggs
1 egg yolk
2 cups hot milk
1 teaspoon vanilla
½ teaspoon almond extract
¼ cup unsalted butter or margarine, cut in small pieces

Sift flour and sugar together in saucepan. Blend in 2 whole eggs, one at a time, and the one egg yolk; slowly add hot milk until mixture is smooth.

Place over low heat and cook, stirring constantly with wooden spoon until the mixture starts to boil and has thickened. Remove from heat immediately; add vanilla and almond extract. Add butter or margarine a little at a time, blending well after each addition. Stir until cool to prevent a film forming on the surface.

Mousse d'abricot

Apricot Mousse

1

Serve this dessert in individual dessert glasses with *langues de chat* (page 330) or *gaufrettes* (found in gourmet shops).

(Serves 6)

4 cups (about 1 pound) apricots, ripe, peeled, and pitted, or equivalent in canned apricots, well-drained
1 cup whipping cream
⅓ cup fine granulated sugar
1 tablespoon apricot brandy or Triple Sec

Purée apricots in blender. Whip cream, blend in sugar and add to apricot purée with 1 tablespoon brandy or Triple Sec; blend lightly but thoroughly. Refrigerate until ice-cold.

Tarte aux fraises   2
Strawberry Tart

(Serves 8)

1 9-inch pâte brisée sucrée *shell, baked*
2 1-pint boxes *fresh strawberries, washed, hulled, drained, and dried*
½ pint *whipping cream*
⅓-½ cup *superfine sugar*
1 teaspoon *grated lemon peel*

Glaze:
½ cup *currant jelly or strawberry jelly*
1 tablespoon *white rum or cognac*

Preheat oven to 400°.

Prepare *pâte brisée;* roll out pastry on floured surface. Lift pastry into pie dish or tart pan; press firmly into pan; prick bottom; turn edges under and flute with fingers. Chill ½ hour. Bake in pre-heated oven for 10 minutes; turn oven down to 350° for a few more minutes (3-5) or until lightly browned. Remove from oven and cool thoroughly.

Prepare glaze: melt jelly over low heat until clear in small sauce-pan; add rum or cognac; blend and set aside to cool thoroughly.

When ready to put tart together, whip cream until stiff peaks form; add sugar and lemon peel; beat a little longer to blend. Spread in bottom of the cooled shell; arrange strawberries on top. Glaze strawberries with jelly mixture and cool until serving time.

Pêches grenadine   2
Peaches with Grenadine

A very pretty dessert. Grenadine is to be found in liquor stores. It is a ruby syrup, originally made from the *grenade* or pomegranate.

(Serves 4)

4 large yellow peaches, ripe but firm, halved and pitted
Boiling water to cover
1 tablespoon sugar
Juice of ½ lemon
1 cup grenadine
½ cup rosé or dry white wine
1 strip lemon rind (thin yellow part) about 1½ inches long
¼ cup slivered almonds
2 tablespoons red currant jelly
1 tablespoon brandy or kirsch
Whipped cream (optional)

Dissolve sugar and lemon juice in boiling water; pour over peaches and let them stay in liquid for 5 minutes. Drain and peel peaches; divide them in halves, discard pits. Set peaches aside.

Mix grenadine and wine in enameled saucepan large enough to hold peaches; bring to light boil; turn down to simmer; place peach halves in hot syrup and continue simmering 8-10 minutes, turning peaches several times with wooden spoon to let them absorb the syrup.

Remove peach halves to individual serving glasses, 2 halves to a glass; sprinkle with almonds.

Blend jelly and 1 tablespoon of the hot syrup in small saucepan; melt over very low heat; as soon as it is liquid, remove from heat; add brandy or kirsch. Ladle some of the syrup over peaches. Cool before refrigerating. Serve with whipped cream if you wish.

Tarte aux fruits   2
Fruit Tart

(9-inch tart; serves 6)

1 9-inch pâte brisée sucrée shell, baked and cooled
1½ cups crème patissière filling
2½-3 cups fresh strawberries, raspberries, currants, cherries,
*   peaches, or apricots*
½ cup currant, strawberry, or raspberry jelly

Clean fruits. If you use cherries, peaches, or apricots, pit and halve them. Fill bottom of baked and cooled shell with cooled *crème patissière*. Arrange fruits over cream filling in a pleasing fashion. Melt jelly over low heat; cool slightly and glaze by brushing melted jelly over the fruit.

Refrigerate until serving time. Because fruits are not cooked, do not prepare too long in advance, so that the fruit will keep its fresh and appealing appearance.

Pommes au four Calville   2
Baked Apple Calville

Calville is the name given to a variety of French apple. Because of its delicious flavor and firm texture, it makes the perfect baking apple. Apples are a wonderful fruit, rich in vitamins and easily digested, especially when baked, making them a perfect food for delicate stomachs. Raw they contain fiber and pectin. For baking purposes here in the United States we can use Rome Beauty apples which can be found from October to June, or Winesaps, a late-season apple, from November to July. If none of these are available, Jonathan is a good substitute; it can be found from September to April.

(Serves 4)

4 large baking apples
1 tablespoon lemon juice
1 cup apricot preserves
½ cup sweet butter or sweet margarine at room temperature
4 teaspoons white rum
⅛ teaspoon nutmeg
4 slices pound cake ¼-inch thick
¼ cup milk
2 beaten eggs
⅓ cup superfine sugar
2 tablespoons butter
2 tablespoons slivered almonds, lightly toasted

Preheat oven to 350°.

Peel apples and plunge them immediately into water with lemon juice added to prevent darkening. Prepare a well-buttered baking dish. Blend apricot preserves, 2 teaspoons rum, and nutmeg in a bowl.

Drain apples, wipe dry, core, and fill each center with some of the softened butter. Place in baking dish; ladle apricot mixture over them; cover with lid or foil; bake in preheated oven 30-35 minutes. Apples should be just on the soft side, and golden, but not so soft that they fall apart.

Meanwhile dip cake slices rapidly in milk, just enough to dampen on both sides; do not let them get soggy. Then dip in beaten eggs; sprinkle with sugar on both sides.

Melt butter in large skillet; place slices in butter over low heat until sugar caramelizes. Turn slices carefully with spatula and coat on the other side.

Place cake slices on warm serving platter; put an apple on each slice; ladle with sauce left over from baking apples. Refrigerate about 3 hours; when ready to serve, flambé apples by igniting 2 teaspoons warm rum in stainless-steel ladle and pouring flaming liquid over apples. Let flames die out; sprinkle almonds over; serve.

Petits batonnets de meringue   2
Meringue Fingers

These *batonnets* (small sticks) are eaten with some desserts, such as mousse, fruit cups, etc.

(Makes 2 dozen)

4 egg whites at room temperature
Pinch of salt
1 cup superfine sugar
1 teaspoon vanilla
1 teaspoon distilled white vinegar

Preheat oven to 250°.

Beat egg whites and salt in large bowl until very stiff and standing in peaks when beater is lifted. Add sugar gradually, 1 tablespoon at a time, beating constantly. Add vanilla and vinegar; continue beating until stiff.

Pipe mixture through a pastry bag with a ¼-inch plain tip onto an ungreased aluminum cookie sheet; make them 3 inches in length, 2 inches apart, or shape with a spoon like fat fingers 1 inch by 3 inches.

Place cookie sheet on middle shelf of preheated oven; bake 1 hour or until a very light brown. With metal spatula scoop fingers off the cookie sheet onto a large piece of foil and cool.

Beignets de pommes   3
Apple Fritters

These fritters are so good you will make them often.

(Serves 3-4)

3 cooking apples
¼ cup sugar
¼ cup kirsch, cognac, or light rum
1 cup all-purpose flour
1 egg yolk
⅛ teaspoon salt
1 tablespoon vegetable oil
⅔ cup whole milk
1 egg white stiffly beaten
Vegetable oil for deep frying

Peel and core apples; slice each apple into 6 slices; place slices in large bowl, sprinkle with sugar; pour kirsch, cognac, or rum over; mix well and let sit for 30 minutes.

Place flour in bowl; in center place egg yolk, salt, oil, and milk; stir until smooth, do not overwork; let rest ½ hour covered with towel; add beaten egg white and blend well. Drain apples; stir this liquid into batter.

Fill deep fryer or deep pan with oil about ½ inch deep; heat to 375°. Pick up apple slices with fork or tongs and dip into batter one at a time; let excess batter drop off. Drop carefully into hot fat and fry a few at a time until golden brown (do not crowd them); turn and fry the other side. Remove with slotted spatula and drain on paper toweling. Sprinkle with sugar.

La bûche de Noël   3
Yule Log

A tradition going back to the time of the Druids.

(Serves 8-10)

Biscuit roll:
4 egg yolks
½ cup sugar, superfine
4 egg whites
⅛ teaspoon salt
1 teaspoon vanilla
⅓ cup sifted all-purpose flour
1 teaspoon baking powder

Mocha filling:
¼ cup confectioner's sugar
1 cup unsalted butter or margarine at room temperature
1 tablespoon instant coffee
1 teaspoon cocoa powder
2 egg whites

Cream for topping:
¼ cup confectioner's sugar
1 tablespoon cocoa powder
2 cups whipping cream

Meringue mushrooms:
2 egg whites at room temperature

1 cup superfine sugar
½ teaspoon vanilla
¼ teaspoon vinegar
Pinch of cream of tartar

The log:
Preheat oven to 375°.

Beat egg yolks until thick and lemon-colored; gradually beat in ¼ cup sugar. Beat egg whites, vanilla, and salt to soft peaks in a different bowl; gradually beat in remaining ¼ cup sugar until stiff; fold egg yolk mixture into egg whites.

Sift flour with baking powder; fold into egg mixture with spatula using up-and-down motion, just until streaks of white disappear; do not over work mixture. Spread mixture into a 15½"x10½"x1" buttered and lightly floured baking sheet. Place in preheated oven and bake 12-15 minutes or until lightly brown. Turn immediately onto a towel sprinkled with confectioner's sugar. Using edges of towel, at narrow end roll cake and towel to form jelly roll. Cool thoroughly. Unroll and spread mocha filling evenly over cake; reroll and chill.

Mocha filling:
Sift sugar with instant coffee and cocoa powder; cream butter or margarine; add sugar-coffee-cocoa mixture and cream again until smooth. Beat egg whites until stiff; fold cream mixture into egg whites; spread on cake.

Cream for topping:
Sift confectioner's sugar with cocoa; whip cream until fairly thickened; gradually add cocoa mixture, beating until soft peaks appear. Cover surface of roll with mixture and pass tines of fork the length of the log, making markings to resemble bark. Place one or two meringue mushrooms on top. (If you want to follow the full tradition, write or print *Noël* in chocolate icing on top of the log.)

Meringue mushrooms:
Preheat oven to 275°.

Beat egg whites until foamy; add sugar 2 tablespoons at a time until peaks form; add vanilla and vinegar and cream of tartar; continue beating until peaks stand upright when beater is held up.

Pastry-bag method: On ungreased teflon cookie sheet pipe mixture through pastry bag fitted with large plain tip to form stems of mushrooms. Form caps with a number 8 tip. Bake at 275° for 20 minutes until set and lightly colored.

Spoon method: Caps — drop meringue by teaspoonfuls, pushing with rubber spatula onto cookie sheet. With spoon form small mounds 1½ inches in diameter; place 1 inch apart.

Stems — drop meringue by teaspoonfuls as above, but form stems by shaping meringue into short, narrow columns, 1½ inches high by ¾ inch thick.

Entremets aux cerises   3
Cold Cherry Soup Dessert

A good dessert that can be served also at the beginning of a summer meal.

(Serves 6)

1¼ pounds fresh cherries
⅔ cup sugar
1 cup water
⅛ teaspoon salt
½ cup heavy cream
½ cup dry red wine such as Bordeaux
1 tablespoon cornstarch
1 tablespoon lemon juice
¾ cup sour cream or yogurt
3 tablespoons kirsch or almond liqueur
6 slices pound cake
3 tablespoons butter

Wash cherries; remove stems; pit and halve. Mix cherries, sugar, water, and salt in saucepan. Bring to a boil over medium heat; reduce to low and cook, stirring slowly with wooden spoon for 5 minutes. Blend in cream slowly.

Add wine to cornstarch; blend until smooth. Add to cream-cherry mixture and blend. Cook over medium heat until thickened. Add lemon juice; stir until blended. Ladle some of the hot mixture into the sour cream in a bowl; mix well; return to the remaining hot mixture and blend well. Simmer 5 more minutes.

Meanwhile melt butter in large skillet over low heat; add cake slices; warm 1 minute; turn them with spatula; warm again. Drain on paper towel.

Pour hot soup into bowl, add kirsch or almond liqueur; serve with warm cake.

Marquise au chocolat   3
Hot Chocolate Soufflé

(Serves 6)

1 cup milk
⅓ cup granulated sugar
3 tablespoons all-purpose flour
Pinch of salt
3 1-ounce squares unsweetened chocolate
1 tablespoon grated orange zeste
1 teaspoon vanilla extract
4 egg yolks
4 egg whites
⅛ teaspoon cream of tartar
2 tablespoons granulated sugar
Crème anglaise (see index)

Preheat oven to 350°.

Butter a 6-cup soufflé dish well. Sprinkle evenly with sugar. Fold a 24-inch piece of kitchen parchment or foil in thirds; butter and sugar it. Wrap around soufflé dish, sugared-side-in to form a crown extending 2 inches above rim; tie with kitchen string; set aside.

Combine the flour, ⅓ cup sugar, and salt in saucepan. Add milk gradually; beat with whisk until blended; add chocolate and cook over medium heat, stirring until chocolate is melted, mixture starts to boil and has thickened. Remove from heat and add orange peel and vanilla. Cool slightly.

Beat egg yolks with a wire whisk in small bowl; add some of the chocolate mixture, then gradually add the egg yolk mixture to the rest of the chocolate combination.

Add cream of tartar to egg whites in large bowl and beat until soft peaks form when beater is lifted. Add the 2 remaining tablespoons sugar, 1 tablespoon at a time, and beat until stiff. Stir ⅓ of chocolate mixture over top of egg whites. With a rubber spatula, gently fold mixture into whites with a down-under-over motion. Add remaining chocolate mixture and fold in gently.

Pour into prepared soufflé dish. Sprinkle evenly with sugar. Place dish in a pan in which boiling water has been added to a depth of 1 inch; place in preheated oven for 45 minutes or until puffed and center is not quite firm. (Soufflé continues baking for a little while after it is removed from oven.)

Serve immediately with *créme anglaise* passed in a serving dish.

Gâteau de marrons   **3**
Chestnut Cake

(Serves 6-8)

1 15½-ounce can purée de marron (*chestnut purée*)
2 whole eggs, lightly beaten
½ cup sugar
1½ cups light cream
3 1-ounce squares semi-sweet chocolate, cut in small pieces
2 tablespoons Cointreau, Grand Marnier, or brandy
1 envelope unflavored gelatin
¼ cup cold water
1-1½ cups whipping cream
1 10-ounce package frozen raspberries, thawed

Force *purée de marron* through ricer or food mill, or blend in electric blender; set aside.

Combine beaten eggs, sugar, cream, and chocolate pieces in top part of double-boiler. Cook, stirring often, over simmering (not boiling) water until chocolate has melted and mixture has thickened (about 8-10 minutes). Add liquor; blend.

Meanwhile place the ¼ cup water in small saucepan and sprinkle the gelatin over; place over low heat and stir until gelatin has dissolved.

When chocolate mixture is ready, spoon some of it into the gelatin; blend well and return this to the rest of the chocolate mixture in the double-boiler; blend thoroughly; add chestnut purée; blend again. Cool slightly; pour into a well-buttered 8-inch ring mold or a cake pan 8½"x4½"x2½". Refrigerate several hours before serving.

When ready to serve, dip mold into warm water 1 minute or 2, place serving plate over mold and invert. Cake will slide onto plate. Refrigerate while you prepare whipped cream and raspberries.

Drain raspberries thoroughly (save syrup to make jelly or sauce). Whip cream. Blend raspberries in whipped cream and serve over cake.

Le gâteau des rois   **3**
The Kings' Cake

In Provence during Epiphany — from the first to the twelfth of January — people celebrate the visit of the Three Kings to the Christ Child by partaking of a feast in which a kind of brioche in the shape of a ring, or crown of the king, is eaten. A *fava* bean or a little porcelain figurine is inserted in the dough before baking; this is called *la fève*. The guest who receives the slice of cake with the *fève* in it is king or queen for a day. This charming custom makes for increased sales of this cake, for the lucky winner is required to buy the crown for the next gathering of friends or relatives.

This same tradition is followed in the northern part of France, where the cake is made of a flaky dough (puff paste), and it is flat in shape instead of crown shaped. It is called *Galette des rois*, and is sold in bakeries with a gold cardboard crown.

(Makes 1 ring)

1 package active dry yeast
¼ cup warm water, 95-100°
½ cup milk
6 tablespoons butter or margarine
½ cup sugar
Pinch of salt
2 eggs, lightly beaten and at room temperature
1 tablespoon grated orange or lemon rind
1 tablespoon vanilla extract
3 to 3¾ cups all-purpose flour
1 egg yolk at room temperature
1 tablespoon water, lukewarm
Candied cherries
Candied green lemon or pineapple
1 fava bean or a very small porcelain figure

Icing:
½ cup sifted powdered sugar
Enough milk or light cream to make a very soft icing
Rock-sugar candy (optional)

Mix yeast and warm water in large mixing bowl; let it stand 5 minutes to proof (that is, until the yeast is working).

Heat milk, butter, and sugar to lukewarm (about 115°) in saucepan; add to yeast and water in bowl with salt, lemon or orange rind, eggs, and vanilla extract; stir to blend. Add 2½ cups of the flour and beat at low speed for ½ minute; add ½ cup of the leftover flour and beat at high speed for 2 minutes, to get a soft dough. If dough is too sticky, add more flour until firm enough to knead.

Turn out onto a floured surface and knead until smooth and elastic, adding more flour if necessary; knead about 6-8 minutes. Form into a ball and place in a greased bowl, turning once to grease it all around. Cover bowl with plastic film and cover it with towel. Let dough rise slowly about 2 hours or until doubled.

Preheat oven to 350°.

Grease or butter large baking sheet.

Punch down dough and turn out onto lightly floured surface; roll it into a 26-inch rope. Join both ends together and seal neatly to make a nice even ring. Place ring on well-greased baking sheet; insert *fava* bean or porcelain figure into the dough; cover lightly with clean towel and let rise until doubled, about 40 minutes.

Beat egg yolk and water; brush surface of cake lightly with this mixture. Place cake in preheated oven and bake 10-12 minutes. If at that time surface is already brown, cover with piece of foil and continue baking 8-10 minutes more or until toothpick inserted in center comes out clean.

Remove cake from oven, and while warm, frost with icing made by blending confectioner's sugar and milk or cream. Arrange candied cherries and green candied lemon on icing to resemble fruits and leaves. Sprinkle with rock-sugar candy. A festive way to bring this cake to the table is to fill the center with holly.

Meringue glacée lyonnaise   3
Chilled Meringue Lyon Style

(Serves 4-5)

1 *quart* granité aux framboises (*raspberry ice; see index, or com-mercial sherbet may be used)*
3 *tablespoons cognac or other brandy*
6 *ounces raspberry jelly or preserve, sieved*
Whipping cream, whipped
Nougatine *(see page 325)*
8-10 *meringue fingers*

Warm jelly or sieved preserves in small saucepan over medium-low heat until just to the liquid state. Blend in cognac or brandy and chill, covered.

Place a scoop of raspberry ice in individual dessert dish. Spoon the jelly-liqueur mixture over ice; cover with whipped cream; sprinkle with nougatine; place one meringue on each side of sherbet, at an angle. Serve immediately.

Les merveilles   3
Marvels

The word *merveilles* means "small wonders." They are also called *oreillettes*, little pillows, which they resemble when cooked.

(Makes 24)

2 cups all-purpose flour
4 egg yolks
1 teaspoon grated lemon or orange rind
1 tablespoon light rum
⅔ cup sugar
Pinch of salt

Place 2 cups flour in large bowl and make a well in the center; add egg yolks, lemon or orange rind, rum, sugar, and salt. With fingers, incorporate flour in egg-sugar mixture and work until a ball of dough is developed.

Sprinkle working surface with remaining flour and knead dough until it is shiny and smooth. Place in cool spot or refrigerator, covered, for 1 hour.

Roll out ¼ the dough at a time to about ⅛-inch thickness, or less; with pastry wheel or knife, cut thin rectangles 3½"x5".

Fill deep-fryer or deep pan with oil ⅔ full. Heat to 350° and drop rectangles of dough, one at a time, carefully, into hot fat; do not crowd (about 3-4 in the fat at once); fry 2-3 minutes or until golden brown and puffed. Remove with slotted spatula; drain on paper toweling. Sprinkle with confectioner's sugar. Serve hot or warm.

Tartelettes aux marrons   2
Chestnut Tartlets

(Makes 12)

12 pâte brisée sucrée *tartlets, baked*
1 recipe for 6 mousse aux marrons *(see index)*

½ cup raspberry jelly
Whipping cream, whipped
*Chocolate shavings from semi-sweet chocolate**

Divide chestnut mousse among the 12 tartlets and spread in bottom. Melt jelly over medium-low heat in small saucepan until melted; spoon over mousse in each tartlet. Decorate with whipped cream and sprinkle chocolate shavings over.

Le moka   3
Moccha Cake   ·

This rich cake may be served at an afternoon tea, a luncheon, or an after-dinner social. (This confection is one of my weaknesses.)

(Makes 8-10 thin slices)

1 tablespoon instant coffee
3 tablespoons hot water
½ cup superfine sugar
2 egg yolks, slightly beaten
8 ounces unsalted butter at room temperature
½ teaspoon rum or brandy
20 (approximately) butter biscuits (Petits beurres or "Social Tea")

Blend instant coffee and hot water; cool thoroughly. (This is called *essence*.) Blend sugar with egg yolks in mixing bowl, working until sugar does not feel granulated any longer.

Add butter, small amount at a time; work with wooden spoon until mixture is smooth and shiny. In warm weather work fast, to prevent butter from melting; it should retain its thick texture. Add 2 teaspoons coffee mixture (*essence*) and rum or brandy; blend thoroughly. Spread a thin layer of this filling in bottom of aluminum loaf pan 7⅜"x3⅝"x2¼", well buttered.

Mix remaining coffee *essence* with 4 teaspoons water and a little

---

*Use large teeth of a cheese-grater to grate semi-sweet chocolate.

sugar in wide bowl. Dip biscuits, one at a time, in sweetened coffee until soft; arrange in a layer over the filling in pan (you will need to break some biscuits in order to cover the bottom completely). Spread another layer of filling ½ inch thick over biscuits; repeat with layer of biscuits and layer of filling, ending with a layer of biscuits (this should take about 16 biscuits).

Place piece of wax paper over top layer of biscuits; press lightly with a weight; leave light weight on top; place in refrigerator for at least 6 hours. When ready to serve, dip bottom of pan quickly in hot water; pass a sharp knife around sides to loosen; invert onto chilled plate. Place 4 remaining cookies in small paper bag; crush to fine crumbs; spread over cake; place cake on serving platter. (Being very rich, this cake should be sliced very thin—a small amount will satisfy!)

Pâte brisée sucrée aux oeufs   2
Sweet Pastry with Egg

(Makes one 9-inch pie crust)

1½ cups all-purpose flour
¼ teaspoon salt
1 tablespoon superfine sugar
6 tablespoons unsalted butter or unsalted margarine, cold
1 egg yolk, lightly beaten
5-6 tablespoons ice water

Preheat oven to 400°.

Sift together flour, salt, and sugar into large bowl; cut butter or margarine in small pieces; add to flour mixture and cut butter in with a pastry blender or the tines of a fork until mixture resembles coarse meal. Work the egg yolk into the flour-butter mixture; knead gently with fingertips, then add water, 1 tablespoon at a time, until dough holds together. Form ball; sprinkle it lightly with flour and chill, wrapped in wax paper, at least 1 hour. Then proceed as usual to roll out dough.

Oeufs à la neige   **3**
Snowy Eggs (Floating Island)

A very old, traditional dessert, still very popular in France. It is refreshing as well as elegant.

(Serves 4-6)

1 quart milk
4 tablespoons fine granulated sugar
6 egg whites
⅛ teaspoon salt
1½ cups fine granulated sugar
6 egg yolks, well beaten
1½ teaspoons vanilla extract
⅓ cup sugar

Stretch a clean towel over one large cake rack and place over a pan so liquid can drain through. Dissolve 4 tablespoons sugar in milk in large heavy skillet; bring to scalding point over very low heat; keep on simmering.

While milk heats, place egg whites and salt in large bowl; beat until foamy; add cup of sugar slowly, 1 tablespoon at a time, and beat until stiff peaks form. With large spoon, scoop out enough meringue to drop large balls into scalded milk; poach in simmering milk 1 minute; turn meringue balls gently and poach 1 or 2 minutes longer. Remove with slotted spoon to towel. Poach until all the meringue has been used up.

Strain milk into large bowl; add more milk to make 3 cups. Beat egg yolks with sugar and salt. Place beaten yolk-sugar mixture in large saucepan (be sure to get every drop by cleaning bowl with rubber scraper). Gradually stir in milk and place over low heat; stir slowly but constantly until mixture starts to thicken, 8-10 minutes. Custard is ready when mixture coats spoon. Remove from heat; add vanilla; pour into large serving bowl; float meringue balls over custard.

Prepare caramel by placing the ⅓ cup sugar in small cast-iron skillet or small heavy saucepan and let it melt slowly over medium-low heat until amber-colored; drizzle on meringue balls. Chill in refrigerator.

Tourte aux blettes   3
Swiss Chard Pie

A surprisingly good dessert tart. It is very traditional in the South, especially in and around Nice. Sometimes a sliced banana is added to the filling.

(Serves 6)

Two-crust pastry dough for *tourte*:
2 cups all-purpose flour
⅛ teaspoon salt
1 tablespoon granulated sugar
1 tablespoon brown sugar
1 stick butter or margarine at room temperature
5 tablespoons ice water

Filling:
1 tart apple, peeled, quartered, and sliced thin
1½ pounds Swiss chard leaves
¼ cup grated Gouda or Cheddar cheese (mild)
¼ cup dry currants or raisins
⅓ cup rum
¼ cup piñon nuts (found in health food or specialty stores)
Salt
2 whole eggs
2 tablespoons olive oil
2 tablespoons granulated sugar

One hour ahead soak currants or raisins in rum to plump; drain before using.

Preheat oven to 375°.

Two 10-inch crusts: Sift flour, salt, sugar, and brown sugar in large bowl; cut butter in with pastry blender or tines of a fork until mixture resembles coarse meal; add just enough water to make dough adhere; form a ball; refrigerate 20 minutes in hot weather (in cold weather dough may be handled without chilling). Divide dough to form 2 balls. Place 1 ball between 2 pieces waxed paper lightly floured; roll into 10-inch circle. Line pie dish or quiche dish with pastry; do not cut around the overlapping edges; set aside.

Filling: Clean chard leaves and dry thoroughly; chop fine. Place chopped chard leaves, apple, grated cheese, drained currants or raisins, piñon nuts, and salt in bowl. Beat eggs slightly; blend with mixture. Fill pastry with this mixture; drizzle olive oil over.

Roll out second ball into another 10-inch circle; place over chard mixture. Pinch edges of pastry together to seal; trim and flute. Cut a hole in center of top crust to let steam escape.

Place in preheated oven and bake 20-25 minutes or until light brown. If crust darkens too fast, cover edges with foil; uncover a few minutes before end of baking time. Sprinkle top with granulated sugar after taking *tourte* out of oven.

Oranges au sabayon   **3**
Individual Orange Soufflé

(Serves 6)

6 California oranges
Juice of ½ lemon
2 egg whites
2 egg yolks, slightly beaten
⅔ cup sugar
1 tablespoon cornstarch
2 teaspoons Cointreau, Triple Sec, or orange-flavored brandy
Whipped cream

Slice ⅓ off top of each orange; with knife, cut or scoop out pulp of oranges, leaving shells whole—they will be used as cups. Put pulp of 4 oranges in sieve and drain the juice into a bowl. Remove the white membrane from the 2 oranges left over and cut pulp into small sections; set aside. Add lemon juice to orange juice; set aside.

Beat egg whites until stiff; set aside. In top of double-boiler blend egg yolks, sugar, cornstarch; beat well with wooden spoon. Slowly add orange and lemon juice until well blended. Place top over simmering water and stir until mixture thickens (about 7-8 minutes); remove from heat; add liqueur and blend. (This is the *sabayon*.)

Fold beaten egg whites into the *sabayon* by lifting whites lightly up and over until no white is showing.

Place reserved orange sections in bottom of orange shells. Spoon the creamy mixture over orange sections. Arrange shells in a pan. Place in refrigerator and chill thoroughly. When ready to serve, arrange each shell in a serving dish and top with whipped cream.

Tarte au fromage   3
Cheese Tart

(Serves 8)

8 ounces cream cheese (Philadelphia, Neufchâtel, or your locally
    made cream cheese), at room temperature
⅓ cup light cream
4 tablespoons sugar
2 egg yolks (large), slightly beaten
1 teaspoon freshly grated orange or lemon peel
1 tablespoon vanilla or orange-flavored brandy
2 egg whites
1 tablespoon sugar
⅓ cup apricot preserves
1 tablespoon cognac, Grand Marnier, or other brandy, or even
    some good whiskey
1 9-inch pâte brisée shell, unbaked

Chill pie shell 30 minutes before baking. Prick bottom and bake at 400° for 15 minutes; remove from oven and cool.

Preheat oven to 350°.

Blend cream cheese, cream, sugar, egg yolks, orange or lemon peel, and vanilla or brandy in a bowl until smooth (blending can be done with an electric beater at low speed); set aside.

Beat egg whites until frothy in another bowl; add one tablespoon sugar and beat again until stiff but not dry. Fold egg whites into cream cheese mixture with a down-up-over motion until no streaks of white are left.

Pour into the prebaked shell and bake in preheated oven 30 minutes; reduce heat to 325° and bake 10-15 minutes longer or until a toothpick inserted in the center comes out clean; set aside to cool. (If edges brown too fast, cover with foil.)

Heat preserves slowly in small saucepan until melted; remove from heat immediately and blend in cognac or substitute; pour this mixture over the cooled top of the cheese tart; cool again and serve.

Tarte aux noisettes   3
Hazelnut Tart

A deliciously rich winter tart. It can be made with filberts if you cannot find hazelnuts. (Filberts are a variety of hazelnuts, slightly larger.)

(Serves 8-10)

1 9-inch pâte brisée *shell, baked*
1 cup ground prepared hazelnuts
½ cup granulated sugar
2 tablespoons water
½ cup dark honey
1 cup whipping cream or heavy cream
2 whole eggs, lightly beaten
Crème chantilly *(recipe below)*

Prepare hazelnuts:
Spread nuts on a heavy cookie sheet and place in 350° oven for 10-15 minutes or until skin turns dark in color (watch toward the end of the ten minutes, as the nuts burn easily). Remove immediately and cool slightly. Place nuts in a towel; fold over and rub to remove loose skin. Grind in food processor or blender.

Filling:
Blend sugar and water in medium-sized heavy skillet; bring mix-

ture slowly to a boil and stir often to dissolve sugar. Cook on medium-high until mixture turns to a light brown; remove from heat immediately as it continues cooking away from heat source; at once add ground hazelnuts and honey; stir in slowly and carefully and blend well. Return the mixture to the stove; cook on medium heat 3 more minutes or until it starts to thicken slightly. Pour a small amount of this mixture into beaten eggs and stir rapidly to blend; return this to the mixture in the pan and blend thoroughly. Cook over medium heat until thickened, 3 more minutes. Pour into prebaked pie shell and cool thoroughly before serving with *crème Chantilly*:

1 cup very cold whipping cream
2 tablespoons confectioner's sugar
1 teaspoon vanilla

Whip cream until double in volume; add sugar and beat again until well blended. Add vanilla; stir and serve.

Tarte aux pommes   3
Apple Tart

(Serves 8)

1 9-inch pâte brisée *shell*
1½ pounds tart apples (Jonathan, Granny Smith, or Winesap)
2 tablespoons lemon juice
½ cup granulated sugar
⅓ cup currant jelly

Apple Syrup:
Reserved apple peelings
½ cup sugar
Lemon peel 2½ inches long
1 tablespoon lemon juice
1 tablespoon brandy

Preheat oven to 350°.

Wash, peel, and core apples; reserve peelings. Slice apples fine and mix with lemon juice and ⅓ cup of the sugar. Set aside.

Roll out dough and line a 9-inch pie plate or tart pan; prick bottom with fork. Arrange apples in shell, reserving enough slices to make a pinwheel on the top layer. Sprinkle remaining 2 tablespoons sugar over top; bake in preheated oven for 35 minutes or until apples are soft.

Prepare apple syrup by placing the reserved peelings and enough water to barely cover in a saucepan; add sugar, lemon peel, lemon juice, and brandy. Bring to brisk boil and continue cooking briskly to reduce the syrup for 20-25 minutes. Strain, squeezing every drop of syrup from the peelings (it will make ⅓ cup or a little more); set aside.

When tart is baked, remove from oven; pour reserved ⅓ cup syrup over fruits; cool at room temperature. Heat currant jelly in small saucepan over low heat until melted. Brush over top of tart to glaze; cool before serving.

Poires framboisées au porto   **3**
Raspberry Flavored Pears with Port

(Serves 4)

4 Bosc or other pears, ripe but firm
Cold water to cover
Juice of ½ lemon
⅔ cup sugar
1 cup water
½ cup port wine
2 tablespoons brandy
1 inch vanilla bean, split, or 1 teaspoon vanilla extract
1 strip orange or lemon peel, 2½" long, fresh or dried
⅓ to ½ cup raspberry jelly or preserves
1 tablespoon brandy or Triple Sec
Whipped cream

Preheat oven to 375°.

Peel pears and square off bottom slightly to be able to stand them up in serving dish. Place in bowl with cold water to cover, and lemon juice, until ready to bake.

Bring water and sugar to a boil in heavy saucepan over medium heat and continue cooking over medium heat for 8 minutes (the liquid should bubble rapidly). Add port wine, brandy, orange peel, and vanilla bean or vanilla extract. Bring back to rapid boil 1 minute longer.

Place pears on their sides in a deep glass or ceramic baking dish; pour hot syrup over; cover tightly with lid or heavy foil; place in preheated oven for 30-40 minutes, depending on ripeness of the pears, until tender but firm; baste twice. Remove pears from syrup with slotted spoon and place standing up, in individual dessert glasses; pour 1 teaspoon of the hot syrup over each; set aside.

Mix jelly or sieved preserves and 1 tablespoon hot syrup in small saucepan; heat slowly until melted; remove from heat; add brandy or Triple Sec. Stir to blend and pour some over each pear. Cool thoroughly; chill in refrigerator at least 2 hours. Serve with whipped cream.

Poires à la crème vanillée 3
Pears in Vanilla Cream

(Serves 8)

4 pears, Bosc or other, ripe but firm, cut in half lengthwise
Cold water to cover
Juice of ½ lemon
⅔ cup sugar
1 cup water
½ cup port wine
2 tablespoons brandy
1 strip orange peel or lemon peel 2½ inches in length
1 inch vanilla bean, split, or 1 teaspoon vanilla extract
1 cup whipping cream
8 teaspoons raspberry jam
8 **Langues de chat** *(Ladyfingers; see index)*
Ice cubes (about 20) in cold water

Crème vanillée:
2 cups milk
4 egg yolks

1 tablespoon flour
4 tablespoons superfine sugar
1 teaspoon vanilla extract

Prepare and poach pears as in *Poires framboisées au porto*, but reduce oven time to 25 minutes. Remove pears from syrup with slotted spoon; place one pear half in each dessert glass. Set aside to cool. Reserve syrup and cool. Combine ice cubes and cold water in a large bowl; set aside.

Prepare *crème vanillée*: Scald milk; cool and skim. Combine egg yolks, flour, and sugar. Add cooled milk and vanilla; blend; pour in saucepan over medium heat, stirring constantly until thick and starting to boil. Place saucepan with custard immediately over ice water in large bowl and continue stirring until custard cools thoroughly.

Whip cream until soft peaks form; add 2 tablespoons reserved cold syrup; whip until stiff; fold into cold custard. Fill each pear center with 1 teaspoon raspberry jam; pour chilled custard over pears and jam; serve with *langues de chat*.

Sweets

The French housewife has never felt the need to make sweets at home, except on special occasions. The confectioners' shops with their rows of wonderful delicacies supply her well. Moreover, in the past her kitchen was not equipped for the complicated processes some of them require. However, some traditional bonbons and cookies are produced in the home on religious feast-days or for special events. The following recipes are a few examples of what the housewife makes in her own kitchen.

Les figues fourrées (les capucins)   1
Stuffed Figs

These delicious and simple-to-make sweets were served in my home at Christmastime.

Make a slash in each dry fig and stuff the cavity with a walnut half, dipped in honey. Roll stuffed figs in powdered sugar and arrange on a pretty serving dish.

Les pralines aux noix   1
Walnut Pralines

(Makes 2 pounds)

3 cups granulated sugar
1¼ cups hot water
1 teaspoon vanilla extract
1¼ cups walnut meat, chopped fine
⅛ teaspoon cream of tartar

Mix all ingredients in large saucepan and cook over medium-high heat, stirring often with wooden spoon, until candy thermometer reaches 238° F. Remove from heat and continue stirring until the mixture loses its shiny appearance, about 5 minutes.

Pour into a well-buttered 8"x8" baking pan. Let cool thoroughly; cut into 1-inch squares.

Truffes au chocolat   2
Chocolate Truffles

This is one of the most delicious candies that has ever been invented!

(Makes about 30)

8 ounces semi-sweet chocolate cut into pieces
1 tablespoon unsweetened cocoa
3 tablespoons warm water
3 egg yolks, beaten slightly
½ cup sweet butter, cut into pieces
Unsweetened cocoa for decorating

Place chocolate pieces, cocoa, and warm water in top of double-boiler; melt over medium heat; do not let water boil or touch the bottom of the upper bowl. Remove from heat; stir mixture; add egg yolks and blend well with wooden spoon. Return to low heat and cook, stirring, for 3 minutes until it reaches the consistency of thick cream. Remove again from heat; stir 1-2 minutes; add butter 1 or 2 pieces at a time, beating until butter is incorporated and mixture is smooth and shiny. Cool, stir once or twice, then refrigerate until firm, about 3-4 hours. (Some seedless raisins soaked in rum and thoroughly drained may be added at this point.)

Pick up particles of chocolate mixture with teaspoon; with your hands form small balls ¾-inch in diameter; roll them in cocoa to coat; place in small candy paper cups and store them in airtight tin can (or omit paper cups). The cocoa gives them the special taste by which these truffles are known. They keep well for weeks, refrigerated.

Galettes sucrées pour le thé   **2**
Tea Cookies

(Makes about 1 dozen)

1 cup all-purpose flour plus 1 tablespoon
⅛ teaspoon salt
½ cup superfine sugar
1 tablespoon milk
1 teaspoon grated lemon rind
2 egg yolks, beaten slightly
8 ounces butter or margarine at room temperature

Preheat oven to 350°.

Sift flour, salt, and sugar in large bowl; blend milk and egg yolks in separate bowl; make a well in flour-sugar mixture; put milk and egg yolks in center.

Cut butter in small pieces; add to milk and eggs; work with fingers, bringing flour gradually in until soft dough is formed. Place on lightly floured surface and work dough until smooth; chill 1-2 hours.

Roll into a circle ⅜-inch thick and 7 inches in diameter; with small round cutter, cut out 12 small cookies. Place on a lightly buttered cookie sheet. Beat egg yolk with 1 tablespoon water; brush surface of cookies with this mixture. Bake in pre-heated oven 40-45 minutes.

Tuiles aux amandes   **2**
Almond Tiles

(Makes about 2 dozen)

⅓ cup butter, softened at room temperature
⅓ cup superfine sugar
½ cup (scant) sifted all-purpose flour
⅔ cup ground almonds
½ teaspoon vanilla extract
½ teaspoon almond extract

Preheat oven to 400°.

Cream butter and sugar together with wooden spoon until light. Beat in flour a small amount at a time; add almonds, vanilla extract, and almond extract; beat until well blended. Drop batter in mounds 3 inches apart with teaspoon; flatten each mound to a 2½-inch circle. Bake 8-10 minutes or until cookies are lightly browned.

Remove cookies immediately with metal spatula, one at a time, to a rolling-pin or bottle to form curved tiles; after a few minutes they will curl and hold their shape. If they cool too fast, return baking sheet to oven for a few seconds. Finish cooling tiles on a rack.

Nougatine   2
Almond Brittle

¾ *cup slivered almonds*
¾ *cup sugar*
2 tablespoons water

Preheat oven to 350°.

Toast almonds by spreading them on a cookie sheet in preheated oven until golden brown, about 5-7 minutes. Watch carefully because the almonds burn easily. Remove immediately to a piece of foil or wax paper to cool.

Place sugar and water in small, heavy saucepan on medium-low heat until sugar turns to a golden brown, 15-20 minutes. Watch toward the end, as the caramel should be a light golden. When you remove it from the heat it will continue darkening for a few seconds. Stir in toasted almonds at once and pour on a piece of foil, spreading the mixture. Cool thoroughly; it will harden.

Break it in chunks and place in paper sack. Crush with a meat mallet or heavy object until it is of the consistency of coarse meal. This is nougatine, to be used as the finishing touch for a number of desserts.

Petits gâteaux secs aux noisettes   **3**
Hazelnut Tea Cookies

These cookies are a perfect accompaniment for tea or coffee. The double ones are so rich that one or two for each guest will suffice.

(Makes 15-16 double or 30-32 single cookies)

3 egg whites from extra-large eggs
1¼ cups sugar
¾ cup ground hazelnuts or walnuts
1 cup fine dry bread crumbs
1 teaspoon vanilla
Candied violets (obtainable at specialty food stores) or walnuts or
*   hazelnuts*

Frosting:
½ cup unsalted butter
1 cup confectioner's sugar
1 teaspoon very strong coffee essence (see Le moka*), cold*
1 teaspoon vanilla

Preheat oven to 300°.

Butter two 13"x9" baking pans; set aside. Beat egg whites until stiff in large bowl (copper or stainless steel); add ¾ cup sugar gradually and continue beating until eggs are shiny and very stiff. Add remaining sugar, hazelnuts or walnuts, bread crumbs, and vanilla; fold gently but thoroughly with spatula. Divide batter; spread into the two buttered pans — batter should be ¼-inch thick. Bake for 15-20 minutes or until set but still soft.

Remove from oven and with round cookie cutter 2 inches in diameter or a glass of same dimension, cut 28-30 rounds, working quickly. Leave rounds in place and return everything to oven to bake 8-10 minutes longer to crisp. With a pointed knife lift rounds and place on cake racks to cool.

Return cake pans with leftover trimmings to oven to brown 8-10 minutes longer; remove and cool trimmings on cake rack. When trimmings are cold, reduce them to crumbs in food processor or place them in a paper bag and crush with rolling-pin; set aside.

Prepare frosting by creaming butter; add confectioner's sugar, a small amount at a time, until smooth; add coffee essence and vanilla; blend.

For double cookies: Spread icing between two cookie rounds to make sandwiches; spread icing around sides of cookies; roll sides in crumbs; spread icing on top and decorate each cookie with a sugar violet or walnut or hazelnut.

For single cookies: Spread icing on each round; decorate.

Les pignolats   2
Small Crescent Cookies with Nuts

The coastal region of the South abounds in piñon pines. Their fruit, piñon nuts, is called *pignoun* in Provençal, *graines de pommes de pin* in French. These small cookies, *pignolats*, are made with piñon nuts and served to company. If you cannot obtain piñon nuts in the health food store, use slivered almonds instead.

(Makes about 30 cookies)

2½ cups all-purpose flour
½ cup unsalted butter or margarine
¼ cup honey (dark if possible)
½ cup granulated sugar
1 egg, lightly beaten
1 teaspoon grated lemon or orange peel
1 teaspoon vanilla
¼ cup light cream
½ cup piñon nuts or slivered almonds
¼ cup honey

Sift flour; set aside. Cream butter or margarine in large bowl; add honey and sugar; blend with electric beater; add egg and blend well, then grated lemon or orange peel, vanilla, and cream; blend in flour and stir until smooth. Form into a ball and refrigerate, covered, at least 1 hour.

Preheat oven to 350°.

When ready to bake, take about 1 heaping tablespoon of dough and roll it between your palms to make a thick sausage-like roll about 2½-3 inches in length. Pinch the end slightly and form into a crescent. Press some piñon nuts or almonds onto the top of each cookie. Place on ungreased cookie sheet, 1 inch apart. Set aside.

Warm the honey in small saucepan until it is very fluid; brush or drizzle a little onto each cookie.

Bake in preheated oven for 15-20 minutes or until a deep golden brown. Remove immediately with metal spatula to a wire rack to cool. Store in metal container, in cool, dry place.

Navettes provençales   3
Provençal Cookies

These small cookies in the shape of little boats are traditionally bought and served at *la Chandeleur*, the first part of February, to honor the three blessed saints, the "Three Marys." Legend has it that they came to Provence to preach the gospel. The small sea-coast town, Les Saintes Maries de la Mer, was named after them.

(Makes about 20)

3 cups all-purpose flour
1½ cups sugar
¼ teaspoon salt
⅓ cup butter or margarine, softened at room temperature
1 tablespoon grated lemon rind
1 teaspoon almond extract
3 eggs, slightly beaten
3-4 tablespoons water
1 egg yolk
4 tablespoons water

Preheat oven to 375°.

Sift flour, sugar, and salt together in large bowl. Make a well in the center and place butter, cut in small pieces, lemon rind, almond extract, eggs, and 3 tablespoons water in it. Work with fingers to blend those ingredients with the flour. Bring in small amount of flour at a time until flour is completely incorporated and dough is smooth and homogenous. (If the mixture seems too dry when you work with it, add 1 more tablespoon water.) Form a ball and divide into 10 equal parts; roll these into long rolls about 5 inches in length. Cut each roll in half; pinch at both ends to make them egg-shaped; place on one or several well greased cookie sheets 1½ inches apart. Make a light incision lengthwise in center with point of knife. Let cookies rest 2 hours in warm place, away from draft.

When ready to bake, brush lightly with egg yolk and water beaten together; place in preheated oven for 25 minutes or until nicely browned. Cool on rack.

Pâte de coings
Soft Quince Candy

3

This soft candy is made at Christmastime. It can also be prepared with apples if quince is unavailable. Use the same proportions, only reduce water to 2½ tablespoons.

(Makes 4-5 dozen)

1½ pounds quince
4 tablespoons water
2 cups granulated superfine sugar
2 envelopes unflavored gelatin
2 teaspoons lemon juice
1 teaspoon grated lemon peel
½ teaspoon vanilla extract
Granulated or powdered sugar

Core quince but do not peel; cut into pieces 1-1½ inches thick. Place in large, heavy saucepan with water; cover and simmer until tender. If liquid has not evaporated, uncover; raise heat slightly and cook until all liquid is gone, stirring with wooden spoon all the while.

Sieve or whirl in blender until soft; mix sugar and gelatin; add to purée; return to saucepan. Bring to light boil; cook, stirring over medium-low heat (about 200° on a candy thermometer) 15-20 minutes or until mixture becomes a solid mass. (Watch carefully, as the mixture scorches easily.) It is done when the spoon cut across the mass shows the bottom easily.

Remove from heat; blend in lemon juice, lemon peel, and vanilla extract. Pour into a well-buttered 8-inch-square baking pan and cool thoroughly; cover with wax paper and let sit at room temperature at least 12 hours.

Cut into squares, rectangles, or cut-out designs made with cookie-cutter. Remove to piece of foil or wax paper to dry a few hours; dust with powdered or regular sugar. Store in covered container.

Langues de chat   3
Ladyfingers (literally, Cat's Tongues)

(Makes about 25)

3 egg whites
Dash of salt
2 tablespoons superfine granulated sugar
3 egg yolks
⅓ cup superfine granulated sugar
Dash of vanilla extract or 1 teaspoon lemon juice
1 teaspoon grated lemon rind
⅔ cup sifted all-purpose flour
Confectioner's sugar

Preheat oven to 325°.

Butter and flour 2 cookie sheets. Shake off excess flour. Beat egg whites and salt to a soft peak consistency. With same beater, beat egg yolks in separate large bowl until thickened and lemon-colored; add the ⅓ cup sugar gradually, beating until mixture is thick, about 3 minutes. Add flour a little at a time, folding with rubber spatula (not electric beater) gently; add vanilla or lemon juice and lemon rind.

Add some of the beaten egg whites gently into the egg mixture and mix carefully; then add the remaining egg white and fold, in an up-down-around motion until all lumps are absorbed.

Pipe mixture onto baking sheet through a pastry bag fitted with a large ½-inch plain tube; make strips 3 to 3½ inches long and space 1½ inches apart. Sprinkle some confectioner's sugar over strips; bake in preheated oven for 12 minutes or until light brown.

Remove immediately to cake rack, sprinkle again with confectioner's sugar, and cool. Store cookies in tightly-covered cookie tin.

Languettes d'orange au chocolat   3
Chocolate Covered Candied Orange

(Makes 20)

4 ounces prepared candied orange peel (see index for Candied Fruits)
4 ounces semi-sweet chocolate
¼ cup sweet butter

After cooling pieces of orange peel, place on cake rack and let stand overnight.

Melt chocolate in double-boiler over gently simmering heat; remove from heat; add butter; stir until blended. Dip each peel in chocolate mixture with a fork; be sure each strip is completely covered. Place one at a time on cake rack to cool thoroughly.

Les Madeleines   3
(Small, shell-like cakes)

Originally from the Limousin region *Madeleines* are now made and sold all over France as well as in the South. The molds for these small cakes are found in the houseware departments of department stores or in specialty shops. You may also use muffin tins, but fill only one-third full.

(Makes 14)

½ cup superfine granulated sugar
3 small eggs (about 4 ounces total)
1 teaspoon vanilla extract
1 teaspoon grated lemon zeste
½ cup cake flour
½ cup melted butter or margarine
Light pinch of salt
¼ teaspoon baking powder (omit for baking at high altitude)

Preheat oven to 350°.

Butter *Madeleine* molds well; dust with flour; shake off excess. Beat eggs in a bowl with sugar, until light and fluffy, with wire whip or electric beater. With wooden spoon work in the flour a small amount at a time until no flour lumps are left. Blend in vanilla and lemon rind; add melted butter or margarine, salt, and baking powder; blend.

Fill molds with this mixture and bake in preheated oven for 20-25 minutes; cakes should be uniformly light brown. Cool 5 minutes on wire rack; turn molds upside down and tap; the cakes should come out easily—if not help them along by lifting gently with point of knife. Cool thoroughly on cake rack; these cakes are better when on the dry side.

To store, place in open container. To be eaten as they are or with jam or jelly.

Fruits confits   **2**
Candied Fruits

½ pound lemon or orange peel (white pulp carefully removed)
1 cup granulated sugar
¼ cup light corn syrup
½ cup water

Cut the peel into strips of desired length (2"x½" is a good size). Cover the peel with cold water in a pan; bring to a boil; reduce to simmer and blanch for 5-8 minutes; drain thoroughly.

Mix sugar, syrup, and water in saucepan. Bring to boil over

medium-high heat; continue boiling gently until candy thermometer shows it has reached "hard-crack" stage (300°); immediately drop strips of peel into syrup; cook 10 minutes.

Remove peels with slotted spoon and place on a buttered cookie sheet. Cool and dry thoroughly.

Can be kept in glass container in dry place for weeks.

Le nougat blanc   3
White Nougat

This deliciously soft candy originated in Montélimar, a small town in Provence. It is said in the Provençal language, *"Ges de Nouve sense nougat"*. (Without nougat there is no Christmas.)

(Makes 32 candies)

Nougatine (can be prepared the day before):
½ cup sliced almonds
½ cup sugar
2 tablespoons water

Preheat oven to 350°.

Spread almonds on cookie sheet and toast in preheated oven until light brown, 8-10 minutes; remove and cool.

Combine sugar and water in small saucepan; dissolve sugar by stirring; place over medium heat and bring to gentle boil; continue gentle boil, without stirring, until a golden caramel forms; remove immediately from heat (do not let it get too dark); add almonds; stir to blend; pour over large piece of foil. Cool thoroughly and break into pieces; pulverize by pounding the pieces in a mortar in a heavy bowl, or pulverize in blender.

Nougat:
3 egg whites
1 cup sugar
½ cup water
1¼ cups honey
½ cup chopped mixed glacéed fruits

Beat egg whites until stiff; set aside. Combine sugar and water in saucepan; bring to boil over medium heat and cook until syrup reaches 290° (hard ball stage); the syrup should bubble gently.

Place honey in another saucepan over medium heat; cook in same manner but stir slowly and constantly until it reaches 290°.

Carefully mix the 2 syrups together in one of the pans; add this resulting syrup in a stream to the beaten egg whites, beating constantly with wooden spoon. Return to saucepan; over very low heat stir in glacéed fruits; blend; remove immediately from heat.

Add nougatine and blend. Pour into 8-inch-square pan lined with piece of foil of the same dimensions, or a piece of well-buttered wax paper. Place another piece of foil or buttered wax paper over, then a square piece of cardboard 8"x8" and weight it with heavy object such as iron, brick, etc. until contents are completely cold. Cut into rectangles 1"x2".

Galettes à l'anis   1
Anise Seed Cookies

(Makes about 7 dozen)

3½ cups all-purpose flour
1½ cups confectioner's sugar
Pinch of salt
2 cups butter or margarine, softened, at room temperature
½ cup almonds, chopped fine
½ cup walnuts, chopped fine
1 tablespoon anise seed, crushed
1½ teaspoons almond extract or vanilla extract

Preheat oven to 350°.

Sift flour, sugar, and salt together; add softened butter or margarine, almonds, walnuts, anise seed, and almond extract; knead with fingers until well blended and workable. Shape into small balls, about 1 inch in size; place on ungreased cookie sheets, 1 inch apart. Bake 10 minutes or until very lightly browned. Remove cookies immediately with spatula onto piece of foil. Cool thoroughly; store in tightly covered cookie jar.

Jellies, Jams, Preserves, and Liqueurs

If I close my eyes I can still visualize my grandmother's kitchen when August came around and it meant jam and jelly time. Raspberries always bring a pang of homesickness to me, as the sweet and delicate flavor of this beautiful fruit lingers on my tongue. I am transported on the wings of thought to the slopes of the French countryside of the Alps, where we would go in joyous groups to gather the ruby fruits.

Like its French counterpart, our countryside still abounds with wild fruits and berries — an almost unbelievable fact in an age of rapidly disappearing wilderness. These little jewels of nature should be treated with all the respect they deserve. This is the reason I have used only sugar, no pectin, in my recipes, so that their delicious flavor is not altered in this process.

Napoleon was indirectly responsible for the invention of canning. He offered a 17,000-franc prize for a method of preserving fruits and vegetables to supplement his troops' unhealthy diet of bread and salted meat. Francois Appert, a chef, won the prize for his technique using airtight, wide-mouth glass containers. In 1852, right before the Crimean War, Chevalier Appert improved the method by sterilizing the jars.

Preservation of food is of primary importance, and the right method of canning will prevent the loss of food. The boiling-water bath is recommended for two very important reasons: It kills micro-organisms that cause spoilage and it inactivates the enzymes which affect the appearance and flavor of the finished product.

This process is also advised for jams and jellies, especially if you cannot keep them in a cool and dry location.

To process canned foods, immerse the filled and tightly-capped jars in rapidly boiling water in a deep kettle or canner with the water one or two inches above the jar tops.

For high-altitude canning add (a) one minute for each thousand feet above sea level to processing times of twenty minutes or less, (b) two minutes per thousand feet to processing times longer than twenty minutes.

Brandy aux cerises   1
Cherry Brandy

(Makes 3 cups)

1 pound cherries, cleaned, stems removed
2 cups brandy
½ cinnamon stick
1 teaspoon coriander seeds, crushed
½ cup sugar

Pit cherries; keep ½ the pits and crush them with clean hammer; reserve crushed pits (woody parts and nuts).

Mash cherries; in large, clean jar combine mashed cherries, pits, brandy, ½ cinnamon stick, coriander, and sugar. Cover tightly; keep in cool place; invert jar daily for a week, or until sugar has dissolved. Then let mixture rest for 1 month.

Strain through several layers of cheesecloth into sterilized serving bottle. Keep tightly covered. Serve in liqueur glasses.

You may use *eau-de-vie* instead of brandy; it is then called *eau-de-vie aux cerises. Eau-de-vie* is also called *marc* in various parts of France.

Liqueur de fraises   1
Strawberry Liqueur

(Makes 1 quart)

1 pound strawberries, picked, cleaned, and hulled·
1 quart good grain alcohol
1 pound sugar
1 vanilla bean

Place strawberries in large sterilized glass jar and cover with alcohol. Mash fruit with clean fork, add sugar, and blend thoroughly.

Slice vanilla bean lengthwise and add to fruit and alcohol mixture. Cover tightly and let the mixture steep 1 month in cool, dry, dark place (a basement, for example). Invert jar daily until sugar has dissolved; then do not touch for remainder of time.

When ready to bottle, sterilize a nice quart bottle; place large plastic funnel in neck of bottle; cover funnel with triple layer of cheesecloth; strain liqueur through. Cork tightly and keep in cool place.

Liqueur de prunes sauvages   1
Wild Plum Liqueur

(Makes 1 quart)

1 pound (approximately) wild plums, picked, cleaned, pitted, and
     halved
2 cups good grain alcohol
2 cups sugar

Place wild plums in large sterilized jar. Mix alcohol and sugar; pour over plums. Cover tightly and steep for 1 month in cool, dry part of house. Invert jar daily until sugar has dissolved; then do not touch for remainder of the time.

When ready to bottle, sterilize a nice quart bottle; place large plastic funnel in neck of bottle; cover funnel with triple layer of cheesecloth; strain liqueur through. Cork tightly and keep in cool place.

Cornichons confits au vinaigre   **3**
French Style Gherkins

(Makes 3 1-pound jars)

30-40 tiny pickling cucumbers, about 1½ inches in length
20 small pickling onions
1 tablespoon peppercorns
3 large fresh sprigs of tarragon or 1 tablespoon dry tarragon leaves
1 quart pickling white vinegar with 4%-6% acetic acid (40- to
*   60-grain strength)*
Coarse pickling salt
Soft water for boiling

Wash and clean cucumbers thoroughly in cold water. Use a soft brush and clean a few at a time. Rinse several times and be sure no soil is left. Discard any soft ones. With sharp knife cut out blossom-end scars and stem ends.

Pour boiling soft water over skinned and cleaned onions; let stand 2 minutes. Meanwhile place cucumbers in a stoneware crock or glass bowl; sprinkle thoroughly with salt and let stand for 24 hours in a cool place.

Next day remove from salt brine; pour boiling soft water over cucumbers; let stand 2 minutes; drain and wipe cucumbers with paper towel; place in a clean stoneware crock or glass bowl.

Drain and wipe onions with paper towel; place them over cucumbers with tarragon and peppercorns. Bring vinegar to boiling point in unchipped enamel, aluminum, or stainless steel pan; pour over ingredients in the crock; let stand 24 hours in cool place.

Seal and process jars for 10 minutes in a boiling-water bath canner or deep kettle. (Capped jars are immersed in boiling water, at least 1 inch above jar tops.)

Vin d'orange   1
Orange Wine

(Makes about 1½ quart)

Zeste *of ½ orange*
1 whole orange
½ lemon, peeled (peeling may be dried for later use)
1 quart good dry white wine   ·
1 pound sugar
1⅔ cups good grain alcohol

Peel orange with vegetable parer to get the *zeste*. Avoid getting white part. Save peeled orange to be eaten later. Dry *zeste* in a 200° oven for 15 minutes.

Meanwhile, slice orange very thin; set aside in large bowl. Slice lemon thin, add to sliced orange in bowl. Add oven-dried orange *zeste*, wine, sugar, and alcohol. Cover tightly and steep or "macerate" in dark, dry, cool place for 40 days. (A basement is good.)

Filter through several thicknesses of cheesecloth in glass bowl and ladle into sterilized bottles. Cork tightly and keep in cool place.

Confiture de coings   2
Quince Marmalade

(Makes about 4½ pints)

3 cups well-ripened quinces, unpeeled, cleaned, cored, and sliced
3 cups sugar
3 cups water
1 tablespoon grated orange or lemon peel

Mix fruits, sugar, and water with orange or lemon peel in heavy copper or enameled kettle; bring to boil over medium heat; continue boiling gently until syrup reaches 220° on candy thermometer or until a drop of syrup on a cold dish feels syrupy to the touch.

Pour into sterilized jars; cool. Seal with wax if you intend to keep for quite a while. If marmalade is to be used in the next few days, cover with rounds of wax paper dipped in alcohol (whiskey, brandy, cognac, etc.) and keep in warmer part of refrigerator.

Confiture de figues   2
Fig Jam

(Makes 3-4 pints)

6 cups fresh whole figs, cleaned and stemmed
3 cups sugar
¾ cup water
Thinly-peeled rind of ½ lemon, diced fine
Juice of ½ lemon

Sterilize jars and a slotted spoon while cooking the jam, set aside on paper toweling with open part down.

Place sugar and water in large copper or enameled saucepan or kettle. Bring to boil over medium heat; add figs and lemon rind; bring back to light boil; lower to simmer and cook 2 hours. Add lemon juice and simmer 10 minutes longer.

Remove figs from syrup with slotted spoon; pack in sterilized jars. Fill with hot syrup; cool and seal. Keep in cool, dry place.

Confiture de cantaloup à l'aigre-doux   2
Sweet and Sour Cantaloupe Marmalade

(Makes about 5½ cups)

4 cups prepared cantaloupe (see below), not too ripe
5 cups sugar
Rind of ½ lemon, thinly peeled and cut into fine julienne
Juice of 1 lemon
½ cup cider vinegar
1 vanilla bean
10 whole cloves

Peel outside skin of melon, leaving some of the greenish flesh; remove the very soft interior, leaving the firm flesh intact. Cut melon in pieces 1½-2 inches thick. Place in colander over a bowl and let fruit drain overnight or at least 8 hours.

Next day, place lemon rind, vanilla bean, and cloves in a cheesecloth bag; add to non-aluminum (copper or enameled) kettle with lemon juice, vinegar, and drained cantaloupe. Bring to a boil; reduce heat and cook, gently bubbling, for 1 hour or until syrup reaches the syrupy stage (220°). Remove from heat; discard cheesecloth bag and its contents; skim foam.

Ladle fruit into sterilized jars until half full. Cook syrup 2 more minutes; fill jar to ¼ inch of top with hot syrup. Seal; sterilize jars. Keep in a cool place.

Sirop de framboises ou de mûres   3
Red or Black Raspberry Syrup

Wonderful for all sorts of desserts: topping for ice cream, to mix with a macédoine of fruits, to glaze tarts.

Juice:
2¼ cups (18 ounces) raspberries
1 cup water

Crush raspberries with potato masher; place in enameled saucepan; add water; bring to very light boil over medium heat; cook 10 minutes. Strain juice through jelly bag or several layers of cheesecloth into a glass or porcelain bowl. Let juice stand in bowl for 24 hours in cool place.

Syrup:
2 cups raspberry juice
3 cups sugar

Next day, place juice and sugar in copper or enameled saucepan. Bring to light boil over medium heat; skim the foam; continue cooking until syrup reaches 235° to 238°. Remove from heat; pour through a sterilized glass or plastic funnel into sterilized bottles; seal. Sterilize in boiling water bath for 10 minutes.

Confiture d'oranges   **2**
Orange Marmalade

(Makes about 4 cups)

6 small oranges, the variety with thin skin and seeds, washed and
    dried
2 lemons, washed and dried
3½ cups (approximately) sugar

Place the whole fruits in cold water; cover and refrigerate overnight to soften the skin. Next day place them in a non-aluminum
kettle with enough water to cover. Bring to boil and boil gently
over medium heat until fruits are soft under pressure. Remove
from heat, place in a colander and drain at least 8 hours.

Cut oranges and lemons in half, then halves into quarters. Remove
seeds and discard; keep juices and add to the bowl.

Measure fruits and juices and add the same amount of sugar (3-3½
cups). Place fruit and sugar back in kettle; stir; bring gently to a
boil and continue boiling, gently, uncovered, until fruits are transparent, 30-40 minutes.

Remove from heat and skim foam. Ladle fruit into sterilized jars to
fill half-way. Cook syrup 2 more minutes and fill jars with syrup.
Seal, sterilize jars.

Abricots à l'eau de vie (marc)   **3**
Apricots Preserved in Alcohol

This is a delicious dessert-drink to serve after a rich meal.

(Makes 2 quart jars)

2 pounds medium-sized, very firm fresh apricots, not too ripe,
    unblemished, cleaned; leave whole (do not remove pits)
18 ounces sugar
2 cups water
2½ cups eau de vie, Calvados, or good grain alcohol

Place the cleaned apricots in large saucepan; cover with 1 inch cold water; bring to boil over medium-high heat. As soon as it boils, remove from heat; with slotted spoon remove fruits and plunge them immediately in a bowl filled with cold water; drain water, peel apricots and set aside.

Blend sugar and water in deep enameled saucepan; bring slowly to light boil over medium heat and continue cooking 3 minutes.

While syrup is cooking remove apricots carefully from water to colander lined with clean towel or paper toweling, to drain. When syrup is ready, drop apricots one by one into hot syrup; return to light boil and cook 2-3 minutes. Do not let apricots get too soft.

Gently remove fruits with clean slotted spoon to clean colander to drain. Reserve syrup. Add alcohol to leftover syrup and blend by stirring with a sterilized spoon.

Divide apricots between 2 sterilized wide-mouth quart mason jars or decorative jars; arrange fruit in bottom; pour syrup-alcohol mixture over them. Be sure fruit is entirely covered by alcohol mixture. Cool, then close tightly. Should remain *at least* 1 month in a cool place.

To serve place one apricot in each serving glass and pour the liqueur over.

Gelée de prunes sauvages   3
Wild Plum Jelly

Pick and wash wild or homegrown plums which are on the not-too-ripe side. Make a slash in each plum with sharp knife. Place them in a large enameled saucepan with just enough water to reach under top layer of fruit. Bring to boil and cook rapidly until plums are tender. Remove from heat and strain juice through jelly bag or several layers of cheesecloth suspended securely over glass bowl. Do not squeeze bag or jelly will be cloudy.

Measure the juice obtained. Add 1 cup sugar to 1 cup juice. Place in enameled saucepan and return to boiling; boil rapidly until jelly thermometer registers 220° for soft jelly, 222° for firmer jelly.

(Watch again for overboil.) Skim once more; remove from heat at once and pour into sterilized jelly glasses. Let jelly cool thoroughly; seal with wax if you intend to keep for quite a while. Keep sealed jelly in dry, cool place. If jelly is to be used in the next few days, cover with rounds of wax paper dipped in alcohol (whiskey, cognac, brandy, etc.) and keep in warmer part of refrigerator.

Gelée de framboises ou de mûres   3
Raspberry or Blackberry Jelly

Place picked and cleaned fruits in an enameled saucepan. Crush berries lightly with potato masher and bring slowly to a light boil; reduce heat to get berries to bubble gently. Cook until soft, stirring often with wooden spoon to prevent scorching at the bottom; this should take 7-10 minutes. Remove from heat. Strain through jelly bag or several thicknesses of cheesecloth suspended over a bowl. Do not squeeze the bag or jelly will be cloudy.

Measure juice obtained; cook only 3-4 cups at a time. For each cup of juice add ¾ cup sugar.

Return to boiling; boil rapidly until jelly thermometer registers 220° for soft jelly, 222° for firmer jelly. (Watch again for overboil.) Skim once more; remove from heat at once and pour into sterilized jelly glasses. Let jelly cool thoroughly; seal with wax if you intend to keep for quite a while. Keep sealed jelly in dry, cool place. If jelly is to be used in the next few days, cover with rounds of wax paper dipped in alcohol (whiskey, cognac, brandy, etc.) and keep in warmer part of refrigerator.

Gelée de raisins sauvages   3
Wild Grape Jelly

One can still find wild grapes in the countryside of Provence. In some areas of Colorado in good years wild grapes ripen; this event is the pretext for some good picnics with the added fun of tracking these delicious little gems and of putting this good jelly aside for the winter. The recipe may also be used for homegrown grapes.

Remove grapes from stems, discard spoiled fruits. Rinse fruit at least twice to remove impurities. Place in enameled saucepan with ⅓ cup water for 2 cups of grapes. Crush lightly with potato masher and bring to gentle boil; cook until grapes are soft, 7-10 minutes.

Drain through jelly bag or several layers of cheesecloth suspended securely over a glass bowl. Do not squeeze the bag or the jelly will be cloudy.

Put juice in large heavy enameled saucepan and bring to boil; boil rapidly 5 minutes (watch carefully; it boils over easily). Skim; add sugar all at once; following these proportions: for each cup of juice add ¾-1 cup sugar. Use less sugar if fruit is on the ripe side, more sugar if underripe.

Return to boiling; boil rapidly until jelly thermometer registers 220° for soft jelly, 222° for firmer jelly. (Watch again for overboil.) Skim once more; remove from heat at once and pour into sterilized jelly glasses. Let jelly cool thoroughly; seal with wax if you intend to keep for quite a while. Keep sealed jelly in dry, cool place. If jelly is to be used in the next few days, cover with rounds of wax paper dipped in alcohol (whiskey, cognac, brandy, etc.) and keep in warmer part of refrigerator.

Plants, Herbs, and Spices

Our ancestors knew from long experience the wonderful properties of the plants and herbs which grew in the surrounding countryside or in their gardens. Travelers had brought from far countries hitherto unknown spices. Soon people learned to cook with them and paid dearly to obtain these precious items.

I grew up surrounded by the delicious scents of plants and herbs. My mother operated an *herboristerie* (herbalist shop), and I learned early to recognize each plant not only in the fields and mountains, but in dried form, stored in the pretty glass jars and boxes neatly lining the shelves of our store. Perhaps it was then that I acquired a love of nature and a "green thumb." I have always grown something green; even as a little girl I had rows of pots on our balcony in the apartment where we lived in sunny Marseille. I could not do without flowers or vegetables in this country — and of course an herb garden.

That we have forgotten or ignored the role the plants play in nature is our loss. They continue to produce their precious essences all around us. A sunny window is space enough to grow some fresh herbs, which will enhance a dish of meat or vegetables or a salad. For some of us who are on low-salt diets, herbs are a life-saver; they will give the palate such delight that the need for salt will be forgotten.

Herbs can be dried or frozen so that they can be at our disposal during the winter months. If you have only a small amount, freeze them. Pick early in the morning before the sun has touched them; rinse well; wipe damp in a clean towel; in small bunches, place in plastic bags and freeze.

If you have a quantity, dry them. Tie the herbs by the stems (after they have been cleaned and the moisture thoroughly shaken out) and hang them in a well-ventilated area away from the sun or other strong light.

Another method is to spread them to dry on paper toweling away from sunlight and strong light in a well-ventilated area. Turn them twice a day. When thoroughly dry (they should crumble when rubbed between your fingers), store them in perfectly clean, dry glass containers or cans, tightly sealed, away from heat sources, windows, or sunny spots. (This is also the way spices should be stored.)

If you follow these suggestions, you will be rewarded by the long shelf-life of your herbs and will enjoy the scents of summer all year long.

PLANTS, HERBS, AND SPICES IN COMMON USAGE IN FRENCH KITCHENS

Allspice (*les Quatre épices*). It is used in cooking meats and poultry and for pickling and in flavoring pies. The oil is the base for some ointments. Allspice contains *piment* from Jamaica, nutmeg, cloves, and cinnamon.

Angelic (*l' Angélique*). The stem of this herb is used in the confection of sweets.

Anis (*l'Anis*). An herb used in cookery, the root especially. The seeds are used to flavor cakes and cookies. A well-known drink, anisette, is made from anis. The herb has carminative properties.

Basil (*le Basilic*). This sweet herb enhances vegetables such as tomatoes, beans, etc. and flavors soups, stews, fish, stuffings, and pastry.

Bay leaf (*le Laurier*). Very pungent, the leaf and berries were used in antiquity. Now, only the leaves are used to flavor broths, soups, stews, meats, fish, and stuffings.

Burnet (*la Pimprenelle*). Used in certain dishes (*bouquet garni*).

Camomile (*la Camomille*). The flower is used in lotions for tightening the skin; it is a good hair rinse for blond people, bringing out the highlights; and brewed in a tea it is good for sluggish gall bladders.

Capers (*les Capres*). The pickled buds are used with salads, sauces, and fish.

Caraway (or *le Carvi*). The seed is used to flavor breads, stews, vegetables, sauerkraut, and cheeses.

Cardamom (*le Cardamome*). The pod is a flavoring for breads, pastries, etc., and is also a pickling spice.

Cayenne (*le Poivre de Cayenne*). This very sharp spice is used in cooking meats.

Celery (*le Céléri*). The plant is of course a vegetable; the seeds are used to flavor fish, soups, stews, and stuffings. It is a good diuretic.

Chervil (*le Cerfeuil*). A pungent herb used in soups, salads, and sauces; delicious in omelets or scrambled eggs.

Chives (*la Ciboulette*). This mild onion adds subtle flavor to salads, eggs, sauces, vegetables, poultry, and meats.

Cinnamon (*la Cannelle*). This is an aromatic spice used in powder or chip form to flavor fruit pies, fruit dishes, cakes, and desserts. It is also used to make oils and incense.

Cloves (*les Clous de Girofle*). The dried buds flavor soups, broths, stews, and meats; the powder is used to flavor fruit dishes. The tubers go into the making of oils, incense and sachets.

Coriander (*la Coriandre*). When ground, it flavors cakes, cookies, pastries, and some sauces and poultry.

Cumin (*le Cumin*). The seed is used for seasoning. The liqueur kümmel is made from cumin.

Curry (*le Curry*). In reality a mixture of several herbs and spices, it is used to flavor sauces and soups.

Dandelion (*le Pissenlit*). This is a "good" weed of many healthful uses: the tender green leaves are used in salad and as a vegetable; the roasted roots are used as a substitute for coffee. It is very rich in vitamin C.

Fennel (*le Fenouil*). The French cook and eat the stem like celery. The leaves flavor fish dishes and pickling vinegar. It is a good diuretic.

Garlic (*l'Ail*). This very fragrant bulb has so many uses in French cookery that it could be declared the "national hero." A good many medicinal properties (including "good for the bladder") are attributed to it. Recently it has been found to lower cholesterol in clogged arteries.

Ginger (*le Gingembre*). The very spicy powder obtained from this rhizome is used in flavoring cakes and cookies.

Juniper (*le Genièvre*). The berries are used in stews, marinades, and the making of gin. It is a diuretic and carminative.

Lemon (*le Citron*). The thin peeling, or *zeste*, and the juice are used to flavor desserts, pies, cakes, marinades, stews, meats, and fish. Rich in vitamin C, it also has medicinal properties.

Licorice (*le Réglisse*). This sweet root is well known for its use in flavoring candies. It was used to help teething babies; they would chew on the hard root, getting not only the sweet juice but relief from sore gums.

Marjoram (*la Marjolaine*). This is an aromatic herb, widely known for its flavoring of meats, poultry, stews, soups, and vegetables. It is also good as a carminative when used in tea.

Mint (*la Menthe*). A very aromatic herb, it is used to flavor drinks, jellies, and vegetables. The tea is good to help flatulence. *La menthe poivrée* (peppermint) makes a very helpful tea which stimulates the appetite.

Mustard (*la Moutarde*). The seeds are the base for "prepared mustard"; the powder flavors dressings, fish, and meat. It was used in a poultice to help fight chest colds.

Nasturtium (*la Capucine*). This plant could also be classified as an herb. The flowers and leaves may be added to salads. The seeds, pickled, are a nice substitute for capers.

Nutmeg (*la Noix de muscade*). This is a nut. Grated it is used in pies, custards, cakes, cookies, and even stews.

Onion (*l'Oignon*). The bulb, like garlic, is a must in cooking; it is so well known there is no need to list the uses.

Orange (*l'Orange*). The thin peeling, or *zeste*, like that of the lemon, is used in flavoring fruit dishes, desserts, marinades, and stews.

Oregano (*l'Origan*). This very pungent herb is very Mediterranean indeed. It is good in salad dressings, tomato sauces, marinades, meat, poultry, and pastas. The tea is a carminative.

Paprika (*le Paprika*). This is a mild kind of Cayenne; it gives eye and taste appeal to soups and stews.

Parsley (*le Persil*). What would we do without this wonderful herb? It is not only decorative but a great condiment for salads, stews, vegetable soups, meats, and fish, and a very rich source of vitamins A and C and magnesium. Containing chlorophyll, it is good for freshening the breath.

Pepper (*le Poivre*). White or black, the seeds are ground to perk up salad dressing and all sorts of dishes.

Pimiento (*le Piment*). It can be red and sweet; or green and hot; it is rich in vitamin C.

Poppy seeds (*les Graines de Pavot*). These tiny seeds are sprinkled on cakes, cookies, and breads.

Rosemary (*le Romarin*). It is a pungent plant used freely in the cuisine of the South of France. It grows wild on the Mediterranean coastline and hillsides of the back country. It is used in marinades, meats, and fish dishes. The tea is a stomachic. In lotions it is an astringent. It is also used in ointments and is a good hair rinse.

Saffron (*le Safran*). Only the stigmas of the flower of this plant are used, thus making it an expensive—but worthwhile—spice.

Luckily only a tiny pinch is necessary to flavor fish soups, chowders, rice, chicken, and sauces.

Sage (*la Sauge*). This herb was well known to and used by the people of antiquity for medicinal purposes, as a disinfectant, a hair dye, in teas, and in cookery. It is still very popular for flavoring meats, poultry, stuffings, and soups.

Shallots (*les Echalottes*). They are a sweet bulb of the onion family, used in fine cookery.

Summer savory and **winter savory** (*la Sariette*). In Provence it is also called *le pèbre d'ail*, or "donkey's pepper" because it is a favorite of those charming animals. Spicy, it lends a tangy flavor to salad dressings, stuffings, meats, soups, and vegetables.

Tarragon (*l'Estragon*). This is a most delicate and versatile herb used in sauces, salad dressings, poultry, soups, and vegetables. It is an essential ingredient in the making of a delicious vinegar. The tea induces sleep.

Thyme (*le Thym*). For me, thyme is equated with "Provence." In summer the sunny hillsides where it grows in profusion are fragrant with it. There would not be much of a Provençal cuisine without it. This wonderful plant was well-known to the ancient Mediterranean civilizations for its medicinal values as well as for its aromatic properties. These days it is still used in medicinal ointments, as a disinfectant, and in the making of mouthwashes. In cooking, it is a must in stews, broths, and stuffings. It is also used in soups, and meat and poultry cookery. The tea is a tonic which excites the appetite and helps prevent flatulence.

Watercress (*le Cresson*). This water-loving plant makes a wonderful, tangy addition to salads, mayonnaise, soups, and sauces. It is also used as *garniture* for meat and poultry dishes. It is a very rich source of vitamins C and E and of iron.

Vanilla (*la Vanille*). The bean or pod is used as a base for the "extract of vanilla" flavoring for all sorts of desserts and baked goods. The pod in its original state can be used as flavoring for *entremets* and *crèmes*. Vanilla is also used in the preparation of sachets and perfumes.

Vervain (*la Verveine*). I include this plant in my list because of its popularity in France as a tea made from the leaves; it helps digestion and induces sleep.

Violet (*la Violette*). This pretty, shy flower, as we know, enters into the making of a subtle perfume; but it is also used in the preparation of a syrup which is not only delicious but is said to be helpful in preventing coughs, and in candy making (candied violets).

How to Use Herbs

The saying "discretion is the better part of valor" applies in the use of herbs. Start with a small amount until you and your family have acquired a taste for the particular herb. The following list indicates the herbs most suitable for various foods.

Eggs	basil, chives, parsley, cress, dill
Soups	bay leaf, thyme, parsley, leeks, cress, marjoram, garlic
Sauces	dill, fennel (fish sauces), parsley, oregano, marjoram
Vegetables	parsley, cress, chives, basil, summer savory, garlic
Salads	basil, parsley, cress, chives, oregano, garlic
Poultry	thyme, tarragon, basil, garlic
Grilled meats	thyme, rosemary, garlic
Pork	sage, garlic
Veal	thyme, bay leaf
Stews	thyme, bay leaf, parsley, garlic
Marinades	thyme, bay leaf, summer savory, garlic, onions, parsley, orange rind
Game birds, rabbits	juniper berries, thyme, summer savory, bay leaf
Fish	fennel, thyme, bay leaf, dill

In using herbs, use about three times as much fresh herb as you would dried; for example: 1 teaspoon dried thyme = 1 tablespoon fresh.

Combinations

Fines herbes (for eggs, omelets, scrambled eggs): chervil, marjoram, summer savory, thyme, parsley

Bouquet garni (for soups, stews, poultry, fish): parsley, thyme, bay leaf, celery leaves, (sometimes) garlic

Quatre épices (for pâtés, terrines, and stuffings):
   1 teaspoon each ground ginger, ground cloves, ground nutmeg
   1 tablespoon ground cinnamon
   Mix in jar with a tight-fitting lid; shake well; keep away from light.

Épices parisiennes (for casseroles, stews, marinades):
  1 tablespoon each ground white pepper, ground ginger, ground
    nutmeg
  3 tablespoons ground cloves
  Mix as for *Quatre épices.*

Épices de Provence (for soups, stews, marinades):
  1 tablespoon each, finely crushed, dried thyme, dried summer
    savory, dried rosemary, whole cloves, dried orange peel, grated
    or powdered nutmeg
  2 bay leaves, finely crushed.
  Mix as for *Quatre épices.* (Only small amount is necessary — ⅛
    to ¼ teaspoon — for stews or soups, 1 teaspoon for marinade)

Vinaigre à l'estragon
Tarragon Vinegar

---

1 quart white distilled vinegar
6-8 large fresh tarragon sprigs about 5 inches in length

Pick tarragon in the morning when dry of dew but not touched by
the sun; this is when the flavor is still locked in the leaves. Rinse
and shake moisture thoroughly; let leftover moisture dry out by
placing the herb on paper toweling. Same day, place sprigs in a
sterilized jar; pour vinegar over. Put cap on tightly and let stand at
least a month before using.

Vinaigre aux aromates
Aromatic Vinegar

---

1 quart red wine vinegar or cider vinegar
Several mixed sprigs of oregano, summer savory or winter savory,
    basil
1 small sprig rosemary

Proceed as with *Vinaigre à l'estragon.*

Moutarde aux herbes
Herb Mustard

9 ounces pure prepared mustard
2 teaspoons finely chopped capers
2 teaspoons tarragon vinegar
½ teaspoon dry rosemary leaves
¼ teaspoon dry thyme leaves
¼ teaspoon dry summer savory
Small piece bay leaf
Pinch marjoram

Blend mustard, capers, and tarragon vinegar in a bowl; set aside.

Pound rosemary, thyme, summer savory, bay leaf, and marjoram to a powder in mortar. Put through a sieve and work with spoon until all the herbs are sieved. Blend this herb powder with the mustard mixture.

Spoon into clean jars and cover tightly. Keep refrigerated.

Index